THE PATENT PROCESS

THE PATENT PROCESS

A GUIDE TO INTELLECTUAL PROPERTY FOR THE INFORMATION AGE

Craig Hovey, PhD

JOHN WILEY & SONS, INC.

Published by John Wiley & Sons, Inc., New York.
Published simultaneously in Canada.

This publication is designed to provide accurate and authoritative information in regard to the subject matter covered. It is sold with the understanding that the publisher is not engaged in rendering legal, accounting, or other professional services. If legal advice or other expert assistance is required, the services of a competent professional person should be sought.

Designations used by companies to distinguish their products are often claimed by trademarks. In all instances where the author or publisher is aware of a claim, the product names appear in Initial Capital letters. Readers, however, should contact the appropriate companies for more complete information regarding trademarks and registration.

Library of Congress Cataloging-in-Publication Data:

Hovey, Craig 1958–
    The patent process : a guide to intellectual property for the information age /
Craig Hovey.
        p.   cm.
    Includes index.
    ISBN 0-471-44217-8 (pbk. : alk. paper)
    1. Patent laws and legislation—United States.   I. Title.
KF3114 .H68 2002
346.7304'86—dc21   2001045609

Printed in the United States of America.

10   9   8   7   6   5   4   3   2   1

*This book is dedicated to my wife, Gloria, and our three
fabulous children, Max, Chloe, and Eve,
the greatest family a man could ever be part of.*

CONTENTS

CONTENTS

CONTENTS

PREFACE

We hear so much more about intellectual property now than we used to that it would be easy to assume it has only recently become an important topic. In fact, intellectual property, which consists of the ideas and mental efforts of individuals, has always been vital. Be it a factory, painting, piece of software, or glass of beer, no tangible human invention could exist if it was not preceded by an intangible notion. Without intellectual property there would be no property at all.

What is different today is that there are so many goods and services, like software, we use on a daily basis where the connection between the function and the ideas that make it possible are much more clear than in the past. For example, when you buy a pair of shoes, you see them as a product with weight and mass that were produced by a company that used a factory, machines, natural resources, and labor to produce them, with most of these being assets that can be seen and measured. If you buy word processing software, however, you have a good that consists of a set of instructions, where an infinite number of copies can be produced simply using a small amount of tangible resources for each. Neither product would be possible without the ideas that came first, but those ideas are much more apparent in the software.

Another important issue that has brought intellectual property to prominence is the need to protect it. Technology has broadened markets and made it far easier to obtain the ideas of others, duplicate them, and make money selling them. If you have taken on the risks and invested the resources necessary to develop a new invention, work of art, brand name, or process you want to keep to yourself, having somebody else come along and make off with it as their own, then profit from selling it to others without ever having had to sweat over it like you did, is not a pleasant experience. Nobody likes having their property taken, be it a car or a description of an invention to be patented. When it becomes easier for property to be taken, then the issue of how to protect it increases in importance.

Another significant factor relates to intellectual property in any time. It is a common misconception that in order for a patent, for example, to be worth pursuing, the invention in question must be something completely unique, complicated, and breathtaking, with anything less being too obvious to be worth the bother. The reality is the opposite. The mind-blowing stuff that seems like a gold mine in its originality may turn out to be something that's too different to have much appeal yet, while the simple advance that makes sense to a wide range of people is a huge hit.

In the course of writing this book I spoke to a lot of people who were in the midst of the patent process or considering it. Over and over I heard people voice a lack of confidence in their creations because there was nothing fancy about them. Usually, however, the reason there was nothing fancy was because the ideas were direct, useful applications of simple technology that seemed obvious after being explained, but had not been produced yet. These are exactly the kinds of things that should be patented. We hear so much about computer-based business process patents (which are only a relatively small number of patents anyway) that those can mistakenly be taken as the standard in terms of the technology involved. Do not underestimate the value of simplicity and obviousness. Many millions of dollars were made from the Super Soaker, in essence a squirt gun on steroids; sure, it looks so easy in retrospect. The challenge is to come up with workable ideas like that in the present, then protect your intellectual property.

Large businesses have their own patent attorneys. This book is written for individuals and small companies. Even at that, its purpose is to provide the reader with a solid introduction to patents and other forms of intellectual property, but not an exhaustive treatment. My experience with the creators of intellectual property is that they want to focus on what they do best (innovate) and not get too hung up on the technicalities of patents, copyrights, and so on. What is necessary is for creators to understand the core issues, which are what I am trying to assist creators with here.

As the creator of intellectual property, you cannot match the expertise of an experienced patent attorney. Your rule of thumb should be that if a piece of intellectual property is worth protecting, particularly with a patent, it is worthwhile paying a qualified person to obtain the best possible protection. Do not risk the future benefits of your great ideas by falling prey to the bad idea of taking care of the legal stuff on your own.

ACKNOWLEDGMENTS

I owe a particular debt of gratitude to Lisa Harrington for making this book possible. I am also very grateful to my agent, Jeff Herman, for bringing the opportunity to my attention. Michael Hamilton, editor, and Kimberly Vaughn, his assistant at John Wiley & Sons, deserve special thanks for displaying patience, support, and tolerance beyond the call of duty.

THE PATENT PROCESS

THE FACE BEHIND
THE MASK

1

The only thing that keeps us alive is our brilliance. The only way to protect our brilliance is patents.

—Edwin Land, founder of Polaroid

Ideas are to the Information Age what iron ore and other raw materials were to the Industrial Age—only you can't put a fence around ideas. The closest thing is a patent.

—Thomas Field Jr.

THE PATENT EXPLOSION

In the year 2000 the United States Patent and Trademark Office (USPTO) received 315,015 patent applications and granted 175,983 patents. This was about an 80% increase over the patent activity of 1990, when 176,264 applications were received and 96,076 patents were granted, and more than 250% that of 1980, when the patent office received 112,379 applications and granted 66,170 patents.

During the mid-nineties, the annual rate of growth in patent applications averaged a bit more than 12% a year. The biggest jump occurred between 1997 and 1999, with the 169,094 patent grants made in 1999 being 36% more than that of the 1997s. The United States Patent and Trademark Office estimates that patent filings could increase to 600,000 by the year 2006. If that happens and the USPTO continues to grant around 72% of them, as they have in the past, then more than 420,000 of those will go on to be granted and issued.

The growth in patents is even more impressive when looked at in a broader historical context. In 1790, the year Congress enacted the initial U.S. patent laws, the first U.S. patent was issued for a means of making potash fertilizer. It took 210 years for the first 6 million patents to be issued, with patent number 6,000,000 being awarded to 3Com, in a special ceremony on December 10, 1999, for its HotSync technology, which permits the synchronization of information between handheld devices and a computer with one touch of a button. If current trends persist, the next 6 million patents could be issued by 2015.

What is driving the explosive growth in patent activity? The primary factors are advances in technology, the creative spirit of people living and working in the United States, the desire to make life better, and a steadily growing population. Together, these factors have fostered a burst of innovation and entrepreneurship, which is reflected in the rapidly increasing number and variety of patents; there is no reason to expect the process to slow down anytime soon.

Having heard so much about business method patents in the past few years, like those for one-click shopping on Amazon.com and reverse auctions at Priceline.com, it would be easy for us to make the mistake of assuming that Internet-based technology is fueling the biggest chunk of the patent boom. It is true that business method patents, which include new ways of providing goods and services using computers, have increased rapidly, but they still represent only a small fraction of patent activity.

The courts began allowing patents for business methods in 1998. These types of patents are controversial, with critics of them claiming that they take merely obvious services and computerize the means of providing them, with nothing genuinely innovative or new being contributed. Proponents of business method patents say they qualify because they represent useful, improved ways of doing business that employ new technology in creative ways. As of this writing, the issue is far from settled and it is impossible to predict the ultimate fate of business method patents.

Bear in mind, though, that the United States Patent and Trademark Office has already raised the bar on business method patents. In the quarter ending on March 31, 2000, 56% of business method patents were granted. In the quarter ending on December 31, 2000, that percentage had dropped to 36%. Some of the drop may be due to people filing weak applications on the off chance they would receive a patent that would prove lucrative, but most of the drop probably follows from the patent office providing examiners more training in the area and now requiring that all approved business method patents be examined by a second pair of eyes.

In the government's fiscal year 2000, which ended on September 30, applications for business method patents rose to 7,000 from 2,821 the prior year. However, the patent office issued only 899 of this type of patent in the same period. While the number of business method patents granted was only a little more than a third of the amount applied for, remember that rate of approval for patent applications as a whole: 72%.

Along with business methods, patents are being issued in a number of other areas that did not exist in the past. Biotech companies were not allowed to receive patents for genetic discoveries until 1980; patents for software were not permitted until 1981. In addition, technological advances have caused existing inventions to become increasingly complex as they continue to be developed. Consider FutureColor, a new color printing press being developed by Xerox. It is about 80 feet long, weighs in at 5,000 pounds, has more than 3 miles of wiring, and contains 85 microprocessors that can perform 270 million calculations per second. Xerox has spent $1 billion dollars developing the product over the past 7 years, has filed 400 patents on it, and FutureColor is not even on the market yet.

In an economy that has become increasingly reliant on information, those who succeed in it, be they lone individuals, small companies, or huge corporations, are the ones able to generate, apply, and market the best ideas. Because ideas are so important, and because new ones are being generated at a much faster pace than at any other time in history, it is no wonder that Thomas Colson, noted patent attorney and CEO of IP.com said in a company press release, ". . . patent applications are being filed at breakneck speed, extending beyond technology and manufacturing innovations to encompass business-related processes and methods. In some cases, ownership of patents, not products and services, is establishing who dominates a market. This is resulting in savvy intellectual property companies—even previously unheard of startups—gaining enormous leverage over competitors."

OVERVIEW OF INTELLECTUAL PROPERTY

Intellectual property can be anything that begins as an idea in the human mind and is developed into an original creation that can be expressed in a tangible form, such as an invention, book, play, secret process, or mark used to brand a product. Following is a brief description of four forms of intellectual property. Each will be considered in greater detail in subsequent chapters.

PATENTS

A patent is a right granted by the government that allows the holder to exclude others from making, using, or selling the invention the patent pertains to. This right lasts for 20 years from the date of application. The term "invention" refers to any new machine, article, composition of matter, process, use, or improvement.

A patent, by legal statute, can be obtained by anybody who "invents or discovers any new and useful process, machine, manufacture, or compositions of matter, or any new and useful improvement thereof . . . ," within the boundaries of law. Congress was given the power to enact patent laws by the Constitution, which states that "Congress shall have power . . . to promote the progress of science and useful arts, by securing for limited times to authors and inventors the exclusive right to their respective writings and discoveries." The first patent law was passed in 1790. Today's laws are based on a general revision that went into effect in 1953; additional revisions were made in 1999 with the American Inventors Protection Act.

There are three kinds of patents that can be applied for: utility, design, and plant. A utility patent covers unique inventions that perform useful functions. Utility patents are the largest and most important category of patent (usually accounting for 90%–95% of the patents applied for in a given year) and will receive the bulk of this book's attention. Design patents cover unique, ornamental shapes of nonnatural objects, things like original building designs or computer icons. Plant patents cover plants, like flowers, that can be reproduced asexually (using grafts and cuttings).

In essence, a patent provides its owner with a 20-year monopoly that can be enforced against anybody who infringes on the patent by making or selling a patented invention without permission. A patent does not confer on the holder any particular right to make, market, or sell the invention, but, by providing the right to exclude others, it provides owners of patents a wonderful opportunity to profit from their innovations during that 20-year period. Without this right, anybody could come along and copy and sell an inventor's original creation, thereby cutting the originators off from the benefits of their labors and greatly reducing their incentive to develop new goods and services.

COPYRIGHTS

A copyright protects the creators of "original works of authorship," whether or not these works have been published. The copyright holder has sole rights to make copies, author derivative works, and perform or display the work publicly.

Copyright protection is limited to the form of expression a work takes and does not cover the subject matter. So, as many people as want to can write books about World War II, but none are permitted to write a book that is identical to another that has already been authored.

Unlike patents, which must be applied for, copyright protection arises automatically, when the original work is put in a fixed form, like a painting or recorded song. It is best to register copyrighted work with the U.S. Copyright Office, however, so that you have a clear record of it in case any dispute as to authorship arises in the future. Copyright protection lasts for the life of the author, plus an additional 70 years.

TRADEMARKS

A trademark is a means of branding a product that both identifies it and distinguishes it from the goods of others. Trademarks come in the form of words, names, symbols, sounds, or any combination of these. While the existence of your trademark can be used to prevent others from using the same, or very similar, marks, it cannot be used to stop competitors from selling the same goods or services.

A good trademark makes your product unique and recognizable, and if the mark is also associated with quality and value, your product stands an excellent chance of being chosen over less-recognizable competitors by consumers. The Nike "swoosh" is an example of a powerful trademark, as was Hula Hoop a few years back. In both cases, established trademarks, which cost little to maintain and are a constant source of free advertising, played an important role in building popular and lucrative brands.

Trademarks can be protected for as long as they are in use. They can easily be registered, either online or by mail, with the U.S. Patent and Trademark Office. This provides an important record should any legal disputes arise in connection with the trademark.

TRADE SECRETS

A trade secret can be almost any form of information, such as recipes, customer lists, business methods, techniques, designs, formulas, and so on that has value for its owner and is not known outside the business. Examples include McDonald's special sauce, Bluetie's (a business services provider) methods for developing applications quickly, or Coca-Cola's formula.

Trade secrets are sometimes chosen over patents because there is no restriction on how long they last, other than a firm's ability to keep them under wraps. If KFC had patented the "11 herbs and spices" recipe used in their chicken, the patent would have expired by now and anybody who wanted to could duplicate it. Because they have successfully maintained their trade secret, the recipe continues as an extremely valuable piece of intellectual property.

There are no requirements to apply for or register trade secrets with any government office. In order for a trade secret to have validity in a legal action, it must be demonstrated that the keeper(s) of the secret made appropriate efforts to secure the knowledge. If somebody else figures out the secret independently, however, and did not steal it, or acquire it by any other illegal means, then there is no recourse.

Many years ago, goods and services were made on a small scale and depended on the skills and knowledge of the people who handled them in the process of creation. Ever since production began on a larger scale and duplication became possible, people have sought ways to protect their original renderings.

Legend has it that Shah Jahan, the emperor responsible for the building of the Taj Mahal, had his soldiers chop off the hands of the craftsmen involved so they could not get together and create another monument like it. Today, in an economy where the basic building blocks of so many innovations consist of information that can be copied, employers would have to chop off employees' and competitors' heads to achieve the same thing. Since this practice would be frowned on, we have to settle for the protections offered by intellectual property law.

The idea behind patent, copyright, trademark, and trade secret rights is to allow inventors to gain rewards from their efforts so that they will be encouraged to continue innovating in the future, something that benefits us all. The downside is that there is a reduction of potential head-to-head competition. The upside is that the competition becomes one of who can innovate and make forward progress most effectively, both as a way to improve on the protected creations of others and for the purpose of developing new inventions that are eligible for the same rights.

Thomas Jefferson said, "If nature has made any one thing less susceptible than all others of exclusive property, it is the action of the thinking power called an idea. . . . No one possesses the less, because every other possess the whole of it. He who receives an idea from me, receives instruction himself without lessening mine; as he who lights his taper at mine, receives light without darkening me." Jefferson saw knowledge as something to be shared freely to everybody's benefit, but in today's world, when applied ideas are what makes or breaks both companies and individuals trying to make it in a competitive environment, intellectual property is every bit as important as factories and natural resources were in the past, and nobody can afford to have it stolen.

The great thing about intellectual property is that those with great ideas have a better chance of succeeding today than ever before, for it is ultimately ideas that distinguish you from others in the marketplace. Dell, started in a dorm room during the 1980s by Michael Dell, sells computers that are not much different from IBM's or Gateway's.

It became the leading PC seller because Dell had ideas in the areas of inventory control, purchasing, procurement, and customer service that were superior to those of the other manufacturers. The fact that his ideas were originally developed with nowhere near the physical assets or financial capital of his big competitors demonstrates how valuable intellectual property, which is based on the quality of your ideas rather than the depth of cash lining your pockets, truly is.

INTANGIBLE ASSETS: VALUING WHAT CANNOT BE SEEN

One of the challenges posed by intellectual property is figuring out what it is worth. You can always have a building or piece of land appraised, and most owners know about what their inventories will sell for. But, because intellectual property is based on ideas, valuing it means predicting how the ideas will fare in an ever-changing marketplace. Not only that, but often an idea's ultimate value is determined by how well it is handled, and who can predict that? And who can guarantee that good ideas will continue to be generated in the future, in order for a firm's true value to keep growing?

David Koretz, the president and founder of Bluetie, an Internet-based business services provider, estimates that 90% of his company's assets are intangible, things that cannot be grasped, weighed, or accurately quantified. Not only are these intangibles in the form of patents, trademarks, and trade secrets, but, even more importantly, they are embodied in the talents and personal qualities of the workforce he has assembled.

Today, Bluetie, a small company that is only two years old, is outperforming everybody in its field in terms of services and applications, with a talent pool and patented processes that cannot be beat. Not only has its intellectual property given it a significant advantage, but the quality of its ideas, and its resulting prospects, enabled Bluetie to attract solid financing and the kind of talent bigger companies envy. In fact, be it a new or old-style company, big or small, in any sector of the economy, the same has always been so. Before any money is raised, buildings erected, land acquired, or software written, there must first be some form of intellectual property in place, even if it be the simplest set of ideas, before anything else gets done.

In the past, a firm's net worth could be calculated as follows:

$$ASSETS - LIABILITIES = NET\ WORTH$$

Assets are what a firm owns or has a claim to; liabilities are what a firm owes to others, and net worth is whatever is left over. Where it is usually not too difficult to estimate, or at least get a good ballpark figure, for the value of physical assets, the challenge posed by intellectual property is that there is no method for putting its value into dollars. First because the inflow of dollars may not occur until the future. Second because, even if intellectual property is causing revenue inflows now, how much, precisely are they? And, even if we know what our intellectual property is worth today, how much will it be worth tomorrow? Maybe our great ideas will suddenly catch on in a big way and their value will skyrocket, or maybe a competitor will make our ideas obsolete and suddenly devoid of value.

The wonderful thing about intellectual property is that anybody can create it. Even if you are dead broke, you still have the opportunity to create something of immense potential solely based on the quality of your own thinking. Turning those thoughts into real goods and services remains a daunting challenge, of course, but the fact that so much of it is based on the creation of assets that do not require vast financial resources means that the opportunities for creative, persistent individuals today are far greater than they have ever been.

A good example of the value of intellectual property in the form of a patent, and how that patent causes the company's value to be assessed, is found in the experience of the pharmaceutical company Eli Lilly, holder of the patent on Prozac. On August 9, 2000 the value of Eli Lilly's stock plummeted 31%, a drop of $38 billion in the value of its stock. The cause was a court decision that their patent would expire two years earlier than the company had hoped. This decision meant that the patent protection that allowed them to keep other companies from making Prozac was going to evaporate, leaving the door open for any competitor with the means and desire to make and sell Prozac, at a price that would be quickly driven down by competition, with profits from selling the drug sure to slump, also.

Though the price difference may be more extreme than normal, here is another example that serves to further illustrate why an early lapse of patent protection had such a big impact on Eli Lilly's stock. Pfizer holds the patent to Fluconazole, an antifungal medication that costs $10 a tablet to buy. In India, where U.S. patent law holds no sway, a company called Cipla sells the same drug for 25 cents a tablet. The price drop for Prozac after the patent expires will not be as great as the difference in selling prices for Fluconazole between the United States and India, but it will certainly be enough that you can see why stockholders were worried in advance.

Bear in mind that a company's stock price reflects an estimate of its future cash flows, good news that makes prospects in the years to come look better, as when we hear of encouraging results from trials of Zovant, a new drug that Eli Lilly is developing to treat septic shock, which caused the price per share to take off based on optimism for future sales. So, too, does news that has a negative impact on estimates of future cash flows cause the price to drop.

Unlike land and buildings, whose value is relatively stable, based on current valuations, and able to be protected with fences and guards, the value of intellectual property is determined by its future prospects, with the best way to guard, maintain, or increase its value being to use it effectively. The barrier to acquiring tangible assets is the money necessary to buy them. The acquisition of intellectual property is limited only by our imaginations and creativity.

FROM A GLEAM IN THE EYE TO A PRODUCT ON THE SHELF

In 1899 the director of the U.S. Patent Office said, "Everything that can be invented has been invented." He believed that his office should be abolished, as there was no longer any need for it. Then came the twentieth century, a period of immense technological progress and innovation that exceeded all prior centuries combined.

Even without the huge technological leaps forward, innovation would still have continued. As humans we have unlimited wants. We never remain content with things as they are for long, always looking for ways to improve on what is. After all, none of us need computers, indoor plumbing, or automobiles in order to survive; we could live just fine eating tree bark and living in holes in the ground, but who wants to do that? The basics necessary to survive are minimal, but what we want is to constantly improve our environment.

Even seemingly mundane articles we take for granted in our everyday lives have been subject to the drive for constant improvement. For example, years ago it was common for people to eat meat with knives only, a process that worked, but one that could be improved. Over hundreds of years the fork evolved in response to the desire for better eating utensils. Gradually, it went from one, to two, to three, to four tines, from a flat shape to a more effective curve, and somebody will probably come along and improve on the current standard, too.

Before there were paper clips, documents were held together with pins (and pins themselves were subject to a long evolution). Over time, experimentation was done with shapes and metals with the goal of coming up with a device that was strong enough to hold papers together, yet flexible enough to accommodate differing amounts of them.

The drive making the things better in the world we inhabit is never ending, so there need be no fear of opportunities for creation and innovation ever drying up.

Patents play a vital role in the process by granting exclusive rights to the creators of new advances. All of us have limited resources of time, energy, talent, and money, and we try to put these resources into the things that we believe will pay off best in the future, be it in terms of satisfaction, money, or anything else an individual holds dear. If we knew that our novel creations would be at risk for being taken away or copied, why bother developing them or making them available to others in the first place? Yes, it is nice to share, but sharing works a lot better when sharers have an opportunity to get something in return, even if it just be recognition for their accomplishment, which is a big part of the reason for the protections offered by intellectual property.

In the United States, from 1977 until today, approximately four of every five patents have gone to corporations. One in five have gone to the individual inventor. If it sounds like individuals are at a disadvantage, consider that many individuals with marketable patent ideas incorporate before filing them, in order to gain more clout in the forms of financing, expertise, and marketing. Also, if you think back to the Xerox example of 400 patents being granted for one new printing press, it makes sense that corporations would hold lots more patents simply because it takes a large organization to undertake such a daunting task.

What is truly remarkable about the patent process is how open it has always been, and remains, to creative individuals. The creativity that allows individuals, or small groups of them, to thrive independently is also found in large corporations where patenting is a vital part of their operations. In 2000, IBM was the leader in patents, as it often is, with 2,907, about 10 for each working day. Not only does IBM patent things they intend to develop themselves, but patent rights also enable them to license protected technology to others. IBM earned more than $1 billion in licensing fees alone in 2000, more than any other company.

It is the novelty and usefulness of your innovation that determines whether or not you get a patent, and the innovation's quality and your ability to follow through that determines its ultimate success or failure. Deep pockets, networks of connections, and pedigrees that would make a show dog blush might help, but it's what you can do that really counts. Between the technology available to individuals today, in the form of computers and the Internet, and with the increased appreciation of the entrepreneurial spirit behind innovation, the opportunities for individuals who wish to patent, and profit from, their innovations is greater than ever.

A case in point is patent number 6,229,430, an invention that analyzes data from the Internet in order to determine if an alarm clock should go off earlier or later than the time it's set for. Based on factors like weather and traffic, the time necessary to get to work is estimated and the wake-up buzzer is adjusted accordingly. The inventor, Mary

Smith Dewey, took a technology that had been around a long time, combined it with a much newer one, and was able to devise an innovation with the potential to appeal to busy people everywhere who would appreciate the chance to grab a little more sleep when conditions permitted. When else in our history have individuals had such wonderful opportunities to create and succeed?

The most prolific individual inventor and patent holder in our country was Thomas Edison, who amassed an incredible 1,093 patents, in diverse areas that ranged from telegraph technology to cement. When we talk of knowledge it is easy to get the mistaken impression that it consists of entirely new things, that everything an Edison patents is based on creating whole new objects that never existed before. In the case of patents, such is not the case. Ninety percent of patents are for inventions that represent an improvement on something that is already in existence, and I bet a big chunk of the remaining 10% are pretty closely linked to existing technology also.

Another great example of an individual patenting an innovation that was an improvement on what existed, then went on to experience terrific success in the marketplace, is found in Lonnie Johnson's Super Soaker. Mr. Johnson's patent was number 4,591,071 and was issued in 1986 (a copy of the application is reprinted in Figure 1.1). Squirt guns had been around for years, of course, but none were like this, a gun that shot out lots more water than others, and shot it a lot farther. Like many patented innovations, it looks like an obvious idea in retrospect. In fact, if you did not know his story, your natural assumption would be that the idea was good, and the market for it so clear, that Lonnie Johnson's Super Soaker must have been an instant hit. Not so. After getting his first patent, Mr. Johnson thought there would be plenty of contact "from people wanting my invention. And, of course, that didn't happen."

Worse yet, he learned that, in order to produce it himself, it would cost $200,000 to make the first 1,000. Though he did not have enough money to do that, he was finally able to license the design to a company that has since been taken over by Hasbro. He gets a percentage of the sales revenue, and, though he does not reveal what that percentage is, you can assume that, based on the approximately $500 million worth of Super Soakers sold so far, he has done pretty well for himself.

Remember the saying about how the world will beat a path to your door if you invent a better mouse trap? It is completely wrong. As the case of the Super Soaker shows us, the reality is that, in addition to inventing a better mouse trap, you are also going to have to beat a path to customers' doors, and those doors just might get slammed in your face if the potential customers are not interested in your invention, be it better or not.

At the recent International Exhibition of Inventions in Geneva,

United States Patent [19]

Johnson

[11] Patent Number: **4,591,071**

[45] Date of Patent: **May 27, 1986**

[54] SQUIRT GUN

[76] Inventor: Lonnie G. Johnson, 1463 E. Barkley Dr., Mobile, Ala. 36606

[21] Appl. No.: 541,896

[22] Filed: Oct. 14, 1983

[51] Int. Cl.⁴ B67D 5/32
[52] U.S. Cl. .... 222/39; 222/79; 222/401; 340/384 E; 340/406; 116/137 R
[58] Field of Search .... 340/384 E, 406; 116/137 R, 139; 222/39, 79, 323, 324, 401

[56]   References Cited

U.S. PATENT DOCUMENTS

1,333,704	3/1920	Brinks	340/406
2,249,608	7/1941	Greene	222/79
2,302,963	11/1942	Lefever	222/39
2,589,977	3/1952	Stelzer	222/79
3,202,318	8/1965	Black	222/39
4,086,589	4/1978	Cieslak et al.	340/384 E

4,214,674	7/1980	Jones et al.	222/401
4,239,129	12/1980	Esposito	222/79

Primary Examiner—H. Grant Skaggs
Attorney, Agent, or Firm—John A. Beehner

[57] ABSTRACT

A toy squirt gun which shoots a continuous high velocity stream of water. The squirt gun is configured as a structure facilitating partial filling with water leaving a void for compressed air. The squirt gun includes a nozzle for ejecting water at high velocity, a pressurization pump for compressing air into the gun to pressurize water contained therein, and a trigger actuated flow control valve for shooting the gun by controlling flow of pressurized water through the nozzle. A battery-powered oscillator circuit and a water flow powered sound generator produce futuristic space ray gun sound effects when the gun is shooting.

9 Claims, 7 Drawing Figures

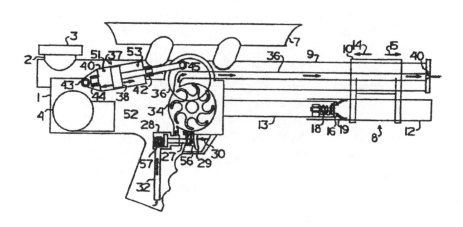

FIGURE 1.1   Super Soaker Patent

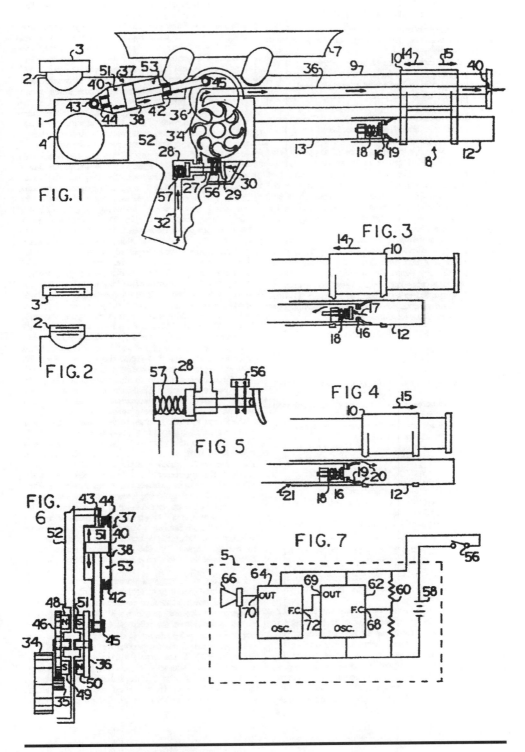

FIG. 1

FIG. 2

FIG. 3

FIG 4

FIG 5

FIG. 6

FIG. 7

FIGURE 1.1 *(Continued)*

1

2

SQUIRT GUN

BACKGROUND AND SUMMARY

The principle utilizing compressed gas as a means for pressurizing water to effect a continuous stream of high velocity waterflow from a nozzle is common practice. However, the embodiment of this principle in a hand-held toy squirt gun having a futuristic space ray gun appearance and including sound effects is novel.

Compressed air is provided by a manually actuated air pump physically mounted underneath the gun barrel. Sound is produced by a battery-powered electronic oscillator circuit. Sound is also produced by a flow actuated sound generator.

To shoot the gun, a trigger is actuated to open a flow control valve and thereby permit pressurized waterflow through a nozzle. The water exits the nozzle and thereby the squirt gun at high velocity. The flow actuated sound generator is functionally coupled in series with the flow control valve and the nozzle to facilitate actuation of the sound generator by flowing water when the gun is shooting.

The waterflow rotates an impeller which is mechanically linked to a vibration means consisting of a piston in a cylinder to effect back and forth motion of the piston and thereby pump air alternatingly through a pair of vibrating reed-type horns to produce sound.

A switch coupled to the trigger is actuated simultaneously with opening of the control valve to switch on the oscillator circuit to produce sound.

BRIEF DESCRIPTION OF THE DRAWINGS

FIG. 1 is a functional diagram of an embodiment of the invention showing actuation of the trigger to shoot the gun.

FIG. 2 shows the resealable cap of the water fill port removed.

FIG. 3 shows actuation of the pressurization pump in the compressive stroke.

FIG. 4 shows actuation of the pressurization pump to resupply air into the pump cylinder.

FIG. 5 shows the trigger actuated flow control valve in a closed state with the control switch for the oscillator circuit in the off position.

FIG. 6 shows additional details of the flow actuated sound generator. The drawing depicts magnetic coupling of motion of an impeller driven gear inside the gun to a flywheel on the outside.

FIG. 7 is a simplified diagram of a battery-powered oscillator circuit.

DETAILED DESCRIPTION AND PREFERRED EMBODIMENT

An in-depth understanding of the present invention can be derived from the following description with reference to the drawings.

FIG. 1 is a configuration drawing showing the major features of the squirt gun. Squirt gun structure means 1 is designed to contain water and air under high internal pressure. Structure means 1 also provides mounting support for various elements of the gun. A water fill port means comprised of port 2 and screw on cap 3 function as a resealable port for opening structure means 1 to put water in the gun and resealing so as to not permit leaks when the gun is operating under high

internal pressure. Screw on cap 3 is shown removed in FIG. 2.

Air reservoir means 7 is designed as a rifle scope means to enhance appearance. It is an integral part of structure 1 and functions to prevent the gun from being completely filled with water. When the gun is held upright with the fill port open, reservoir 7 is above the maximum water level determined by the position of fill port 2 and contains air to insure there is always a volume inside the gun into which air can be compressed.

A manually operated pressurization pump means comprised of pressurization piston means 13, check valve means 16, seal 19, spring 18 and a movable member means comprised of grip 10 and pressurization cylinder means 12 functions to compress air into structure means 1 and thereby air reservoir 7. Grip means 10 provides hand-held support for the gun and is movably coupled by concentric cylinder mounting to gun barrel means 9 to permit sliding along the length of the barrel. Gun barrel 9 and piston 13 are integral parts of structure means 1 and provide additional internal volume for containing air and water. Air pump cylinder 12 forms the bottom portion of grip 10. Compressed air is pumped into structure means 1 by moving grip 10 and cylinder 12 back and forth along the barrel in a pump shotgun type action as depicted by arrows 14 and 15. The compressive stroke is in the direction of arrow 14 as shown in FIG. 3. As cylinder 12 is moved further onto piston 13, pressure inside cylinder 12 increases and opens check valve 16. The compressed air flows into structure means 1 as illustrated by arrow 17. Check valve 16 is normally held closed by spring 18. The refill stroke of cylinder 12 is shown in FIG. 4. As cylinder 12 is moved in the direction of arrow 15, piston 13 is withdrawn from cylinder 12 and ambient air is sucked into cylinder 12 past seal 19 as depicted by arrows 20 and 21. The gun is pressurized by repeating this cycle with back and forth motion of grip 10 along barrel 9. The maximum pressure reached inside the water gun is determined by the ratio of the maximum volume to minimum volume created inside pump cylinder 12.

As shown in FIG. 1, to shoot the water gun, control valve means 28 is opened by pressing trigger means 29 in the direction of arrow 30. Control valve means 28 is coupled to structure means 1 and includes movable shaft means 27 which extends external to structure means 1. Trigger means 29 is attached to shaft means 27. With valve 28 open, pressurized water flows into conduit means 32 and up through valve 28 from the bottom of the gun as the compressed air in the top part of the gun and in reservoir 7 expands. Pressurized water flow exiting valve 28 impinges impeller means 34 causing impeller 34 to rotate as pressurized water flows through to conduit means 36. The pressurized water flows through conduit 36 to nozzle means 40 and exits the gun at high velocity.

Futuristic space ray gun sounds are produced by a flow actuated sound generator means. The flow actuated sound generator means includes impeller 34, which is configured operably in series with valve 28 and nozzle 40 as described. Impeller 34 functions as a flow responsive means for extracting operating power for the sound generator from the pressurized water flow. Referring to FIG. 6, the flow actuated sound generator further includes vibration means 37, and a coupling means comprised of a first rotatable structure means represented by gear 46, a second rotatable structure means represented by flywheel 36, first magnetic means

---

FIGURE 1.1 *(Continued)*

3

48 and 49, and second magnetic means 50 and 51. Pinion 35 is attached to impeller 34, and mounted such that it meshes with gear 46 to mate impeller 34 to gear 46. Magnets 48 and 49 are fixed to gear 46, and magnets 50 and 51 are fixed to flywheel 36. Magnets 48, 49, 50 and 51 are mounted such that the mutual attraction of opposite poles maintain a fixed relative orientation of flywheel 36 to gear 46 so that rotation of gear 46 causes rotation of flywheel 36. The magnetic coupling allows relatively low torques produced by impeller 34 to be efficiently coupled to flywheel 36 without friction losses associated with a pressure seal around a shaft. There is no hole through wall 52 which could cause loss of pressure. Wall 52 functions as a baffle means which prevents leakage through impeller 34. Vibration means 37 is comprised of a horn pump means which is represented by horn cylinder means 40 and horn piston means 38, and a horn vibrator means represented by a reed means which includes first reed vibrator means 42 and second reed vibrator means 44. Cylinder 40 is attached to wall 52 at pivot joint 43. Piston 38 is mounted inside cylinder 40 and mated to flywheel 36 at pivot joint 45. As flywheel 36 rotates when the gun is shooting, it moves piston 38 back and forth inside cylinder 40 causing air to be alternatingly pumped in and out of cavities 51 and 53 past reed vibrators 44 and 42, respectively. When piston 38 is moving in a direction forcing air out of cavity 53, air passes out past reed 42 causing reed 42 to vibrate creating a high pitch sound. Air is simultaneously sucked into cavity 51 past reed 44. With continued rotation of flywheel 36, motion of piston 38 is reversed forcing air out of cavity 51 past reed 44 and thereby producing a high pitch sound. Air is simultaneously sucked into cavity 53 past reed 42. The cycle is repeated continuously producing pulsating high frequency sound to create futuristic effects when the gun is shooting. Vibration means 37 is isolated from the pressurized water within structure 1 to allow efficient coupling of the sound vibrations it produces to the ambient air surrounding the gun.

Additional sound is produced by an electronic sound generator means represented by battery-powered oscillator circuit means 5 shown in FIG. 7. Circuit means 5 is housed in compartment 4 which is attached to structure means 1 as shown in FIG. 1. When trigger 29 is moved in the direction of arrow 30 to shoot the gun, switch means 56 is closed simultaneously and oscillator circuit 5 is switched on. As shown in FIG. 5, when trigger 29 is released, spring 57 closes valve 28 and allows switch 56 to open.

Referring to FIG. 7, battery-powered oscillator circuit means 5 is comprised of an electrical power source means represented by battery 58, and an electronic oscillator means represented by series resistor voltage divider 60, first oscillator means 62, second oscillator means 64, and a sound transducer means represented by speaker 66. The on-off state of circuit 5 is controlled by switch 56. When switch 56 is closed, operating power from battery 58 is coupled to oscillators 62 and 64 and voltage divider 60. Voltage divider 60 supplies a fixed voltage to frequency control voltage input means 68 of oscillator 62. Oscillator 62 operates at a significantly lower frequency than oscillator 64. The varying voltage at output 69 of oscillator 62 is coupled to frequency control voltage input means 72 of high frequency oscillator 64. The voltage at output 70 of oscillator 64 drives speaker 66. The high frequency at output 70 of oscillator 64 varies with the control voltage at input 72 and

4

drives speaker 66 to produce varying high frequency sound to create futuristic space ray gun effects.

What is claimed is:

1. A toy squirt gun for shooting a continuous stream of water, comprising:

(a) a structure means for containing water and air under high internal pressure, said structure means being configured to facilitate partially filling with water leaving an internal volume for compressed air, a water fill port means, a pressurization pump means, a trigger means, a flow control valve means, a battery-powered oscillator circuit means, a flow actuated sound generator means and a nozzle means;

(b) said fill port means being attached to said structure means and including a removable cap corresponding to an aperture in said structure means, whereby said fill port means provides access for partially filling said squirt gun with water, the cap being resealable so as to not permit leakage when said squirt gun is operating under high internal pressure;

(c) said pressurization pump means being operably coupled to said structure means, providing hand-held support for said squirt gun and operating to compress air into said structure means, said pressurization pump means including a movable member means for facilitating manual actuation thereof;

(d) said nozzle means being coupled to said structure means, said flow control valve means being fluidly coupled via a passageway within said structure means to said nozzle means, said control valve controlling flow of pressurized water to said nozzle means; to shoot said squirt gun said trigger means being manually actuated to open said control valve means and thereby permit pressurized water flow through said nozzle means, said water flow exiting said nozzle means and thereby said squirt gun at high velocity;

(e) said flow actuated sound generator means including a rotatable impeller means mounted integral and within said structure means and interposed between said control valve means and nozzle means and adapted to rotate when flowing water moves from said control valve means to said nozzle means, and also including vibration means mounted externally on said structure means and operably coupled to said impeller means for activation upon rotation of said impeller means; wherein said vibration means comprises a horn cylinder means, a horn piston means, a first reed vibrator means and a second reed vibrator means, said first and second reed vibrator means being attached to said cylinder means, said piston means being positioned inside said cylinder means, rotation of said impeller means causing said horn piston means to cycle back and forth inside said horn cylinder means and thereby alternatingly force air through said first and second vibrator means causing said first and second vibrator means to vibrate and produce pulsating sounds; and

(f) said battery operated oscillator circuit means being attached to said structure means and including a switch means for controlling on and off states of said circuit means, said switch means being coupled to said trigger means to simultaneously switch said circuit means to an on state when said trigger means is actuated to shoot said squirt gun, said

---

FIGURE 1.1 *(Continued)*

circuit means operating to produce pulsating sounds when switched to an on state.

2. A toy squirt gun for shooting a high velocity stream of water as disclosed in claim 1 wherein said structure means further includes a rifle scope means mounted parallel to said barrel means to enhance the appearance of said squirt gun.

3. A toy squirt gun for shooting a high velocity stream of water as disclosed in claim 1 wherein said air reservoir means comprises a rifle scope configuration mounted parallel to said barrel means.

4. A toy squirt gun for shooting a high velocity stream of water as disclosed in claim 1 wherein said pressurization pump means is mounted underneath said barrel means.

5. A toy squirt gun for shooting a continuous stream of water, comprising:

(a) a structure means for containing water and air under high internal pressure, said structure means being configured to facilitate partially filling with water leaving an internal volume for compressed air, a water fill port means, a pressurization pump means, a trigger means, a flow control valve means, a battery-powered oscillator circuit means, a flow actuated sound generator means and a nozzle means;

(b) said fill port means being attached to said structure means and including a removable cap corresponding to an aperture in said structure means, whereby said fill port means provides access for partially filling said squirt gun with water, the cap being resealable so as to not permit leakage when said squirt gun is operating under high internal pressure;

(c) said pressurization pump means being operably coupled to said structure means, providing hand-held support for said squirt gun and operating to compress air into said structure means, said pressurization pump means including a movable member means for facilitating manual actuation thereof;

(d) said nozzle means being coupled to said structure means, said flow control valve means being fluidly coupled via a passageway within said structure means to said nozzle means, said control valve controlling flow of pressurized water to said nozzle means; to shoot said squirt gun said trigger means being manually actuated to open said control valve means and thereby permit pressurized water flow through said nozzle means, said water flow exiting said nozzle means and thereby said squirt gun at high velocity;

(e) said flow actuated sound generator means including a rotatable impeller means mounted integral and within said structure means and interposed between said control valve means and nozzle means and adapted to rotate when flowing water moves from said control valve means to said nozzle means, and also including vibration means mounted externally on said structure means and operably magnetically coupled to said impeller means for activation upon rotation of said impeller means;

(f) said battery operated oscillator circuit means being attached to said structure means and including a switch means for controlling on and off states of said circuit means, said switch means being coupled to said trigger means to simultaneously switch said circuit means to an on state when said trigger means is actuated to shoot said squirt gun, said

circuit means operating to produce pulsating sounds when switched to an on state.

6. A toy squirt gun for shooting a continuous stream of water at high velocity, said squirt gun comprising:

(a) a structure means for containing water and air under pressure, a pressurization pump means configured to facilitate manual actuation thereof for compressing air into said structure means, a trigger means and a flow control valve means for facilitating manual control of shooting of said gun, a fill port means for providing access for partially filling said structure means with water, a nozzle means for increasing the velocity of said water flow stream as said stream is ejected from said gun when said gun is shooting;

(b) said structure means being configured as a gun in appearance and including a barrel means and an air reservoir means as integral parts thereof; said air reservoir means functioning to prevent said gun from being completely filled with water to insure there is always a volume inside said structure means into which air can be compressed;

(c) said pressurization pump means including a movable member means for facilitating manual actuation thereof and check valve means for permitting one-way flow of compressed air into said structure means, said movable member means being movably coupled to said structure means along said barrel means and being manually actuatable in a back and forth motion to effect pumping of air into said structure means, and said check valve means being fluidly interposed between said movable member means and said structure means and adapted to permit air flow into said structure means and to restrain air and water flow out of said structure means;

(d) said pressurization pump means further comprising a pressurization cylinder means attached to said movable member means, and a pressurization piston means attached to said container, both oriented parallel and adjacent said barrel means, said pressurization piston means being configured to extend into said pressurization cylinder means such that back and forth movement of said movable member means along said barrel means moves said piston means in and out of said cylinder means to effect pumping of air into said structure means;

(e) wherein said pressurization piston means comprises an integral part of said structure means and is hollow so as to provide additional volume for containment of pressurized air and water; and wherein said check valve means is operably mounted to said pressurization piston means and functions to facilitate one way flow of compressed air into said structure means from said pressurization cylinder means;

(f) said fill port means being attached to said structure means and including a removable cap corresponding to an aperture in said structure means, whereby said fill port means provides access for partially filling said squirt gun with water, the cap being resealable so as to not permit leakage when said squirt gun is operating under high internal pressure; and

(g) said control valve means being fluidly coupled via a passageway within said structure means to said nozzle means, said control valve controlling flow of pressurized water to said nozzle means.

FIGURE 1.1 *(Continued)*

7

7. A toy squirt gun comprising:

(a) a gun shaped container for holding water and air under pressure, including a barrel portion with a nozzle in its free end, and a passageway within said barrel communicating between said nozzle and the contents of said container;

(b) said container including an access port for filling said container with water;

(c) a removable cap for sealing said access port;

(d) said container including an air reservoir portion which extends upward beyond the height of said access port, said air reservoir being located such that air will be trapped therein when said container is filled with water;

(e) means operably coupled to said container for manually pressurizing the contents of said container;

(f) a control valve operably mounted within said passageway for opening and closing said passageway, including a shaft connected to said valve which projects externally of said container;

(g) a trigger operably connected to said container and the externally projecting portion of said control valve shaft and adapted to open said control valve upon manual activation thereof;

(h) an impeller rotatably mounted within said passageway between said control valve and nozzle, said impeller adapted to rotate upon the movement of fluid within said passageway;

(i) a mechanical sound generator mounted to said container and magnetically connected to said impeller, said sound generator producing a sound in response to rotation of said impeller; and

(j) an electronic sound generator mounted to said container and electrically connected to said trigger for activation upon pulling of said trigger.

8. A toy squirt gun comprising:

(a) a gun shaped container for holding water and air under pressure, including a barrel portion with a nozzle in its free end, and a passageway within said barrel communicating between said nozzle and the contents of said container;

(b) said container including an access port for filling said container with water;

(c) a removable cap for sealing said access port;

8

(d) said container including an air reservoir portion which extends upward beyond the height of said access port, said air reservoir being located such that air will be trapped therein when said container is filled with water;

(e) means operably coupled to said container for manually pressurizing the contents of said container, including:

a hollow piston portion mounted on said container and projecting therefrom, the hollow portion thereof communicating with contents of said container;

a check valve operably mounted in the free end of said piston for retaining air in said piston injected through said valve;

a hollow pressurization cylinder with one closed end, fitted on said piston like a sleeve for axial slidable movement, the inside diameter of said cylinder being slightly greater than the outside diameter of said piston to allow the entrance of air within said cylinder upon axial movement of said cylinder away from said container; and

flexible seal means mounted on the end of said piston between the walls of said piston and cylinder and adapted to allow one way movement of air into said cylinder when said cylinder is moved axially away from said container;

(f) a control valve operably mounted within said passageway for opening and closing said passageway, including a shaft connected to said valve which projects externally of said container; and

(g) a trigger operably connected to said container and the externally projecting portion of said control valve shaft and adapted to open said control valve upon manual activation thereof.

9. The squirt gun of claim 8, further comprising:

an impeller rotatably mounted within said passageway between said control valve and nozzle, said impeller adapted to rotate upon the movement of fluid within said passageway; and

a mechanical sound generator mounted to said container and magnetically connected to said impeller, said sound generator producing a sound in response to to rotation of said impeller.

* * * * *

FIGURE 1.1 *(Continued)*

visitors may actually have been treated to a better mouse trap, named "The Rat Pack," though, again, the trap had to make a path to them. The idea of its inventor, Michael Lynch, was to create a less messy, more humane way to get rid of rodents. The trap works simply: A curious rat walks into a cardboard tube, then bites into a sack of thick fluid that will suffocate it where it stands. Then the homeowner simply buries the rat-filled, biodegradable tube, without having to deal with a messy body or guilt at visible signs of a nasty extinction. The trap recently went into production, with an estimated selling price of $1.15 each. Though how the trap will ultimately fare on the market is unknown, at this point its potential appears similar to that of the Super Soaker; a good idea that works, is reasonably priced, and has a well-thought-out appeal to consumers.

Not all patented inventions begin their lives with such good prospects. For example, patent number 4,605,000, shown in Figure 1.2, is for a Greenhouse Helmet. The intent of this device is to allow the wearer to breathe in oxygen given off by plants. The invention functions by having an individual's head placed in a clear, sealed enclosure, which looks like a space helmet, that is also occupied by a number of small plants. These plants produce fresh oxygen that is available to the wearer. The assumption is, I assume, that the benefits of consuming superior air outweigh the costs of the device, which include having to tolerate the reactions of other people, along with the price tag. For all I know, the Greenhouse Helmet may work just great, but I do not think there was ever much of a market for it.

The prospects of other innovations are harder to predict. At the same exhibition that featured The Rat Pack, there was this intriguing invention: a pair of glasses equipped with a motion-detecting chip that gives off an alarm if the eyes of the wearer close for more than three seconds. Sounds like a great idea for keeping people from nodding off at the wheel, but how will it sell?

Same for the new sneaker fitted with a pump to flush out the bad air and keep one's feet dry. Nice idea, but predicting how it will be received by consumers is nearly impossible. Having a surefire idea is not among the requirements for getting a patent.

Because it is so difficult to predict the future value of an innovation, individuals and companies often seek patents to protect things they think could be important. Even if they have no clear, or efficient, use at present, gambling that they never will can be a steep chance to take. As we see in Chapter 2, timing a new good or service with the evolution of the market it is intended for is crucial. Today's obscure idea might be all the rage tomorrow. Besides, even if you do not have a practical use for a particular innovation, somebody else just might, and they also just might be willing to pay to license it from you someday.

United States Patent [19]

Anguita

[11] Patent Number: 4,605,000

[45] Date of Patent: Aug. 12, 1986

[54] **GREENHOUSE HELMET**

[76] Inventor: **Waldemar Anguita,** 83 N. Henry St., Apt. 1-L, Brooklyn, N.Y. 11222

[21] Appl. No.: **688,821**

[22] Filed: **Jan. 4, 1985**

[51] Int. Cl.⁴ A62B 7/00
[52] U.S. Cl. **128/201.25**; 2/424; 2/205; 2/171.2; D29/9; D2/322; 446/27
[58] Field of Search 2/209.1, 410, 424, 205, 2/171.2; 128/201.23, 201.22, 201.25, 201.19, 201.26, 201.29; D29/9; D2/322, 323; 446/27

[56] **References Cited**

U.S. PATENT DOCUMENTS

737,373 8/1903 Eagle et al. 128/201.23

2,888,011 5/1959 Penrod et al. 128/201.23

FOREIGN PATENT DOCUMENTS

348733 5/1937 Italy 128/201.25
42409 1/1908 Switzerland 128/201.19
442224 2/1936 United Kingdom 128/201.19

Primary Examiner—Henry J. Recla
Attorney, Agent, or Firm—Richard L. Miller

[57] **ABSTRACT**

A greenhouse helmet is provided and consists of a dome containing plants secured within the dome worn completely over the head of a person so that the person can breathe in the oxygen given off by the plants.

6 Claims, 3 Drawing Figures

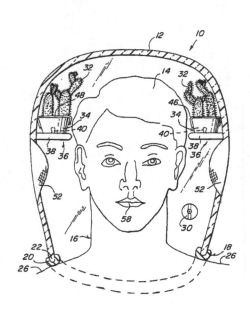

FIGURE 1.2 Greenhouse Helmet Patent

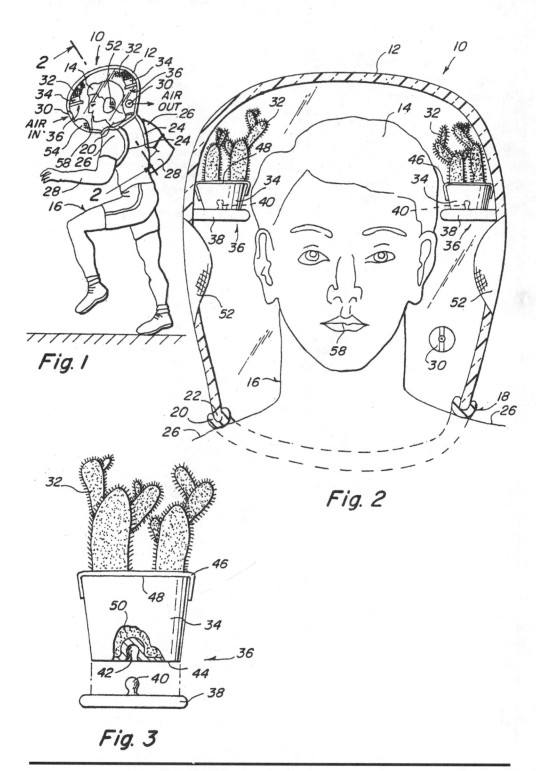

Fig. 1

Fig. 2

Fig. 3

FIGURE 1.2   (Continued)

GREENHOUSE HELMET

BACKGROUND OF THE INVENTION

The instant invention relates generally to enclosure devices and more specifically it relates to a greenhouse helmet that incorporates small plants into a sealed helmet to be worn over the head of a person.

Numerous enclosure devices have been provided in prior art. For example U.S. Pat. Nos. 3,903,642 and 3,995,396 are terrariums adapted to just hold plants and not designed to be worn over the head of a person, while U.S. Pat. No. 4,331,141 contains a variety of devices for protection of organs of respiration that are worn to cover the nose and mouth of a person but are not designed to contain plants within.

SUMMARY OF THE INVENTION

A principle object of the present invention is to provide a greenhouse helmet designed to contain plants secured within and the helmet worn completely over the head of a person so that the person can breathe in the oxygen given off by the plants.

Another object is to provide a greenhouse helmet that has air filters so that ambient air containing carbon dioxide will be filtered therethrough and mixed with the carbon dioxide breathed out by the person to be used by the plants.

An additional object is to provide a greenhouse helmet that will contain hearing and speaking devices so that the person can hear within and speak out through the helmet.

A further object is to provide a greenhouse helmet that is economical in cost to manufacture.

A still further object is to provide a greenhouse helmet that is simple and easy to use.

Further objects of the invention will appear as the description proceeds.

To the accomplishment of the above and related objects, this invention may be embodied in the form illustrated in the accompanying drawings, attention being called to the fact, however, that the drawings are illustrative only and that changes may be made in the specific construction illustrated and described within the scope of the appended claims.

BRIEF DESCRIPTION OF THE DRAWING FIGURES

The figures in the drawings are briefly described as follows:

FIG. 1 is a side view of the invention in use on a person.

FIG. 2 is an enlarged cross sectional view taken along line 2—2 in FIG. 1.

FIG. 3 is still further enlarged partially exploded front view with parts broken away of one of the shelves and potted plants.

DETAILED DESCRIPTION OF THE PREFERRED EMBODIMENTS

Turning now descriptively to the drawings, in which similar reference characters denote similar elements throughout the several views, FIGS. 1 through 3 illustrates a greenhouse helmet 10 that has a transparent dome 12 worn completely over a head 14 of a person 16. The dome 12 is fabricated from anti-fog material so that the person 16 can see therethrough.

A device 18 for securing the dome 12 to the person 16 has insulation 20 formed around lip 22 of the dome to seal the dome around the head 14 of the person. A pair of straps 24, 24 are affixed to the lip 22 of the dome extending around shoulders 26, 26 and arms 28, 28 of the person 16.

A pair of air filters 30, 30 are for adequately filtering ambient air that has carbon dioxide in and out of the dome 12. One filter 30 is mounted within front of the dome allowing the ambient air in and the other filter 30 is mounted within rear of the dome allowing the air breathed by the person 16 out.

Plants 32, each within a pot 34 are placed within the dome 12. The carbon dioxide of the ambient air will mix with carbon dioxide breathed out by the person 16 to be used by the plants 32 to produce oxygen to be breathed in by the person 16.

A device 36 as best shown in FIG. 3 is for securing the plant 32 and pot 34 with the dome 12. The device 36 is a shelf 38 that has a snap-on male member 40 affixed to top thereon. The shelf 38 is transversely affixed within the dome. The pot 34 has a female socket 42 formed within bottom 44 thereof so that the female socket 42 can snap on the male member 40. A cloth 46 covers top 48 of the pot 34 allowing the plant 32 to extend upwards therefrom while keeping dirt 50 within the pot 34.

A pair of hearing devices 52, 52 and an audio device 54 are also provided. Each hearing device 52 is mounted to a side of the dome 12 adjacent an ear 56 of the person 16 so that the person can hear within the dome.

The audio device 54 is mounted to front of the dome 12 adjacent mouth 58 of the person 16 so that the person can speak out through the dome.

While certain novel features of this invention have been shown and described and are pointed out in the annexed claims, it will be understood that various omissions, substitutions and changes in the forms and details of the device illustrated and in its operation can be made by those skilled in the art without departing from the spirit of the invention.

What is claimed is:

1. A greenhouse helmet which comprises:
   (a) a transparent dome worn completely over the head of a person;
   (b) means for securing said dome to said person;
   (c) means for adequately filtering ambient air having carbon dioxide in and out of said dome to meet the needs of the person;
   (d) means for resting at least one plant within a pot placed in said dome so that carbon dioxide of said ambient air will mix with carbon dioxide breathed out by said person to be used by said plant to produce oxygen to be breathed in by said person in addition to the ambient air; and
   (e) means for securing said plant and pot upon said resting means within said dome.

2. A greenhouse helmet as recited in claim 1, wherein said dome is fabricated from anti-fog material so that said person can see therethrough.

3. A greenhouse helmet as recited in claim 2 wherein said means for securing said dome to said person includes:
   (a) insulation formed around lip of said dome to seal dome around said head of person; and

FIGURE 1.2 *(Continued)*

4,605,000

3

(b) a pair of straps affixed to said lip of said dome extending around shoulders and arms of said person.

4. A greenhouse helmet as recited in claim 3 wherein said filtering means includes a pair of air filters, one said filter mounted within front of said dome allowing said ambient air in and other said filter mounted within rear of said dome allowing said air breathed by said person out.

5. A greenhouse helmet as recited in claim 4 wherein said means for securing said plant includes:

(a) a shelf having a snap-on male member affixed to top thereon, said shelf transversely affixed within said dome;

4

(b) said pot having a female socket formed within bottom thereof so that said female socket can snap on said male member; and

(c) a cloth to cover top of said pot allowing said plant to extend upwards therefrom while keeping dirt within said pot.

6. A greenhouse helmet as recited in claim 5 further comprising:

(a) a pair of hearing devices each said hearing device mounted to a side of said dome adjacent an ear of said person so that said person can hear within said dome; and

(b) an audio device mounted to front of said dome adjacent mouth of said person so that said person can speak out through said dome.

* * * * *

FIGURE 1.2 *(Continued)*

INNOVATIONS AND ENTREPRENEURS

2

The man with a new idea is a crank—until the idea succeeds.
—Mark Twain

Never look for your work in one place and your progress in another.
—Epictetus

The processes of innovation and entrepreneurship are often used as interchangeable terms, but they are not the same thing. An innovator, or group of innovators, can do most of their work in isolation; an entrepreneur needs to find the right congregation and give them a good preaching. The successful innovator is the person who figures out how to make a better mousetrap. The successful entrepreneur puts it together in an attractive package, carts it off to market, and earns profits by presenting and selling it at the right price to consumers who have been convinced of their need for that new mousetrap.

An innovation will get you a patent, which provides a 20-year No Trespassing sign to protect your creation with. But, because it is a rare patent whose very existence will cause consumers to blaze a trail to your door and pound on it until you agree to sell, that innovation will remain dormant until the magic of entrepreneurship is applied to it.

Though no patent is possible without innovation, entrepreneurial skills are crucial to bringing the process to a successful conclusion. For even if your focus is purely on innovation, with no intention of your ever doing more with your original creation than selling it to somebody who will take it the rest of the way, you still have to find that person to buy it, and you still need to convince them that your innovation is worth pursuing.

The recent surge of Internet companies who have failed is a good example of what happens when innovation progresses without the right dose of entrepreneurship to go with it. Lots of companies came on the scene whose technological prowess allowed them to create a bounty of great services and sites. Problem was, few of them had any realistic notion of how to make money doing it, or even produce the cash flows necessary to survive more than a year or two.

At the same time, if your intent is to focus on the entrepreneurial side and leave it to others to get their hands dirty, you better have the ability to appreciate the true value of novel innovations, for, without this talent for recognizing potential, none of the other tools in the entrepreneurial skill set will do you much good.

Peter Drucker, who wrote what I believe to be the best book available on the subject, *Innovation and Entrepreneurship* (Harper & Row, 1985), makes the relationship clear, saying, "Innovation is the specific instrument of entrepreneurship. It is the act that endows resources with a new capacity to create wealth. Innovation, indeed, creates a resource." It is this new resource, a change from what went before it, that can be patented. Then comes the time for the application of entrepreneurial skills. In Drucker's words again, "Entrepreneurs see change as the norm and as healthy. Usually, they do not bring about the change themselves, but—and this defines entrepreneurs and entrepreneurship—the entrepreneur always searches for change, responds to it, and exploits it as an opportunity."

Innovation and entrepreneurship should be considered as different stages of the same journey, a trip that starts with an idea and ends with a product (patented, for our purposes) that improves the lives of everybody involved. This chapter looks at both legs of the journey. Some people are equally adept at both, others at one and not the other. For anybody embarking on the journey, it is vital that they know where their strengths lie, and recognize the need to find others who can help them carry the load when they need another shoulder.

John Jordan, of Cap Gemini Ernst & Young's Center for Business Innovation, says that "Innovation is the pirate ship sailing into the yacht club." True, and an entrepreneur is at the helm.

INNOVATION: THE PRACTICE OF IMPROVEMENT

Innovation occurs when technology (applied knowledge, or know-how) is used to create a new or improved product or process. Innovation can come with the application of new genetic discoveries to the treatment of disease or the application of information technology to existing methods of doing business that can be made over into novel, Internet-based applications. An innovation can be as basic as figuring out how to make a cheap pen that still writes when held upside down, or simply finding a way to make an existing product with cheaper material or to produce it more efficiently.

Enterprises based on innovation not only do new things, they also earn greater returns than those based on existing goods and services. As pointed out by *The Economist* in a 1999 survey of innovation, a study of 17 successful innovations made in the 1970s showed them to have an average annual return of 56%, compared with a 16% average annual return for all U.S. business in the past 30 years. It is no surprise, then, that innovation receives so much attention.

Innovations are based on changes in the world around us, and represent additional changes themselves. Peter Drucker identified seven sources of opportunity that result from change. The first four occur within organizations and industries, and I think they can be applied to individuals, too; the remaining three originate in the outside world.

1. The unexpected success, failure, or outside event.
2. The incongruity between what reality was thought to be and what it actually is.
3. The need for better processes.
4. Changes in an industry or market that catch people by surprise.
5. Changes in the population.
6. Changes in perception, mood, and meaning.
7. Any form of new knowledge.

In each of the seven, the key is that something new is going on that alert innovators have the chance to respond to. As will be seen in the examples that follow, the vast majority of successful innovations are the simple ones that look obvious in retrospect, the ones we look at and say "I could have come up with that!" Remember the statistic from Chapter 1: 90% of patents are for improvements on things that already exist. The innovations that go on to be successful are the ones that match changing conditions so well that we gaze back and view them as a natural outgrowth of what went before. At the time, however, their rightness was too new to be widely perceived.

For an example, let's go back to Lonnie Johnson's Super Soaker. These supercharged squirt guns had an immediate appeal when they hit the market, and what could have been more obvious? Here was a squirt gun that shot out lots more water, lots farther, than any other that came before it. Kids loved the Super Soaker, as did the adults who bought them. Yet there was nothing about the Super Soaker's technology that had kept it from being invented years before. Take a look back at the patent for it that is reproduced in Figure 1.1. A fairly simple idea, so why was the timing right for the innovation when it hit the market? Maybe because it appealed to the children of baby boomers, a growing population of kids with parents willing to spend money on cool, new toys?

Again, the Super Soaker looks like an innovation that had great prospects for success from the get-go but do not forget, as we saw in Chapter 1, that the reality was not so easy. Now look at another patent, (Figure 2.1), and see if you can evaluate its chances for success without the advantage of hindsight. The patent for this is fairly recent, and if any are on the market as of this writing, I am not aware of them.

The innovation is a motorized infant stroller. We have all seen, or maybe ourselves have been, people struggling to push a baby stroller in a mall while, at the same time, carrying bags, boxes, or other children. A stroller that can move on its own power seems like a great idea. So why weren't these zipping around mall corridors years ago? Why is the timing right now? Maybe there are good reasons why motorized strollers have not become popular yet, or maybe it is simply that nobody has done it in a way that appeals to parents who are the prospective buyers. Who can say if this stroller will be a hit or miss in the marketplace?

Just because an innovation appears obvious yet has not been implemented before, does not mean there is any problem with it. In the mid-eighties the first minivan was introduced by Chrysler, a vehicle that was a cross between a station wagon and a full-sized van. Once minivans became available, they were an immediate hit. There is no reason the minivan could not have been developed years earlier, which illustrates the point that great opportunities are not snatched up the minute they become possible.

As another illustration, think of a potato peeler, a basic gizmo that there is not room to do anything with, right? By the early 1990s potato peelers had been around for many years and most of us, if we thought about them at all, would assume that their days as objects of innovation were long past. Not so. Sam Farber, whose wife had arthritis and struggled with conventional utensils, decided to make one that was easier to manipulate for people with the same, or similar, physical limitations. He did it simply by making a fatter handle that was easier to hold and use. From there, he went on to create a line of kitchenware that applied the same principles to a range of different devices. How many years was that opportunity there before he did something about it?

An even simpler example is Dan Mahler's lug nut remover, which uses a simple lever to make removing a lug nut easy, rather than the horrible chore it had been for countless people in the past. Millions of us have struggled with them, but why did it take so long for Mahler's innovation to come about?

Part of the explanation comes in Dan's occupation as the owner of

United States Patent [19]

Mackert, Sr.

[11] **Patent Number:** **6,148,942**

[45] **Date of Patent:** **Nov. 21, 2000**

[54] **INFANT STROLLER SAFELY PROPELLED BY A DC ELECTRIC MOTOR HAVING CONTROLLED ACCELERATION AND DECELERATION**

[76] Inventor: **James M. Mackert, Sr.**, 870 Hartford Dr., Elyria, Ohio 44035

[21] Appl. No.: **09/177,072**

[22] Filed: **Oct. 22, 1998**

[51] Int. Cl.[7] **B62B 9/08**; **B60K 1/00**

[52] U.S. Cl. .... **180/65.6**; 180/65.8; 188/69; 192/15; 192/17 R

[58] Field of Search .... 180/65.6, 65.1, 180/65.5, 315, 343, 907, 188, 65.8; 280/47.38, 642, 654, 647, 650; 192/16, 17 R, 19, 219, 220, 15; 188/20, 31, 69

[56] **References Cited**

U.S. PATENT DOCUMENTS

555,949	9/1896	Stallard et al.	.... 180/907 X
675,392	6/1901	Keating .	
1,172,456	3/1916	Hoadley .	
1,747,560	2/1930	Weathers .	
2,004,470	8/1935	Michal .	
2,728,431	2/1955	Keck	.... 192/17 R X
2,742,973	4/1956	Johannesen	.... 180/65
3,077,794	2/1963	Candellero	.... 192/17
3,506,100	4/1970	Tomozawa	.... 192/19
3,754,616	8/1973	Watland .	
3,907,051	9/1975	Weant et al. .	
3,908,776	9/1975	Dudley	.... 180/65
3,955,639	5/1976	Cragg	.... 180/65 X
4,050,533	9/1977	Seamone	.... 180/6.5
4,199,036	4/1980	Wereb	.... 180/6.5
4,209,073	6/1980	Enix .	
4,407,393	10/1983	Youdin et al. .	
4,412,688	11/1983	Giordani .	
4,416,107	11/1983	Hoff	.... 192/17 R X
4,483,405	11/1984	Noda et al.	.... 180/907 X
4,629,044	12/1986	Post et al.	.... 192/17 R X
4,759,418	7/1988	Goldenfeld et al.	.... 180/65.1
4,807,716	2/1989	Hawkins	.... 180/65.1
4,823,900	4/1989	Farnam	.... 180/907 X
5,156,226	10/1992	Boyer et al. .	
5,199,520	4/1993	Chen	.... 180/65.5
5,253,724	10/1993	Prior	.... 180/907 X
5,280,935	1/1994	Sobocan .	
5,293,879	3/1994	Chen .	
5,307,890	5/1994	Huang .	
5,370,408	12/1994	Eagan	.... 280/47.38 X
5,370,572	12/1994	Lee	.... 280/647 X
5,601,297	2/1997	Stein	.... 188/20 X
5,622,375	4/1997	Fairclough	.... 280/642
5,669,620	9/1997	Robbins	.... 280/657 X
5,685,798	11/1997	Lutz et al.	.... 180/65.6 X
5,692,760	12/1997	Pickering .	
5,713,585	2/1998	Curtis .	
5,873,425	2/1999	Yang	.... 180/65.6
5,984,334	11/1999	Dugas	.... 280/650 X
5,988,012	11/1999	Arnoth	.... 280/647 X

Primary Examiner—Michael Mar
Attorney, Agent, or Firm—Joseph H. Taddeo

[57] **ABSTRACT**

A self-propelled motorized infant stroller powered by DC electric motors with safely controlled acceleration and deceleration. As a discrete safety function, the controlled acceleration and deceleration prevents the child occupant from lurching, either forward or backward, upon the starting or stopping of the baby carriage. A single speed control dial establishes the setting of the desired traversing speed. The propulsion system is safely controlled through the use of a set of dual handle switches that both must be simultaneously depressed to start the propulsion system. A safety seat harness is used to protect the infant occupant from sliding or climbing out of the carriage seat. Additional safety is provided by a parking brake system to prevent accidental propulsion or any unforeseen stroller movement, particularly when stopped on an inclined surface.

11 Claims, 11 Drawing Sheets

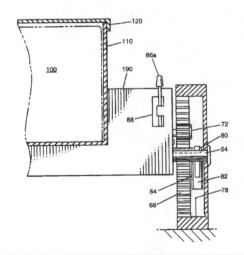

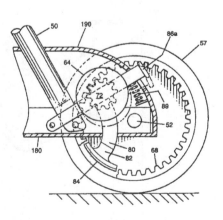

FIGURE 2.1   Baby Stroller Patent

27

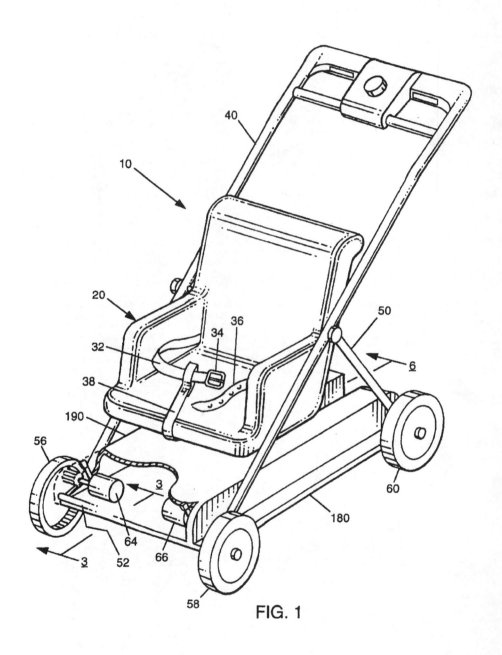

FIG. 1

FIGURE 2.1   *(Continued)*

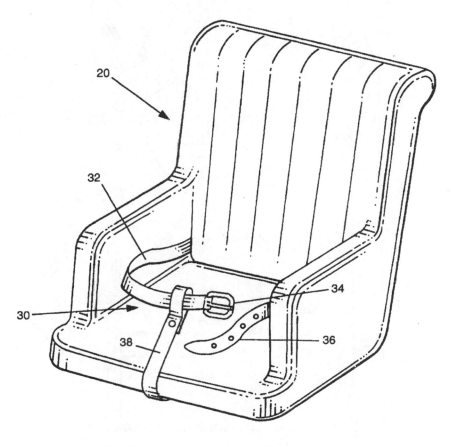

FIG. 2

FIGURE 2.1   *(Continued)*

U.S. Patent   Nov. 21, 2000   Sheet 3 of 11   6,148,942

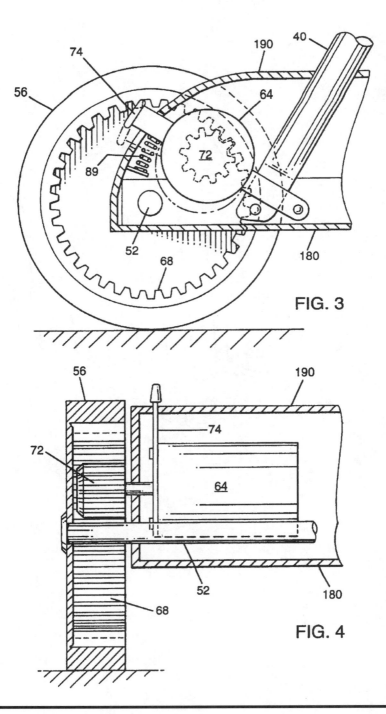

FIG. 3

FIG. 4

FIGURE 2.1 *(Continued)*

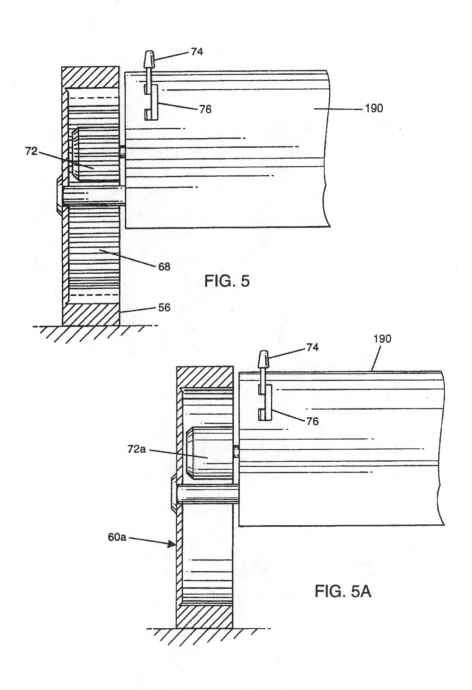

FIG. 5

FIG. 5A

FIGURE 2.1   *(Continued)*

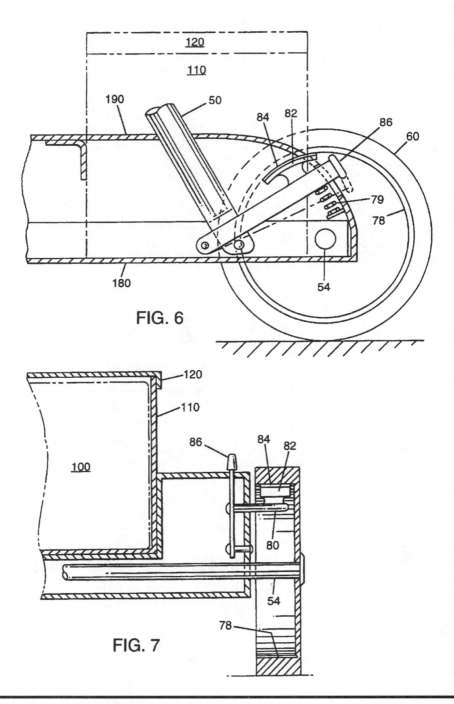

FIG. 6

FIG. 7

FIGURE 2.1 *(Continued)*

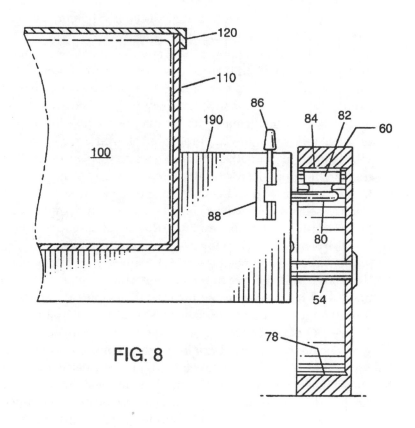

FIG. 8

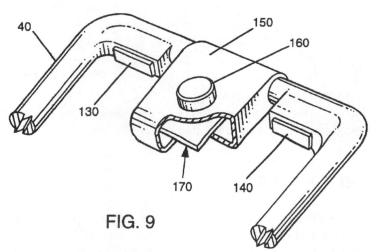

FIG. 9

FIGURE 2.1   *(Continued)*

a car repair shop. Usually, when individuals come up with a novel, yet simple and widely useful, innovation like his, it is an outgrowth of their strengths. Accumulated experience, skills, market knowledge, curiosity, and attention to the unmet needs, or potential wants, of consumers is behind many a patent.

Just because something is innovative, even if it is in your area of expertise, does not mean there will be a market for it, however. The risk that innovators always face is that their creations, no matter how appealing or useful to the inventor, may never catch on with most anybody else. The gentleman who patented a method for preserving the dead, as seen in Figure 2.2, probably believed there would be people who wanted to put deceased loved ones on display, rather than hiding them in the ground. Now, this patent was issued in 1905 and I have yet to walk into anybody's living room and see what the patent drawings portray, so I assume it never caught on. But, maybe in the future it will become fashionable to have a home display of ancestors, who knows?

The combination of a toy dog and vacuum cleaner (see Figure 2.3), while somebody somewhere might want one, is another innovation that looks workable yet never made it as a popular household appliance. And the patent for the physical development apparatus, which looks like it could give you the last stretch you would ever need (see Figure 2.4) does not seem a likely candidate for inclusion when your gym decides it is time to bring in a new set of exercise equipment.

As long as people continue to populate the earth and have the desire to make better lives for themselves, innovation will continue. Because humans are infinitely creative and possess unlimited wants, there will always be plenty of room for the new and improved. Technological and social changes have sparked wave after wave of innovation, with each having more of an impact than the last.

Though, as Drucker tells us, ". . . whatever changes the wealth-producing potential of already existing resources constitutes innovation," entrepreneurial talents are needed to spot that potential and turn it into a reality. If you want to enjoy the wealth your innovations can be used to produce, be sure to take advantage of whatever form of intellectual property protection best suits them.

ENTREPRENEURS ARE US

Oftentimes entrepreneurs are portrayed as superpowered, romantic figures who take heroic, high-stakes shots in the dark, the odds be damned, banking that fate will smile on them. The reality is the opposite. When practiced properly, entrepreneurship is far less risky than most of us think. What gives the impression of entrepreneurship's in-

No. 748,284.

Patented December 29, 1903.

UNITED STATES PATENT OFFICE.

JOSEPH KARWOWSKI, OF HERKIMER, NEW YORK.

METHOD OF PRESERVING THE DEAD.

SPECIFICATION forming part of Letters Patent No. 748,284, dated December 29, 1903.

Application filed October 13, 1903. Serial No. 176,922. (No specimens.)

To all whom it may concern:

Be it known that I, JOSEPH KARWOWSKI, a subject of the Czar of Russia, residing at Herkimer, in the county of Herkimer and State of New York, have invented certain new and useful Improvements in Methods of Preserving the Dead; and I do declare the following to be a full, clear, and exact description of the invention, such as will enable others skilled in the art to which it appertains to make and use the same, reference being had to the accompanying drawings, and to the figures of reference marked thereon, which form a part of this specification.

This invention relates to certain new and useful improvements in methods of preserving the dead; and it has for its object the provision of a means whereby a corpse may be hermetically incased within a block of transparent glass, whereby being effectually excluded from the air the corpse will be maintained for an indefinite period in a perfect and life-like condition, so that it will be prevented from decay and will at all times present a life-like appearance.

To this end and to such others as the invention may pertain the same consists in the steps of the process whereby this result is attained, all as more fully hereinafter described, shown in the accompanying drawings, and then specifically defined in the appended claims.

The invention is clearly illustrated in the accompanying drawings, which, with the figures of reference marked thereon, form a part of this specification, and in which—

Figure 1 is a front elevation of the corpse as it appears after the first step has been taken in carrying out my process. Fig. 2 is a perspective view of the completed glass block, showing the corpse incased therein; and Fig. 3 is a like view of the transparent block of glass, the same being shown as incasing a human head.

In carrying out my process I first surround the corpse 1 with a thick layer 2 of sodium silicate or water-glass. After the corpse has been thus inclosed within the layer of water-glass it is allowed to remain for a short time within a compartment or chamber having a dry heated temperature, which will serve to evaporate the water from this incasing layer, after which molten glass is applied to the desired thickness. This outer layer of glass may be molded into a rectangular form 3, as shown in Fig. 2 of the drawings, or, if preferred, cylindrical or other forms may be substituted for the rectangular block which I have illustrated. In Fig. 3 I have shown the head only of the corpse as incased within the transparent block of glass, it being at once evident that the head alone may be preserved in this manner, if preferred.

It will be at once noted that a body preserved in this way may be kept indefinitely, as the body being hermetically inclosed within the outer glass covering it will be impossible for air to reach it, and hence it will be effectually preserved from decay. The glass surrounding the corpse being transparent, the body will be at all times visible.

Having thus described my invention, what I claim as new, and desire to secure by Letters Patent, is—

1. The process of preserving the dead, which consists in first surrounding the corpse with a coating of sodium silicate or water-glass, and then surrounding the same with an outer coating of molten glass, substantially as shown and described.

2. The process of preserving the dead, which consists in first providing a corpse with a surrounding coating of sodium silicate, evaporating the water from the coating so applied, and afterward incasing the same in molten glass, substantially as described and for the purpose specified.

In testimony whereof I hereunto affix my signature in presence of two witnesses.

JOSEPH KARWOWSKI.

Witnesses:
ALEXANDER JAWOVOSKI,
TOZED TOWOVOWSKI.

FIGURE 2.2   Preservation Patent

No. 748,284.   PATENTED DEC. 29, 1903.

J. KARWOWSKI.

METHOD OF PRESERVING THE DEAD.

APPLICATION FILED OCT. 13, 1903.

NO MODEL.

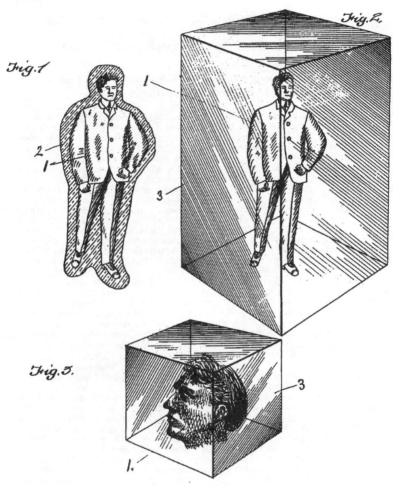

Witnesses

Inventor

Joseph Karwowski,

Attorney

FIGURE 2.2   *(Continued)*

United States Patent [19]

Zaleski

[11] **3,771,192**

[45] **Nov. 13, 1973**

[54] **COMBINATION TOY DOG AND VACUUM CLEANER**

[76] Inventor: Anne Margaret Zaleski, 314 57th St., Pittsburgh, Pa. 15201

[22] Filed: Mar. 16, 1972

[21] Appl. No.: 235,290

Related U.S. Application Data

[63] Continuation-in-part of Ser. No. 8,963, Feb. 5, 1970, abandoned.

[52] U.S. Cl. 15/330, 46/116
[51] Int. Cl. A47l 5/12
[58] Field of Search .... 46/116; 15/257, 323, 15/327 D, 327 E, 328, 330, 335

[56] **References Cited**
UNITED STATES PATENTS

2,367,437   1/1945   Salt 15/323
3,002,215   10/1961   MacParland .... 15/328 X

2,421,958   6/1947   Moretti .... 46/116 UX

FOREIGN PATENTS OR APPLICATIONS.

387,961   2/1933   Great Britain 118/268
355,905   9/1961   Switzerland 15/323

Primary Examiner—Billy J. Wilhite
Assistant Examiner—C. K. Moore
Attorney—William J. Ruano

[57]   **ABSTRACT**

A toy dog closely resembling a real dog and having a hollow interior in which is mounted a vacuum cleaner having a suction hose which is retractable from the tail end of the dog. This enables vacuuming a dog after a hair cut and grooming without causing fear to the dog, inasmuch as the vacuum cleaner noise is greatly muffled by such enclosure. The vacuum cleaner is convertible to a blower and air issuing from the tail end can be heated so as to serve as a dryer.

5 Claims, 5 Drawing Figures

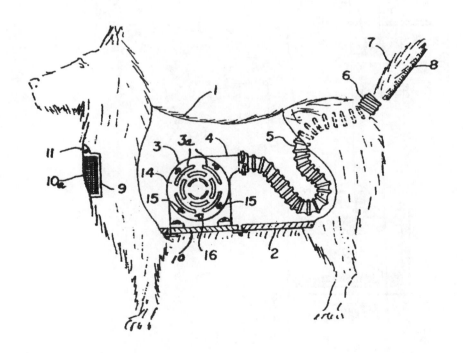

FIGURE 2.3   Dog Vacuum Patent

PATENTED NOV 13 1973

3,771,192

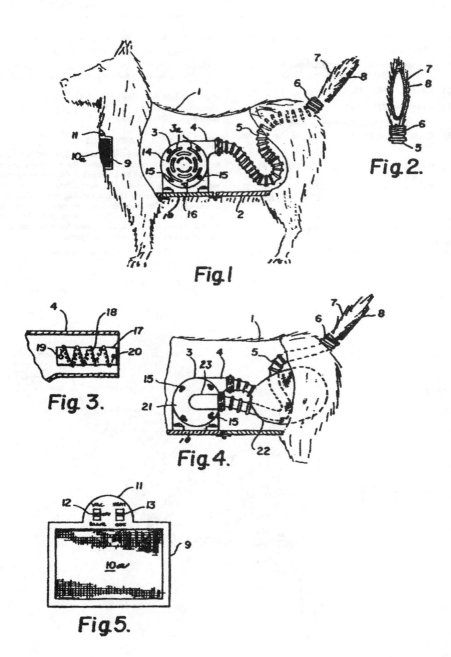

Fig. 1

Fig. 2.

Fig. 3.

Fig. 4.

Fig. 5.

FIGURE 2.3   *(Continued)*

3,771,192

1

COMBINATION TOY DOG AND VACUUM CLEANER

This invention relates to a vacuum cleaner for grooming dogs and similar pets and is a continuation-in-part of the invention described in my application Ser. No. 8963 filed Feb. 5, 1970, and now abandoned. More specifically, it relates to a toy dog and vacuum cleaner combination for overcoming fear in a live dog. In the past, vacuum cleaners have been devised for use on dogs for cleaning clipped hair and the like. These have not met with success because of the fear instilled in a dog at the sight of a vacuum cleaner and because of its very loud noise.

An object of the present invention is to provide a novel combination of a toy dog and vacuum cleaner enclosed completely within the body of a toy dog so as to overcome the abovenamed disadvantages.

A more specific object of the invention is to provide a vacuum cleaner in a toy animal for muffling the sound of the cleaner and which animal has a body portion which contains air inlet and outlet openings for the vacuum cleaner, — the tail of the dog being retractable and usable as a suction nozzle.

Other objects and advantages will become more apparent from a study of the following description taken with the accompanying drawing wherein:

FIG. 1 is a side view of a toy dog with the vacuum bag 22 and cover plate 21 removed and with parts of the body shown broken away to more clearly illustrate an enclosed vacuum cleaner when used as a blower and dryer.

FIG. 2 is a top view of the tail 7;

FIG. 3 is an enlarged view of the heater in housing 4 shown partly broken away;

FIG. 4 shows the vacuum cleaner construction inside body 1 for vacuum cleaning; and,

FIG. 5 shows the vacuum-blower and heater controls of FIG. 1.

Referring more particularly to FIG. 1, numeral 1 is an enclosure of sound deadening material in the shape of a toy dog or other animal, preferably of the general configuration and appearance of the particular pet to be groomed. Numeral 2 denotes the bottom or stomach portion of the toy dog which is provided with a removable or pivotal door 10 for access to the interior.

Enclosed within the toy animal is a vacuum cleaner 3 of any well known type which includes a motor and blower (not shown) and a vacuum bag 22, for collecting cut hairs while grooming the dog and a flexible hose 5 which terminates in a screw collar. Collar 6 carries a tail 7 in the form of an oval housing with an oval nozzle or opening 8 with a brush or comb therearound to be applied to a dog. Collar 6 may screw into the rear end of the body for normally holding the tail 7 or hose 5 in place.

Nozzle 8 serves, selectively, as a vacuum inlet, for sucking in hairs that are clipped or are loose on the dog's body, or for blowing air, such as warm air, for drying the dog after a bath. To convert from a vacuum cleaner as shown in FIG. 4 to a blower as shown in FIG. 1, hose 5 is disconnected from connection 23 and reconnected to connection 4 and the end cover plate 21 and vacuum bag 22 are removed from the motor housing by a slight rotation of the pin and slot connection 15 so as to expose a plurality of arcuate shaped air inlet holes 3a.

2

If desired, a hole 16 may be provided in end plate 14 to receive a locking pin (not shown) on the inside of cover 21. Air enters the dog interior through inlet grill 10a supported in frame 9 detachably connected at 11 to the dog housing.

Also the tail 7 may be filled with flea powder or talcum powder while nozzle 8 is closed with a plate having small holes (not shown), — or it may be used simply as a brush if bristles are applied to the perimeter of nozzle 8.

When the end plate 21 and vacuum bag 22 are removed so as to provide a blower as shown in FIG. 1, the air forced through outlet 4 may be heated therein by a heating coil 18 mounted on an insulator 17 and having terminals 19 and 20 which are energized when switch 13 is at the upper position.

When it is desired to use the device as a vacuum cleaner, as shown in FIG. 4, hose 5 is removed from outlet 4 and connected to inlet 23 and the tail 7 or nozzle, partially covered with hairs to simulate a tail, is pulled out or retracted, after unscrewing its screw collar 6 with respect to the threaded end portion of hose 5, and may be extended or retracted a considerable length of the hose to enable the nozzle 8 to be moved about the outside body surface of a real dog, or other animal, particularly after its hair is cut and trimmed.

After completion of the vacuum cleaning, the dog's tail 7 is either pushed back into the position shown or may be automatically retracted thereto by the use of any well known retractable reel, such as used for air hoses in service stations.

If the cleaner is to be used as a blower and dryer after a dog's bath, vacuum bag 22 and end plate cover 21 are removed to change the structure from that shown in FIG. 4 to that shown in FIG. 1 and switch 12 is moved downwardly and switch 13 upwardly to insert the heater 18 in the circuit. If desired, a separate blower and vacuum device may be used instead.

An outstanding advantage of the above described combination toy dog and vacuum cleaner is that the vacuum cleaner and blower are not only completely concealed from view, but the disturbing noise emanating therefrom is greatly muffled by being inside the toy dog so as not to make a sufficient noise as to frighten the real dog or other animal.

Another advantage is the very convenient manner of retracting the suction nozzle from the toy dog body when it is to be used to vacuum-clean or blower-dry a real dog after his hair has been cut and trimmed.

It will be readily obvious that other shapes of dogs, not shown, may be used instead, preferably one to correspond to the particular type dog to be groomed so that he will feel more friendly toward it. Of course, cats or other pets may be similarly simulated in the toy animal configuration. Thus it will be seen that I have provided a novel combination and arrangement of a toy animal, such as a dog, and vacuum cleaner and blower for completely concealing and muffling the noises of a vacuum cleaner and blower within the confines of the body of a toy animal.

While I have illustrated and described a single specific embodiment of my invention it will be understood that this is by way of illustration only and that various changes and modifications may be contemplated within the scope of the following claims.

I claim:

FIGURE 2.3 *(Continued)*

No. 762,832.

Patented June 14, 1904.

UNITED STATES PATENT OFFICE.

KILION L. MINGES, OF ROCHESTER, NEW YORK, ASSIGNOR TO THE
CARTILAGE COMPANY, OF ROCHESTER, NEW YORK, A FIRM.

PHYSICAL DEVELOPMENT APPARATUS.

SPECIFICATION forming part of Letters Patent No. 762,832, dated June 14, 1904.

Application filed September 23, 1903. Serial No. 174,318. (No model.)

To all whom it may concern:

Be it known that I, KILION L. MINGES, of Rochester, in the county of Monroe and State of New York, have invented certain new and
5 useful Improvements in Physical Development Apparatus; and I do hereby declare the following to be a full, clear, and exact description of the same, reference being had to the drawings forming a part of this specification
10 and to the numerals marked thereon.

My present invention is designed to provide an improved apparatus that is particularly useful in carrying out certain exercises formulated for the development and treatment of
15 the human body; and it consists in certain novel combinations and arrangements of parts to be hereinafter more fully described, and pointed out in the claims hereunto annexed.

In the accompanying drawings, Figure 1 is
20 a diagrammatic view illustrating one embodiment of my invention as applied to the body of a patient; and Fig. 2 is a detail view, enlarged, showing the head and body supports removed.

25 To facilitate an understanding of my present invention, reference will be had to the herein-shown embodiment, wherein 1 designates a supporting-yoke, carrying a pulley 2, through which is rove a cord 3, having one end thereof
30 fastened, as at 4, to a ceiling or other convenient support, its opposite end passing over a relatively stationary pulley 5 and terminating at a suitable distance below it, balls 6 or other devices for affording a firm and conven-
35 ient grasp for the hand being provided at predetermined intervals on said rope between the extremity thereof and the relatively fixed pulley 5. Both arms of the yoke 1 carry at their extremities an upturned or curved hook
40 7 7, each provided with a pair of recesses 8 8, and into the inner pair of recesses thus formed are adapted to rest the rings 9 9, carried upon the extremities of the band 10, that is arranged to rest beneath the chin of the patient, a bind-
45 ing, of felt or other suitable material 11, being preferably provided to prevent abrasion of the skin. A head-strap 12, having one end thereof

fixed to one of the rings 9 and the opposite end free and passing through a buckle 13, at-
50 tached to the ring at the opposite side of the yoke, is also provided to coöperate with the band 10, perforations being provided in the free end of said strap at suitable intervals to receive the tongue of the buckle to enable the
55 length of said strap to be adjusted to accommodate itself to the head of the particular patient under treatment. This device is adapted to be fitted to the head of the patient in the manner shown in Fig. 1, the band 10 be-
60 ing passed beneath the chin and the strap 12 passed around the rear of the head and tightened to the desired degree to firmly retain the device in position and, if desired, assist the band 10 in sustaining the weight imposed
65 upon it.

A body-supporting strap 14, having a loop 15 at one end resting in one of the recesses 8 8 of the yoke 1, is adapted to be passed around the body and beneath the arms of the patient,
70 the opposite end thereof being free and provided with a linked chain or other adjusting device 15ª, adapted to engage the hook at the opposite side of the yoke, whereby the length of said strap may be adjusted as desired by
75 hooking different links of said chain upon the hook of the yoke.

Each foot of the patient is adapted to be passed through a stirrup 16 16, each attached to a cord 17 17, passing through fixed staples
80 or pulleys 18 18 and connected to the arms of a yoke 19, which in turn is attached to a cord 20, passing through a pulley 21 and connected to a yoke 22, carried by the register or indicator 24, the parts being so arranged that
85 the degree of tension upon the cord 20, and consequently the amount of tension upon the body of the patient, will be indicated by the pointer 23 of the indicator 24, which latter may be any suitable device capable of regis-
90 tering the amount of force exerted upon it by the cord 20.

An apparatus constructed in accordance with my invention may be advantageously applied in various ways to the body of the patient

---

FIGURE 2.4 Physical Development Patent

2   762,832

undergoing a course of physical treatment to produce the desired effect in each particular case, and in the present embodiment I have illustrated one form of the appliance as usu-
5 ally employed to produce a stretching action throughout the entire body and limbs to induce growth in the height of the patient, the feet of the patient being inserted in the stirrups 16 16, attached to the cords 17 17, which
10 in turn are connected by the yoke 19 and cord 20 to the indicating device 24 in such a manner that the amount of force exerted upon said stirrups by the patient's feet, tending to draw them upwardly, may be read upon the
15 graduated dial of the indicator by the patient without assistance. The band 10, supported by the yoke 1, passing beneath the chin of the patient, is adjusted into position, and the strap 12, passing behind the head, is tightened
20 until the desired adjustment has been secured, and as the looped end 15 of the body-support 14 is attached to one arm of the yoke the adjusting-chain 15ª may be brought up and hooked upon the opposite arm of the yoke in
25 such a manner that a predetermined proportion of the patient's weight will be supported thereby when a lifting strain is exerted upon said supports.

In practice it is desirable that almost the en-
30 tire weight of the patient should be sustained by the body-support at the beginning of the treatment, leaving the comparatively small amount of force remaining to be exerted upon the head to produce a tension upon the patient's
35 neck and contiguous parts, the proportion of weight sustained by the body-support being gradually reduced at proper intervals during the treatment by adjusting different links of the chain thereof upon the hook of the yoke,
40 as desired. As the cord 3, passing through the pulley 2 of the yoke, is so arranged that the end thereof is in a position to be conveniently grasped by the patient, it is obvious that the services of an attendant are rendered
45 unnecessary in the manipulation of the appliance, the patient being enabled to haul upon the cord to any desired degree to produce the desired tension, and as the indicator 24 is so located that a reading thereof may be had at
50 any time by the patient the resisting force exerted upon the legs of the patient may be regulated as required.

An appliance of this character is especially designed to assist physical exercises for the
55 purpose of increasing the height or promoting growth in a person by acting upon the cartilage of the system by stretching or subjecting the body and limbs of the patient to a tension, and while I have illustrated the pres-
60 ent embodiment as applied to such a purpose and including certain details in construction to obtain such an end it is to be understood that the same may be applied to the patient

in a different manner, or certain parts of the appliance may be omitted to obtain the de- 65
sired results in any particular case, or a modified form of the appliance may be employed, if found desirable, to meet the requirements of varying conditions, all of which forms will come within the scope of my invention. 70

I claim as my invention—

1. An appliance of the character described, comprising a support attached to the upper portion of the patient's body, resistance devices attached to the lower portion thereof, 75
a register connected to said devices and adapted to indicate the amount of force exerted thereon by said devices, and means attached to said support for producing a stretching action upon the patient's body. 80

2. An appliance of the character described, comprising a support to engage the head and a supplemental support to embrace the body of the patient, resistance devices adapted to be attached to the lower limbs of the patient 85
and connected to a register for indicating the amount of force exerted thereon by said devices, means attached to said supports for producing a stretching action upon the body of the patient, and adjusting means carried 90
by the body-support for permitting the relative proportion of force exerted by said head and body support to be varied as desired.

3. An appliance of the character described, comprising a support adapted to embrace the 95
head and a supplemental support to embrace the body of the patient and assist the head-support in sustaining the weight of the patient's body, means for adjusting the relative proportion of weight sustained by each sup- 100
port, and means for sustaining the weight imposed upon said supports.

4. In a physical development appliance, the combination with a support having a band adapted to rest beneath the chin, and an ad- 105
justable strap attached thereto and adapted to be passed behind the head of the patient to cooperate with said band in exerting its force upon the patient's body, a supplemental support engaging the body of the patient and 110
having an adjusting device thereon, means connected to said supports for lifting the body of the patient, and devices adapted to be attached to the lower limbs of the patient and connected to a register for producing a 115
resistance to the lifting of the body and thereby exert a stretching action thereon, the amount of which will be indicated by said register.

5. An appliance of the character described, 120
comprising a support adapted to engage the head, and a supplemental support embracing the body of the patient, lifting devices attached to said supports having a rope accessible to the patient for lifting himself, adjust- 125
ing means carried by the body-support for

FIGURE 2.4 *(Continued)*

41

762,832   8

varying the relative proportions of the weight sustained by said head and body support, and devices attached to the lower limbs of the patient and connected to a register adapted to
5 indicate the amount of resistance exerted upon the patient's limbs while being lifted, and consequently the degree of tension or stretching action produced upon the body of the patient.

KILION L. MINGES.

Witnesses:
    G. WILLARD RICH,
    CLARENCE A. BATEMAN.

FIGURE 2.4   *(Continued)*

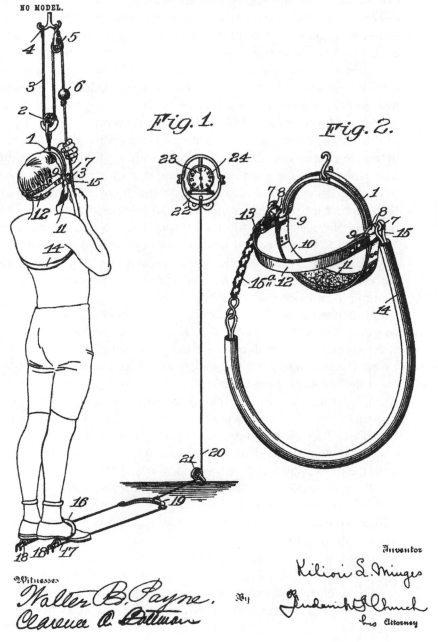

No. 762,832.

PATENTED JUNE 14, 1904.

K. L. MINGES.
PHYSICAL DEVELOPMENT APPARATUS.
APPLICATION FILED SEPT. 23, 1903.

NO MODEL.

Fig. 1.

Fig. 2.

Witnesses
Walter B. Payne.
Clarence A. Dittman

Inventor
Kilion L. Minges
Frederick T. Church
his Attorney

FIGURE 2.4 *(Continued)*

herent riskiness is the fact that so many people embark on ventures with little idea of how to function in their markets. True entrepreneurs, in contrast, take on new ventures only when they are convinced, after examining them thoroughly, that these represent their best available opportunities, rather than being just another run at a windmill. In this sense, the entrepreneurial process should begin well before the patent process, especially if you intend to market your innovation.

Entrepreneurs spot opportunities that others have not seen or acted on yet. They take advantage of these opportunities by developing new and improved goods and services and presenting them to the markets where those untapped opportunities exist, with the goal of earning profits. Entrepreneurs may be responsible for creating the underlying innovations, they may have the initial idea that sparks the innovations that evolve into new goods and services, or they may come in contact with an existing innovation and grow it into a tangible product. They then present it to the right audience, with patents serving as an essential form of protection to help keep others from stealing that audience.

David Koretz, the president and founder of, Internet-based business services provider Bluetie, is a good example of an entrepreneur who uses patents to protect his innovations and to assure clients that his unique products cannot be had elsewhere.

When doing business in the past, he had been frustrated with the length of time it took to send documents back and forth, not to mention the costs involved. It costs around $15 to have Federal Express deliver a document overnight; couriers, if the recipient is close enough, are faster but still expensive; e-mail is cheap but insecure, and even existing Internet services for sending documents require software that does not offer adequate document protection. As a result of these factors, Dave had the inspiration for Secure Send, a service that would encrypt documents and send them to Bluetie clients on the Internet, with the process taking mere seconds, and costing very little.

Prior to embarking on the long and difficult process that would make Secure Send a reality, Dave knew from his own experience and additional market research that there was an enormous potential market for the product. With Bluetie subscribers paying around $25 a month for a broad array of services, of which Secure Send would be just one, all a subscriber had to do was use it twice and the savings would cover the entire cost for all services for a whole month. Beyond that, Dave had a good idea what it would cost to make Secure Send operative and, knowing the extent of its appeal, could go into it knowing that his prospects for covering his costs, then going on to make money on it, were very good. He could not eliminate all risk, but he reduced his risks to the point that developing Secure Send into a viable product was a hard idea to beat.

Without a patent to protect his innovation, Dave would have had little incentive to pursue it. Why spend all that time, money, and energy on Secure Send if somebody else could simply copy it and sell it themselves, once it was operable? Not only does the patent benefit Dave by giving him a monopoly on his invention, it also benefits Bluetie subscribers who find this aspect of doing business now becoming much cheaper, faster, and easier.

Though he had the idea for it and oversaw the creation process from beginning to end, David had plenty of other people in his company, like some great software engineers, who did the bulk of the hands-on work and technical innovation. As an entrepreneur, David was the one who spotted the opportunity, developed an idea for taking advantage of it, made his idea into an attractive product, then began bringing that product to the people he knew could use it.

Talk as we may about all the capacities possessed by entrepreneurs, among the most important attributes are maintaining faith in their endeavors, even when nobody else has any, and the ability to gut it out long enough for their innovations to catch on, even when money and hope are rapidly dwindling.

From drawing board, to patent application, to patent issue, to marketable product, to acceptance by a sizable body of consumers is a long, tough, unpredictable ride, not one for wallflowers or the faint of heart. Almost anybody can get a patent, but the person who goes on to grow one into something special is rare.

To demonstrate the point, I am going to use the story of a woman, Kitty Van Bortel, who started off with one $200 used car she sold from her home and went on to become the largest and most successful Subaru dealer in the country. One of the reasons I chose her, in addition to Kitty being an extraordinary person, is that she succeeded based on implementing simple, obvious ideas that, with no patent or trade secret protection, can be used by anybody. In fact, other people have tried the very same things she does. The difference is that Kitty has followed through in ways that the others have not been able to.

Prior to forming her own dealership, Kitty was a manager at a large local dealership and was doing very well. She went for a promotion that one of her male peers was also seeking. He got it, which was not a problem, but then he fired her because he did not want a woman on his management team. That was a problem.

Instead of finding another position where she would be working for somebody else, and at risk for the same kind of outcome, she decided to go into business for herself. With very little money, she started off selling inexpensive used cars. Gradually she raised the quality of the cars, then secured a Subaru franchise.

Throughout, her idea was to treat customers, particularly female customers, who are still badly treated so often in male dominated dealerships, with honesty and respect. Her prices are always stated up front, be it in person, over the phone, or on the Internet. No manipulations take place, no last minute gouging that has given auto dealers such a bad name. Her salespeople are trained to treat customers with the greatest courtesy; no pressure, just service. Kitty herself says that "Anybody could do what I do," but none of her competitors do. Sure, every once in a while somebody will attempt it, but they never get it right.

It was faith and perseverance that got her through the tough times early in her business, the same qualities that enabled her to stick with her methods until they paid off. The point here is that what matters most is having solid, innovative ideas that appeal to your market, then having the flexibility, faith in yourself and the future, and guts to make it all work. A patent provides you a valuable opportunity in the rights to exclusive use of your innovation. The personal qualities possessed by Kitty are what enable you to succeed no matter how many people have access to your innovation.

To Create a Superstar

With technology making an ever-broader range of goods and services available to an audience who is rapidly increasing in size, those with even small advantages in their appeal to consumers can reap huge benefits. For anybody thinking of seeking a patent on an innovation they intend to either sell themselves or license to another, this is an important fact.

In the early 1980s, Sherwin Rosen, an economist from the University of Chicago, wrote an excellent paper called *"The Economics of Superstars."* The phenomenon he was examining was the incredible amounts of money a handful of people at the top of their fields, such as actors, athletes, and CEOs, made, while the rest of the field, the runners-up, along with people who performed arguably more important functions, such as teachers and nurses, earned far less.

In order for superstar earnings to occur, he found that two things had to be present:

1. Communications technology that makes it possible to distribute the superstar's wares to a broad audience, as occurs when a football player competes in a superbowl or a musician puts out a CD.

2. The superstar must have more appeal, talent, or skill than the competition.

The difference, however, only has to be slight in order to reap huge rewards in comparison to competitors who are close. Tiger Woods, for example, is the best golfer playing today, but he is only a bit better than numerous other great golfers. That small difference enables him to win more tournaments than they do, often by a close margin (and he loses plenty), which translates into annual earnings, especially from endorsements, that are miles beyond what any other golfer can hope for. Julia Roberts, who has an appeal that survives even bad movies, commands huge sums of money to appear in a film, despite the existence of hundreds of actresses who could do a wonderful job at a fraction of the cost. Because there is such demand for what the limited supply of superstars have to offer, even though their advantages may be slight, stratospheric revenues are generated when a lot of people are willing to pay a bit more for what they perceive as the best.

What does this have to do with patents? A few things. First of all, bear in mind that your invention does not have to be head and shoulders above the competition; it just has to have an edge that others do not. As a prospective inventor, it is easy for you to become discouraged by the notion that the only successful creations grow from spectacular leaps forward made by giants, leaving the rest of us mortals lost somewhere back in their dust.

The reality is that a simple, small, appealing step forward that nobody else has made yet has a good chance of sparking consumer enthusiasm in ways that the big leaps, which may not even be understood by more than a few people for years to come, cannot match. With a few obvious exceptions, it would be difficult to find many masters of high tech who have outearned Lonnie Johnson and his Super Soaker.

Given the ongoing development of information technology and its penetration into more and more areas of life, the superstar paydays that used to be confined to people like writers, musicians, and athletes are becoming available in all kinds of new areas. Maybe you can be the one to do it in yours.

As an example, say you are an English professor at a small college, where your salary is limited because you can reach only a small number of students per semester. One day, you get tired of driving that Yugo you cannot find parts for anymore and go into business for yourself, creating and patenting an online method for teaching writing that helps freshman everywhere, at a reasonable cost, get through English 101 with far less suffering than is usually the case. Even if other similar services are available, if yours is marginally better there is the possibility of tapping into an enormous market that is constantly being replenished by new students. Now you have gone from obscurity to superstardom. Not only that, but with a patent to protect your innovation for 20 years, you have an additional advantage of having a monopoly all to yourself, an edge that even Brad Pitt might envy.

HISTORY OF INTELLECTUAL PROPERTY

3

PATENTS

The first person to be granted a patent was Antonius Marini, of the Republic of Venice, in 1443. Though his invention was not new, he requested the right to build flour mills for each of Venice's 24 boroughs, with nobody else permitted to build a flour mill that operated without water, for 20 years. The senate agreed to the monopoly on the condition that one of his mills be tested to confirm that it worked as Antonius Marini claimed it did. The mill operated as it was supposed to and Marini was granted exclusive rights to waterless flour mills for 20 years.

Though not as formal, another example of exclusive rights can be found in Venice nearly 150 years earlier. In 1297 a decree was passed declaring that any physician who made a medicine based on his own secret would have that secret protected by all members of his guild, who were required to swear an oath not to pry into it.

The most famous inventor from Venice to receive a patent was a professor of mathematics at Padua, Galileo. His creation was a machine that raised water and used it to irrigate land. Galileo claimed that the power of a single horse was enough to dispense water that could irrigate crops through 20 spouts. His exclusive rights also lasted 20 years, with an additional provision that anybody who infringed on them would be fined 300 ducats and have their machines taken.

In the third century B.C. one of the earliest recorded references to a patent right was made by the Greek historian Phylarchis in his work, *Banquet of the Learned*. He wrote about a Greek colony, Sybaris, its people known in 500 B.C. for being fond of living well and indulging themselves. Phylarchis told of how a cook who came up with a novel dish of particular excellence was rewarded with a one-year monopoly that prohibited anyone else from preparing the dish during that time period. Such a monopoly provided an incentive for people "to labor at excelling in such pursuits."

Even where monopolies were not tolerated there was usually the recognition that creative citizens were valuable and should be rewarded for their contributions. The Roman emperor Constantine, in A.D. 337 decreed that artisans of particularly important trades, such as chariot makers, engineers, and locksmiths, who lived in cities would be exempt from all civil duties. Emphasis was put on those craftsmen who instructed their sons and worked to perfect their talents in their leisure time.

Much of our patent system in the United States had its origin in England. The English patent system came into its own during the years of Queen Elizabeth I's sovereignty in the sixteenth century. Though exclusive rights had been granted by other rulers in past centuries, she granted monopolies and privileges to inventors to a much greater extent than had occurred before. Prior to her years in power, English kings and queens had granted monopolies to family members and friends as favors, in addition to dispensing monopolies as a means for raising money when the cash necessary to operate their kingdoms was running short. Though these monopolies were very expensive to buy, in comparison to today's fees, the privileges they provided to holders could result in the accumulation of great wealth.

Throughout the Middle Ages monopolies were granted for a variety of things; maybe a municipality would buy the right to collect a toll on merchandise that passed through town, or to be the only ones able to hold a fair or market in town. Guilds were examples of monopolies that were popular in this period. Merchants and manufacturers would organize them for their mutual protection and acquire exclusive rights to their local area by purchasing them from the Crown. Guilds were also used as a means to attract workers, since the restriction on competition enabled them to earn a better living. For example, Edward II offered protection to German miners to attract them to England, and both Edward II and Edward III did the same for artisans they wanted to attract to England for the practice of the artisans' trade. When the English wanted to develop a cloth industry, special privileges were given to dyers, fullers, and weavers. To protect English industry, Edward III prohibited his subjects from wearing foreign cloth.

Though these protections were similar to patents in providing exclusive rights, they were meant to promote the establishment of particular trades, not inventions. Early examples of what are more closely related to the patents of today can be found in the letter of protection granted in 1440 to John Shiedame for a new method of producing salt, or the rights granted to John of Utynam for the production of colored glass, with nobody else able to make it without his permission for a period of 20 years. In return, John had to instruct others in the art so that they could engage in the making of colored glass after the 20-year term expired.

As to who was the original inventor of the process for making colored glass, it is not known if John of Utynam was or not. Until 1977 though, British law gave patent rights to whoever was the first to introduce and find a commercial use for an unpublished patent, whereas the U.S. system has only recognized the actual inventor. A precedent-setting example of rewarding an inventor with a patent happened in 1559. Giacopo Acontio was afraid that others would copy his inventions for a new kind of furnace and "wheel machines" so he petitioned Queen Elizabeth I for protection, saying "Nothing is more honest than that those who by searching have found out things useful to the public should have some fruits of their rights and labors, as meanwhile they abandon all other modes of gain, are at much expense in experiments, and often sustain much loss."

Even with patents like these that foreshadowed modern patent law, there were plenty of abuses in the granting of monopoly rights, which were often given more with an eye to rewarding friends and family members and to raising money than to protecting and encouraging innovation. Walter Raleigh was granted the power to license tavern keepers, though that surely was not a process he had invented. In addition, the patent examination process did not formally exist yet, were it had to be shown that an invention would work before it could be patented. This kept the door open for patents like the one granted in 1575 for the transformation of iron into copper and lead and antimony into mercury, none of these ever having been possible. It was also possible for good ideas to be turned down. John Harrington sought a patent for the water closet and was turned down. As a result that innovation was not introduced for another 150 years, thereby depriving generations of potential users an ideal location for reading the newspaper.

In Queen Elizabeth I's time 54 patents were granted. The process became more formalized in 1624, during the reign of James I, with the passage of the Statute of Monopolies. This act has served as the basis of both English and U.S. patent law. The statute barred the grant of monopoly for anything but new inventions, but whoever petitioned for one was not guaranteed a patent automatically, with it still being necessary to rely on the good graces of the king.

As had England before them, the American colonies sought to attract people with specific skills. To get them to settle there, the colonies frequently offered payments and subsidies, granting monopolies on occasion to craftsmen who were familiar with the English system. The General Court of Massachusetts issued the Body of Liberties in 1641, which prohibited the practice of granting monopolies, with an exception being made for new inventions that were profitable for the country. They granted their first patent in 1641, to Samuel Winslow for a new process for the manufacture of salt, mandating that others were barred "from making this article except in a manner different from his." In 1646 Joseph Jenkes received the first patent for machinery, on his invention of "engines of mills to go by water."

Prior to the patent act of 1790, which made the patent process a federal one, states were responsible for issuing their own patents, which depended on the grant being made by somebody in a position of power.

When the Constitutional Convention began meeting in 1787, the delegates sought a means of preventing the abuses seen in the English system of granting monopolies, many of which had carried over to the American colonies. The focus was on developing a federal system that protected inventors and authors by giving them exclusive rights to their works. Article I of the Constitution said, in part, that Congress shall have the power "to promote the progress of science and useful arts, by securing for limited times to authors and inventors the exclusive right to their respective writings and discoveries." This was the first constitutional recognition that the property rights of individuals extended to works of their intellect and that society would benefit from the protection of these.

In a speech to Congress during the Second Session of 1790 George Washington recognized the "expediency of giving effectual encouragement" for new and useful inventions from abroad and the necessity of providing support "to the exertions of skill and genius in producing them at home." President Washington signed the first patent act on April 10, 1790. Now, instead of separate states applying their own standards, a patent board was put together and given the responsibility of reviewing and issuing patents. The board was made up of the secretary of state, the secretary of war, and the attorney general. Thomas Jefferson and George Washington signed the first U.S. patent.

Initially, the pace of patent issues was slow, with 3 issued in 1790, a jump to 33 in 1791, 11 in 1792, and only 10 in 1793, when a new act was passed and the rate of issues began to rise. In 1835, 752 patents were issued. When the Patent Act of 1836 became law, the U.S. Patent Office was established as a separate bureau that had its own commissioner. With only a few modifications, the Patent Act of 1836 remained in force until 1951, when most of the features we still have today were put in place. The biggest single change may be in patent protection being extended to plants in 1930. Previously, this was not available to plant breeders or discoverers of new varieties. Luther Burbank, a horticulturist, had lamented that, "A man can patent a mouse trap or copyright a nasty song, but if he gives to the world a new fruit, he will be fortunate if he is rewarded by so much as having his name connected with the result."

The range and creativity seen in U.S. patents has been extraordinary. As intended, the exclusive rights to manufacture and sell their inventions has provided innovators and entrepreneurs with the incentive to bring goods to market that have had an enormous impact on our society and the rest of the world. As an illustration, here are the 15 "outstanding great inventions" produced from the beginning of the formalized United States patent process through the end of the nineteenth century, as selected by the National Committee for the U.S. Patent Law Sesquicentennial Celebration in 1940.

Inventor	Invention	Date
Eli Whitney	Cotton gin	1794
Robert Fulton	Steamboat	1811
Cyrus H. McCormick	Reaper	1834
Samuel F.B. Morse	Telegraph	1840
Charles Goodyear	Vulcanization	1844
Elias Howe Jr.	Sewing machine	1846
C. Latham Sholes	Typewriter	1868
George Westinghouse	Air brake	1869
Alexander Graham	Bell Telephone	1876
Thomas Edison	Phonograph	1878
Thomas Edison	Incandescent lamp	1880
Nikola Tesla	Induction motor	1888
Charles Hall	Aluminum production	1889
Ottmar Mergenthaler	Linotype	1890
Thomas Edison	Motion picture projector	1893

In Akron, Ohio, inventors are inducted into the National Inventor's Hall of Fame each year. As extraordinary as the preceding list is, the pace and impact of innovation is even greater today. It would be fascinating to look forward and see a list of the outstanding great inventions of the twenty-first century.

The driving force behind innovation has always been the desire to make life better, to make improvements on and add to what is, and then, instead of resting there, to push on with new creations that were unthinkable even a few years earlier.

As an example of improving on what is, then using an advance to initiate new ones, consider the achievements of Joseph Burns, a glass cutter by trade. When cutting bread with a regular knife, he found the result to be unsatisfactory, the bread often torn, squashed, or otherwise not in desirable shape. His idea was to create a blade that would make the cutting easier and produce a more appetizing result. Lots of people try to create the greatest thing since sliced bread; Joseph Burns invented the serrated blade and made it possible to slice bread better.

What he did was to go to the local hardware store and buy a dozen blank knife blades, which he then brought home and started working on with his grinding wheel. His idea was to produce a blade with a cutting edge featuring a new type of surface that made slicing easier and more predictable. He produced a dozen blades and brought them back to the hardware store, where they quickly sold out. Seeing that there was a potential market for his invention, Joseph Burns patented it.

In 1919 he founded Burns Manufacturing. With exclusive rights to the serrated cutting edge, he built a factory that produced them for other companies. These companies would provide the blades and Burns Manufacturing would give them the appropriate edge (see Figure 3.1). Other firms could also license the technology from Burns, for a negotiated fee, and produce the serrated blades for themselves.

After developing the serrated blade, Joseph Burns applied it to a variety of new innovations, from variations on cutting tools, to a grapefruit corer, to a fire hose nozzle. Now, that nozzle may sound pretty far afield of his area of expertise, but it really was not. By relying on the irregular serrated shape, it was possible to dispense water in a conical fog pattern that was effective in combating fires.

Those with inventive turns of mind, like Burns, are often able to turn their intellects on a variety of areas with creative results. The keys are the desire to improve on what is and the practical ability to do so in a way that makes good sense to other people. For example, Burns wondered if it was really necessary to use up so many trees at Christmas time, with millions of them being chopped down for the holiday, only to be discarded a couple of weeks later. His idea was to develop a tree that could be used over and over again, brought out for the holiday season then put away until the next year, thus saving trees and time and making the whole process a lot easier. His idea was ahead of the technology of the time, however, and artificial Christmas trees did not come out on the market for a few more years.

UNITED STATES PATENT OFFICE.

JOSEPH E. BURNS, OF SYRACUSE, NEW YORK.

CUTTING-TOOL.

1,388,547.
　　　　Specification of Letters Patent.　　Patented Aug. 23, 1921.

Application filed September 25, 1919.　Serial No. 326,364.

To all whom it may concern:

Be it known that I, JOSEPH E. BURNS, of Syracuse, in the county of Onondaga, in the State of New York, have invented new and useful Improvements in Cutting-Tools, of which the following, taken in connection with the accompanying drawings, is a full, clear, and exact description.

This invention relates to certain improvements in edge tools or cutting blades, including knives of all characters and is closely related to the invention of my copending application, Ser. No. 296,995, filed May 14, 1919.

The object of the invention is to produce an improved and highly efficient cutting blade and in my copending application, I have described a method of serrating edge tools by the use of a properly shaped grinding wheel formed of suitable abrasive material and the invention of this application relates specifically to the formation and relative disposition of the grooves ground at the edge of the tool to form these serrations so that the knife cuts easily and rapidly when moved in either longitudinal direction.

Other objects and advantages relate to the details of formation, arrangement and construction of the tool as hereinafter described and claimed.

In the drawings—

Figure 1 is an elevation of a knife suitable for cutting bread, the grooves and serrations at the edge being illustrated more or less diagrammatically.

Fig. 2 is an enlarged illustration of a portion of the knife of Fig. 1 showing the inclined grooves and the serrations or teeth formed thereby.

Fig. 3 illustrates a method of forming the serrations by the use of a rotary grinding wheel indicated in dotted lines.

I have illustrated my invention as applied to a knife adapted for cutting bread and it consists in the formation of a plurality of series of substantially parallel grooves intersecting the edge of the knife and forming a plurality or series of serrations or teeth inclined in opposite directions with respect to a lateral axis of the knife. The series of serrations may be and are preferably separated by a plain or unserrated portion which as a result of the opposite inclinations of the adjacent grooves is of keystone shape, the adjacent plain portions having their taper extending in opposite directions as a result of the opposite inclination of the adjacent grooves, serrations or teeth.

Each series of grooves may comprise any suitable number to form any desired number of serrations or teeth and in the illustration I have shown five series of grooves and the number of grooves in each series may be the same or may vary as desired and the spaced distance of each series may vary as desired or may be uniform throughout.

Perhaps the preferred method of forming the edge as shown in the figures is by the use of a rotary grooving wheel formed with a plurality of circumferentially extending parallel ridges, the number of said ridges being equal to the desired number of grooves to be formed to constitute a single series. By the use of such a wheel all of the grooves of one series may be ground simultaneously and by this method the spacing and formation of the grooves is rendered perhaps more uniform than otherwise would be the case. However, such method of forming a plurality of grooves simultaneously is not essential to my invention. It will be noted that the teeth of series 1 incline rearwardly and the teeth of series 2 incline forwardly of the knife —A—, that the teeth of series 3 and 5 also incline rearwardly while the teeth of series 4 incline forwardly and that the said series of grooves or serrations are spaced by plain portions 6, 7, 8 and 9, all of substantially keystone shape, approaching triangular formation. The taper or plain portions 6 and 8 being opposite the taper of the plain portions 7 and 9.

The inclination of the grooves —10— will shape the forward portion —12— of the tooth or serration —11— so that its edge —14— is substantially perpendicular to the longitudinal axis of the knife while the rear portion —13— of the tooth is obliquely inclined to a material extent with reference to the forward portion.

The portion of tools adjacent their cutting edge is usually tapered in cross section as shown in Fig. 3 and I believe that the grinding of a plurality of substantially parallel grooves on such a tapered edge portion is new and I have claimed the same in my said copending application and I further contemplate as new the grinding of a plurality of grooves upon such an edge when said grooves are inclined with respect to the lateral axis of the tool.

In practice I have found that by forming

FIGURE 3.1　Cutting Tool Patent

54

J. E. BURNS.
CUTTING TOOL.
APPLICATION FILED SEPT. 25, 1919.

1,388,547. Patented Aug. 23, 1921.

Fig. 1.
Fig. 2.
Fig. 3.
Inventor
By Joseph E. Burns
Attorneys'

Copy provided by USPTO from the CSIR Image Database on 07-02-2001

FIGURE 3.1 ***(Continued)***

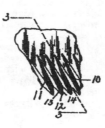

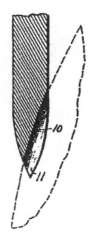

2   1,388,547

the knife as shown in Fig. 1, it cuts rapidly and easily when drawn in either direction and its efficiency for the purpose described is materially increased.

5   Any suitable number of series of grooves and serrations may be formed on the blade and the number of grooves in each of the series may be varied and the spaced distance of the series may be varied and the relative 10 inclination of the grooves in the several series may be varied, all within the scope of my invention as set forth in the appended claims.

What I claim is:

15   1. An edged tool provided with a plurality of series of obliquely disposed grooves forming a plurality of series of relatively fine accurately shaped ground teeth, the grooves of each series being inclined with respect to the edge of said tool in a direc- 20 tion offset to the direction of inclination of the adjacent series of ground grooves.

2. An edge tool provided with a plurality of series of obliquely disposed grooves, form- ing a plurality of series of relatively fine 25 accurately shaped ground teeth, the grooves of each series being inclined with respect to the edge of said tool in a direction offset to the direction of inclination of the adjacent series of ground grooves, and key-stone 30 shaped, smooth edged parts separating adjacent series of ground grooves.

In witness whereof I have hereunto set my hand this 13th day of September, 1919.

JOSEPH E. BURNS.

Witnesses:
H. E. CHASE.
E. A. THOMPSON.

FIGURE 3.1 *(Continued)*

COPYRIGHTS

As with patents, copyright law in the United States has its roots in English common law, though the original intent in England was different. When William Caxton opened England's first print shop in 1476, the Crown worried that the growth of the book trade and knowledge being disbursed more widely could promote religious and political ideas that would influence the public in undesirable ways. As a result, they decided to regulate the printing industry in order to exert control over what kind of written material was produced and sold.

Restrictions on the right to print included:

- The issuance of royal grants and patents that provided the exclusive right to print certain books.
- The demand that the author's and printer's names appear in each copy.
- The requirement that a printed copy of each work be submitted to the sovereign's private collection.

In 1557 the Stationer's Company of London was established. It was a trade association of printers and booksellers that had a royal patent to print books for sale in England. Nobody could print books for sale without its approval, and it kept a register in which printers and booksellers were required to enter the title of all books purchased from authors and other members. This helped to demonstrate claims of priority in legal actions, but also allowed the company to fulfill its responsibility to keep track of heretical writers and see to it that they were punished when they went too far. The association also destroyed books they thought to be undeserving of publication, burning them before they got into the wrong hands.

Though the existing laws were effective in censoring works, it was not until the time of Queen Anne, in 1709, that authors were given copyright protection in a legal statute that sought to protect their property rights, instead of merely controlling what was written and distributed. The act states, "Whereas printers, booksellers, and other persons have of late frequently taken the liberty of printing, reprinting, and publishing books without the consent of the authors or proprietors . . . to their very great detriment, and too often to the ruin of them and their families: for preventing therefore such practices for the future, and for the encouragement of learned men to compose and write useful books . . ." and gave authors a 14-year period of sole rights to their works, which could be renewed for another 14 years. The act when on to say, ". . . if any bookseller, printer, or other person whatsoever, shall print, reprint, or import any such book or books, without the consent of the proprietor . . . then such offender shall forfeit such book or books to the proprietor of the copy thereof, who shall forthwith damage and make wastepaper of them; and further, that every such offender shall forfeit one penny for every sheet which shall be found in his custody."

European countries followed England's lead on copyright law, as did the United States. Before the federal Constitution was in force, 12 of the 13 colonies had passed copyright acts; then the first federal Copyright Act was issued in 1790. It covered books, maps, and charts for 14 years, which could be renewed for another 14 years, as was the case with English law. U.S. copyright law was periodically updated through the time of the Copyright Act of 1909. Not until the Copyright Revision Act of 1976 was copyright law significantly updated, though it still contained most features of the original body of copyright law.

As advances in technology made it possible to put an increasing range of creative works in the fixed form required to secure a copyright, the law has been adapted to forms that could not have been foreseen when enacted, such as computer software and compact discs. To date, the law has proved to be remarkably flexible.

TRADEMARKS

Considering that trademarks are much easier to manage than patents and copyrights, and do not require literacy for their administration, it is no surprise that they have been around much longer than other forms of intellectual property. Because pottery is the most commonly found relic that survives past civilizations, it is here that a particularly rich array of trademarks can be found. Bees, other animals, hearts, religious symbols, and a lion's head are among the estimated 6,000 different Roman potters' marks that have been identified. In inventiveness and intent many would fit right in with today's trademarks. Marcus Rutilus Lupus, for example, was an oil lamp maker who used an imprint of a wolf's head as a trademark (*lupus* means wolf in Latin). Hundreds of years later, the rock band Steppenwolf also made use of a wolf's head as a symbol.

Pottery markings have been found from as far back as the Stone Age. Cave drawings from the same period, approximately 5000 B.C., show pictures of animals with marks on their flanks to show ownership. Jars buried in tombs from the First Dynasty Egyptian kings have been uncovered that show the marks of their makers. These marks could also be used to identify the maker in case their workmanship was poor. Building stones, roof tiles, and bricks were stamped with the names of those who made them, too.

The earliest records of trademarks being used in an economic sense, as they most commonly are today, come from the Roman civilization of 500 B.C. to A.D. 500, when trademarks were used by the makers and sellers of products like cheese, lamps, wine, medicines, and ornaments. From A.D. 500 until the end of the eleventh century, the Dark Ages, there is little information available on the use of trademarks. From the twelfth century onward, the Middle Ages through today, trademarks have been very common. Guilds usually mandated that anything made by a craftsman show both the symbol of the guild and the mark of the individual who produced the article.

In English law the first known statute applying to trademarks comes from 1266, when bakers were required to have their own marks for each type of bread they made. In the fifteenth and sixteenth centuries armorers, metal workers, paper workers, weavers, printers, tanners, and smiths used trademarks to identify their goods, and tough laws existed to punish whoever copied somebody else's trademark. Once an innkeeper was hanged for trying to sell a cheap wine as Rudesheimer. In addition to merchants, it became common for well-off families to develop their own form of trademark, the coat of arms, many of which we continue to see today.

When mass production and distribution had grown to a considerable level, as a result of the Industrial Revolution, in the mid-nineteenth century, trademarks became much more valuable as a tool of commerce, a tool used to assure customers that all goods bearing the mark would be of the same high quality. Under the first federal trademark act of 1870, 121 trademarks were registered; by now the number has grown to more than 3 million.

THE POWER
TO PATENT

4

TO PROTECT WHAT IS YOURS

Patents are vehicles used by the government to provide inventors with property rights that cover original intellectual creations. These rights do not guarantee anybody a market for their innovations or provide the means to develop them. Rather, a patent's power lies in the capacity its holders possess to take legal action against parties who are making and selling the holders' inventions without permission, which is patent infringement.

Having a patent means you have staked a claim and can run intruders off your territory, with you being the only one allowed to mine it for a 20-year period. That does not mean you will automatically strike it rich; that part is up to you, but it does provide you with a powerful weapon to ward off, or use against, any squatters who come along with the intention of taking over what is yours.

Tangible property is much easier to secure because the essence of the measures used are to keep the property out of the wrong hands. Ideas, however, which form the basis of any intellectual property that is patented, cannot be kept out of the wrong heads, nor can they be removed once they have found their way in. In fact, since patent applications are published, with some exceptions, by the U.S. Patent Office 18 months after being received, the core ideas become available to all who want them fairly soon. As a result, legal protections for patents focus on deterring infringement and providing legal recourse in the event infringement occurs.

PATENT POWER: HELP OR HINDRANCE?

Without patents, the incentive to take chances and innovate would be greatly diminished. Who wants to go to all the trouble of creating something, only to witness another person step in, run with the invention, and reap the rewards? That would be like buying a new car, then watching your neighbor drive off in it the next day, never to return.

All successful economies have solid systems of property rights in place. Even in the freest market your freedom to do what you wish with your own resources ends where the next person's legal rights and property begin. In today's economy, where so many of a firm's assets are intangible, the laws governing intellectual property are often far more important than the laws keeping other people from stealing the building. If, like Bluetie's David Koretz, you find yourself in a business where 90% of your firm's assets are intangible, it behooves you to do the best possible job of protecting them.

The process that begins with an inspiration, becomes an idea, is turned into an innovation, leads to a patent, and results in a marketable product that other people want, is a long, tough, risky road that calls for huge investments of time, energy, talent, and sweat, all of these being limited resources most of us would prefer to do other things with if we could not be assured of the protections afforded intellectual property. With a patent, the owner has a monopoly that lasts for 20 years from the date of the initial patent application, usually plenty of time to take advantage of, or create, any opportunities the invention might have.

Critics of patents claim they stifle competition and creativity, but that is not true. Patents are designed to prevent the theft of intellectual property and provide the patent holder offensive rights against anybody who wrongfully appropriates that property. Competitors are always free to come up with their own inventions, so long as they are unique and do not stray onto the staked claim of another.

For the typical toiling-in-the-garage individual inventor, patent protection gives them a chance to get a foothold in their industry. For example, in the early 1980s Phil Baechler wanted to figure out a way he could jog with his infant son. The strollers available at the time were not up to the task, and running with a baby in your arms does not work too well, unless you really need to be running away from something.

In short (see babyjogger.com for more information on the company), he combined a reinforced old stroller with bicycle tires and, with a few other modifications, had something that worked. About a year later he had a version he could market and Phil's baby joggers quickly became a popular product. Without the protection of patents,

---

CASE STUDY Bluetie's Secure Send

As you recall, we were introduced to Bluetie, a business services provider led by its dynamic president and founder, David Koretz, in the first two chapters. Now we begin a series of short case studies using Bluetie's experience with one of their patented innovations, Secure Send, that are designed to illustrate different aspects of the patent process.

After David hit on the idea for Secure Send, it took him and his crack team approximately 18 months to develop it to the point where it was a viable service that could be offered to customers. From there, Bluetie still had to market it and keep the technology operational. When all the labor, hardware, and overhead costs are added together, Secure Send becomes a very expensive proposition. Sure, based on what we learned about it in Chapter 2, its prospects were excellent from the start, but would Bluetie have gone to all the trouble and expense of making the idea a reality without knowing that a patent could be used to protect their creation? Probably not.

Like many other information based products, Secure Send requires a steep initial investment of financial capital and high-quality talent, not a combination many new firms possess to the necessary degree. But, once it is operational, plenty of firms have the capacity to copy it and use it as their own.

With the protection of a patent, Bluetie, as a young business, has exclusive rights to the technology, along with legal remedies if anybody else trespasses on their territory. The result is a dynamic firm who offers its clients a service that makes their operations run smoother and easier. Competitors, while they cannot pirate Secure Send, are free to develop competing technologies.

Though patent protection lasts for 20 years from the date of application, no firm in the economy's information sector expects to have an advantage over their competitors for that long, but even if they secure a lead of two, three, or five years before a sharp competitor figures out a way to beat what they have to offer, they also have time to capture a good-sized chunk of the market, and start working on the next step themselves.

---

a firm with the necessary capital could easily have come along, taken his ideas and innovations, and used their greater marketing clout to steal his thunder.

Just because Phil patented his innovation, others were not prevented from also creating their own devices to run a baby around in. If you do a search on "baby joggers" or "running strollers" on the USPTO site (www.uspto.gov), you will see that plenty of activity has taken place in that area. The Baby Jogger has done so well because the original design was excellent, it had a natural appeal, and the company has continued to improve on the basic design and add additional models and accessories. They did not need to run everybody out of the market or bar anybody from entering. The patent for the Baby Jogger merely provided a means for taking offensive action should anybody misappropriate their particular innovation.

As the parents of three children, who range in age from 2 years to 13 years, my wife and I have owned three different Baby Joggers, each better than the last, which demonstrates how good companies build on the initial advantages offered by a patent.

Though a patent gives its owner an exclusive 20-year monopoly, these monopolies do not serve to stifle creativity, rarely result in price gouging, or outlaw competition. Monopolies are a problem only when nobody is allowed to introduce substitute products (such as a running stroller unique enough to get its own patent) that allow consumers additional choices. If you introduce a patented invention that is a huge success on the market, you can be sure that, patent or not, others will be well motivated to find a way around your No Trespassing sign.

Bear in mind also that, in the process of applying for a patent, you must show how the invention in question will work, and patents that are granted, along with most patent applications, are public property available to whoever wants them. So part of the exchange that takes place is that, in order to secure patent rights, patent applicants must share their ideas freely. Without patents, inventors would be likely to keep more of their ideas as secrets in order to protect themselves. As it is, ideas becoming freely available educates and inspires others to make their own improvements.

It must be stressed that particular results cannot be patented. This means that if you patent and market a smokeless cigar, others cannot be prevented from achieving the same goal; they are just barred from doing it in the way you have already claimed.

THE LAW OF THE LAND

The Constitution of the United States gives Congress the power to create and enact patent laws, stating that "Congress shall have the power . . . to promote the progress of science and useful arts, by securing for limited times to authors and inventors the exclusive right to their respective writings and discoveries." The first patent law was enacted in 1790 and has been updated periodically since then, the most recent update being the American Inventors Protection Act of 1999, part of which mandated that patent applications filed from November 29, 2000 onward, would be published in 18 months.

Patent law tells us what kinds of things may be patented and the conditions that must be met in order to obtain a patent. The U.S.

Patent and Trademark Office was created as a distinct entity within the Department of State in 1802 to administer the law and grant patents. It has been part of the Department of Commerce since 1925.

A patent is a property right the government grants to innovators who meet the proper requirements. It gives the holder of a patent "the right to exclude others from making, using, offering for sale, or selling" the innovator's creation in the United Sates; nor may anybody import it from outside the country. This right lasts for 20 years from the time the patent application was filed.

Despite administering laws concerning the granting of patents and performing a broad range of other duties related to patents, the USPTO does not enforce patents or decide on cases of possible infringement. They also do not become involved in promoting particular patents or their applications, nor do they decide on how a patent should be utilized.

The protection of a domestic patent applies only to the United States and its possessions and territories, but patent protection covering much more of the world is available (see section on foreign patents in Chapter 5).

What a patent does not do is give its owner any particular rights to make, sell, or license their innovations. All of these depend on the initiative of the patent holder. Being able to exclude others from pirating your innovations is indeed a powerful protection, but it is one that has little value until the innovation is developed and presented to the right market in the right way.

CLEARING THE HURDLES

Before going through all the trouble of applying for a patent, it is important to first make sure that your invention is patentable. You may have a truly great idea and are convinced throngs of consumers will fall over each other to get their hands on it, but if the basic requirements are not met, no patent will be issued, no matter how great your inspiration is, and you will have wasted a lot of time, energy, and money.

Three basic conditions must be met in order to get a patent and can be identified in the form of the following questions that will be examined in detail next.

1. Is the invention new?

2. Is the invention useful?

3. Does the invention work?

The law states that anybody who "invents or discovers any new and useful process, machine, manufacture, or composition of matter, or any new and useful improvement thereof, may obtain a patent," provided they meet the legal requirements. As you can see, because of the broad nature of the language used, an enormous range of possibilities can qualify. For example, a "process" can be almost any method, act, or series of steps that give a unique result. Usually, patented processes are in industrial or technical areas. "Machines" are devices that accomplish something useful. "Manufacture" covers tangible goods that can be produced, and "composition of matter" refers to the combination and make-up of ingredients used. When you add them all up, it becomes clear that just about anything we can make, or any process we can dream up, is covered, so long as it is legal (In 1954 the Atomic Energy Act outlawed the patenting of inventions used for nuclear weapons, for example).

Is the Invention New?

To be awarded a patent, it is not necessary to invent something that is completely new in the sense that nothing like it has ever been seen before. Rather, the newness requirement in patent law can be interpreted more as instruction that an innovation be sufficiently novel and nonobvious and that it can be clearly distinguished from similar items. Ninety percent of patents issued are for improvements, and if you looked closely at the rest, most of those involve improvements, too. Bear in mind, though, that what one refers to as an improvement must really provide some kind of solid advance. Merely changing a color, substituting one similar material for another, changing the shape, altering the size, and rearranging components in ways that do not alter how the invention functions, do not qualify.

Under patent law, an improvement is considered "new" if it meets the criteria for a patent being issued. The condition required is better thought of as being that of novelty, meaning that an invention has to be different enough from what has gone before that it is unique in its own right. An easy way to establish the dividing line is to consider what cannot be patented. This happens when "the invention was known or used by others in this country, or patented or described in a printed publication in this or a foreign country, before the invention thereof by the applicant for patent," and it also happens when "the invention was patented or described in a printed publication in this or a foreign country or in public use or on sale in this country more than one year prior to the application for patent in the United States. . . ."

Is the Invention Useful?

To be useful an invention must have a purpose, something it does or can be used to accomplish. Usefulness is such a broad requirement that a use for almost anything could be found that qualifies. There are plenty of innovations that lots of us view as useless, such as ties and dress shoes that are devoid of traction, but the useful criteria is not a subjective judgment.

If an invention is illegal or obviously unsafe, it cannot be patented, be it useful or not. So, should you invent an ATM card that can be used to strip cash from any machine anywhere, do not bother filing a patent.

Does the Invention Work?

An idea itself, no matter how good or marketable, cannot be patented. Patent law requires that an invention fulfill the condition of operativeness. What this means is that your creation must really work. If people could merely patent ideas without figuring out how to implement them, the patent office would be flooded with all kinds of notions, from the plain ridiculous to those that are sent in the hope of establishing a prior claim just in case somebody else in the future figures out how to actually do it.

For example, it would be great if there was a machine that turned beer bellies into muscles, but until the workings of it can be described to the satisfaction of a skeptical patent examiner, no one need rush out a patent application for it. My own great idea is a force-field diaper that zaps away all unwanted output without leaving any evidence behind, or harming the baby. As a parent who has done lots of time changing diapers, I know how enthusiastically this innovation would be greeted, but until I can figure out how to put my brilliant observation into practice, a patent is out of reach.

According to patent law, an inventor will not receive a patent if "the invention was known or used by others in this country, or patented or described in a printed publication in this or a foreign country, before the invention thereof by the applicant for patent." A patent will also be denied if "the invention was patented or described in a printed publication in this or a foreign country or in public use or on sale in this country more than one year prior to the application for patent in the United States. . . ." So it does not matter whether the invention has ever been produced or sold; so long as there was knowledge of it at some point in the past, and it is not being kept secret now, no patent will be issued for it.

The legal term for already existing documentation is "prior art." As you will see in Chapter 5, doing a thorough search for prior art is important, not just prior to filing a patent application (and a patent examiner will also do their own search), but even before you get too far along in working on an invention. Unless you just enjoy the process, it could be a real heartbreak to spend months working away at home, in your limited spare time, to develop an inventory processing system for your refrigerator that tracks when you are close to running out of something important (like that beer you still hope can be made waistline friendly) and orders more from the store for you, only to discover that the system was recently patented (patent number 6,204,763 by Masahiro Sone, for the company Jujitsu).

This does not mean you cannot go ahead with your invention. If the patent term has expired, anybody who wants to can make and market the invention; they just have to be willing to do so without the protection a patent affords. Another avenue is to focus your efforts on making a significant enough improvement on that previously described invention so that you can get a patent on your own advances.

As broad as the criteria for patents are, other limits include laws of nature, physical phenomena, and abstract ideas. So, I cannot get a patent on the process of changing tides in the ocean, the way a toenail grows, or faith in the Holy Ghost, no matter how sincerely I might believe that they are all my inventions. Nor can I get a patent for just having an idea for a new machine or process.

Though the criteria for getting a patent has remained constant, technology has not, so there is always the challenge of applying them to inventions that could not have existed when these conditions were first developed. Fortunately, the requirements that an invention be new, useful, and functional have proven broad enough to cover the advances we have seen to date. The challenge is to adapt them to changing times.

Business method patents are a fairly new and controversial area for patenting, though still a much smaller portion of patent activity than all the attention it receives might make you think. As seen in the first chapter, the U.S. Patent Office has responded to the recent influx of business method patents by providing patent examiners additional training and having these types of patents looked at by more than one person. As a result, they are being issued at a much slower rate now, with only about a third of the Internet-based business process patent applications being granted at present, in comparison with more than two-thirds of patent applications in general being granted.

Though still an issue of contention, by looking at the claims in the most famous business application patent to date, for Amazon.com's one-click ordering, we can see where the owners can claim that the process satisfies the requirements of newness, usefulness, and being able to function. The patent (Figure 4.1) is a good example of how a simple function can be accomplished in an innovative way by using novel applications of technology.

US005960411A

United States Patent [19]
Hartman et al.

[11] Patent Number: 5,960,411

[45] Date of Patent: Sep. 28, 1999

[54] **METHOD AND SYSTEM FOR PLACING A PURCHASE ORDER VIA A COMMUNICATIONS NETWORK**

[75] Inventors: **Peri Hartman; Jeffrey P. Bezos; Shel Kaphan; Joel Spiegel**, all of Seattle, Wash.

[73] Assignee: **Amazon.com, Inc.**, Seattle, Wash.

[21] Appl. No.: **08/928,951**

[22] Filed: **Sep. 12, 1997**

[51] Int. Cl.[6] **G06F 17/60**
[52] U.S. Cl. **705/26**; 705/27; 345/962
[58] Field of Search 705/26, 27; 380/24, 380/25; 235/2, 375, 378, 381; 395/188.01; 345/962

[56] **References Cited**

U.S. PATENT DOCUMENTS

4,937,863	6/1990	Robert et al.	380/4
5,204,897	4/1993	Wyman	380/4
5,260,999	11/1993	Wyman	384/4
5,627,940	5/1997	Rohra et al.	395/12
5,640,501	6/1997	Turpin	395/768
5,640,577	6/1997	Scharmer	395/768
5,664,111	9/1997	Nahan et al.	705/27
5,715,314	2/1998	Payne et al.	380/24
5,715,399	2/1998	Bezos	705/27
5,727,163	3/1998	Bezos	705/27
5,745,681	4/1998	Levine et al.	395/200.3
5,758,126	5/1998	Daniels et al.	395/500

FOREIGN PATENT DOCUMENTS

0855659 A1	1/1998	European Pat. Off.	G06F 17/30
0855687 A2	1/1998	European Pat. Off.	G07F 19/00
0845747A2	6/1998	European Pat. Off.	G06F 17/60
0883076A2	12/1998	European Pat. Off.	G06F 17/60
WO 95/30961	11/1995	WIPO	G06F 17/60
WO 96/38799	12/1996	WIPO	G06F 17/60
WO 98/21679	5/1998	WIPO	G06F 17/60

OTHER PUBLICATIONS

Jones, Chris. "Java Shopping Cart and Java Wallet; Oracles plans to join e–commerce initiative." Mar. 31, 1997, Info-World Media Group.

"Pacific Coast Software Software creates virtual shopping cart." Sep. 6, 1996. M2 Communications Ltd 1996.

"Software Creates Virtual Shopping Cart." Sep. 5, 1996. Business Wire, Inc.

Terdoslavich, William. "Java Electronic Commerce Framework." Computer Reseller News, Sep. 23, 1996, CMP Media, Inc., 1996, pp. 126, http://www.elibrary.com/id/101/101/getdoc . . . rydocid=902269@library__d&dtype=0–0&dinst=. [Accessed Nov. 19, 1998].

"Internet Access: Disc Distributing Announces Interactive World Wide." Cambridge Work–Group Computing Report, Cambridge Publishing, Inc., 1995, http://www.elibrary.com/id/101/101/getdoc . . . docid=1007497@library__a&dtype=0–0&dinst=0. [Accessed Nov. 19, 1998].

(List continued on next page.)

Primary Examiner—James P. Trammell
Assistant Examiner—Demetra R. Smith
Attorney, Agent, or Firm—Perkins Coie LLP

[57] **ABSTRACT**

A method and system for placing an order to purchase an item via the Internet. The order is placed by a purchaser at a client system and received by a server system. The server system receives purchaser information including identification of the purchaser, payment information, and shipment information from the client system. The server system then assigns a client identifier to the client system and associates the assigned client identifier with the received purchaser information. The server system sends to the client system the assigned client identifier and an HTML document identifying the item and including an order button. The client system receives and stores the assigned client identifier and receives and displays the HTML document. In response to the selection of the order button, the client system sends to the server system a request to purchase the identified item. The server system receives the request and combines the purchaser information associated with the client identifier of the client system to generate an order to purchase the item in accordance with the billing and shipment information whereby the purchaser effects the ordering of the product by selection of the order button.

26 Claims, 11 Drawing Sheets

FIGURE 4.1   One-Click Shopping Patent

OTHER PUBLICATIONS

Nance, Barry, "Reviews: A Grand Opening for Virtual Storefront With Middleware." Jun. 1, 1997, CMP Media, Inc. 1997, p. 80, http://www.elibrary.com/getdoc.egi?id=117 . . . docid=1257247@library_a&dtype=0–0&dinst=0. [Accessed Nov. 19, 1998].

"Go–Cart Shopping Cart Software Features." 1996 GO International, Inc. http://www.go–cart.com/features.html. [Accessed Nov. 19, 1998].

"PerlShop Manual (version 2.2)." 1996, ARPAnct Corp. http://www.w3u.com/grokksoft/shop/perlman.html. [Accessed Nov. 19, 1998].

"Sax Software Announces Sax NetSell; Sax NetSell's design–time ActiveX controls make Internet commerce easy."1997, Sax Software Corp.

Baron, Chris and Bob Weil, "Implementing a Web Shopping Cart," *Dr. Dobb's Journal,* Sep. 1996, pp. 64, 66, 68–69, and 83–85.

Hoque, Reaz, "A Shopping Cart Application with JavaScript," *Web Techniques,* May 1998, pp. 63, 65–66, and 68.

FIGURE 4.1   *(Continued)*

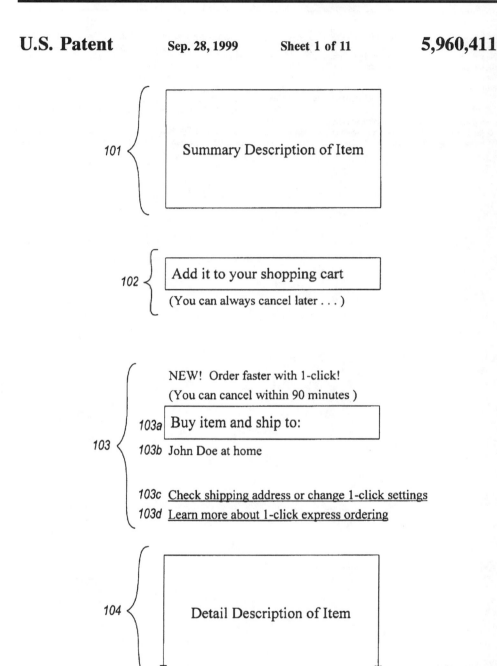

Fig. 1A

FIGURE 4.1   *(Continued)*

Thank you for your 1-click order!

A quantity of 1 of [the item] will be shipped to you
as soon as possible. We will do our best to
minimize your shipping costs by combining your
1-click orders into as few shipments as possible.

Please continue browsing.

Review or change your 1-click orders

105

Summary Description of Item

101

⋮

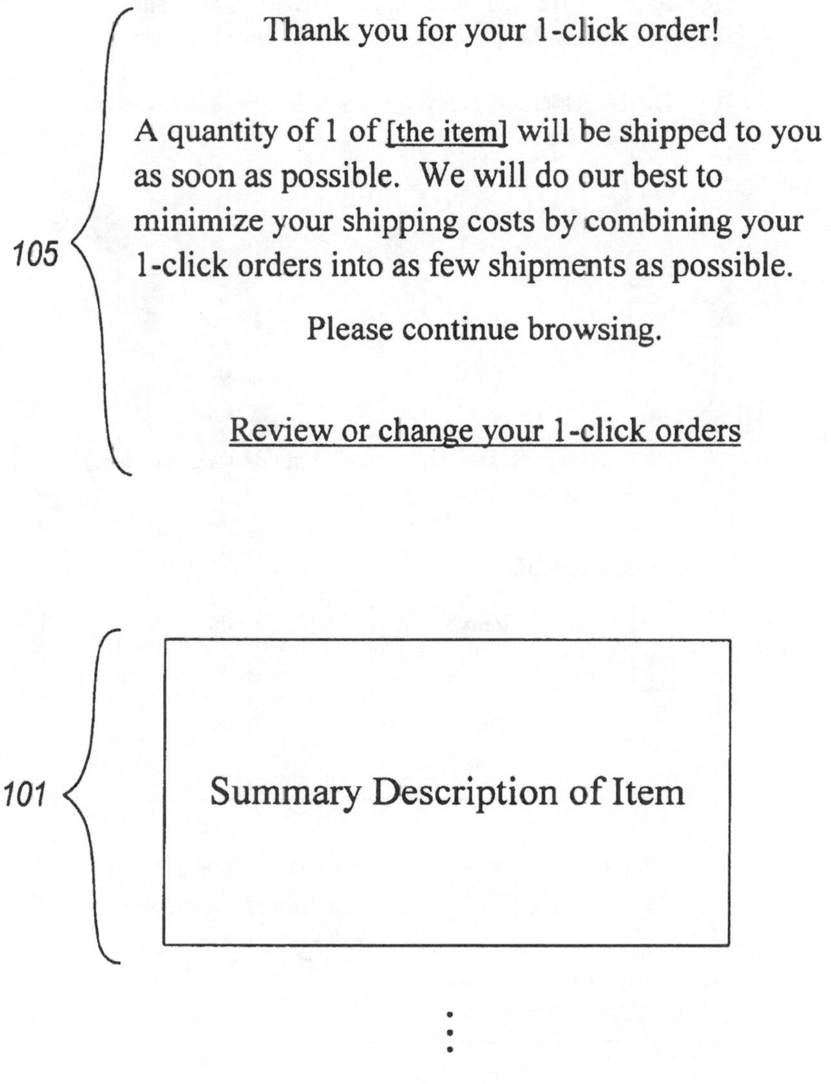

Fig. 1B

FIGURE 4.1   *(Continued)*

71

Summary of 1-Click Express Orders

Press this button if you [Changed Quantities] of any item
below. If you don't press it, your changes won't "stick."
You can set the quantity to 0 (zero) to cancel an item.

The 1-click orders below (available in 3 or fewer days)
will be shipped together.

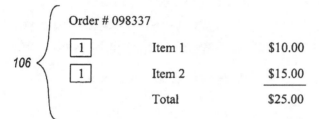

106
Order # 098337

1	Item 1	$10.00
1	Item 2	$15.00
	Total	$25.00

The 1-click orders below (available in one week or more)
will be shipped together.

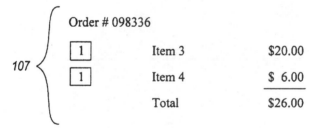

107
Order # 098336

1	Item 3	$20.00
1	Item 4	$ 6.00
	Total	$26.00

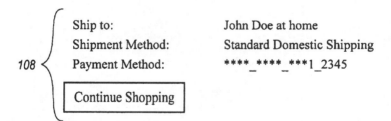

108

Ship to: John Doe at home
Shipment Method: Standard Domestic Shipping
Payment Method: ****_****_***1_2345

[Continue Shopping]

1-Click Express shipping policies

Fig. 1C

FIGURE 4.1   *(Continued)*

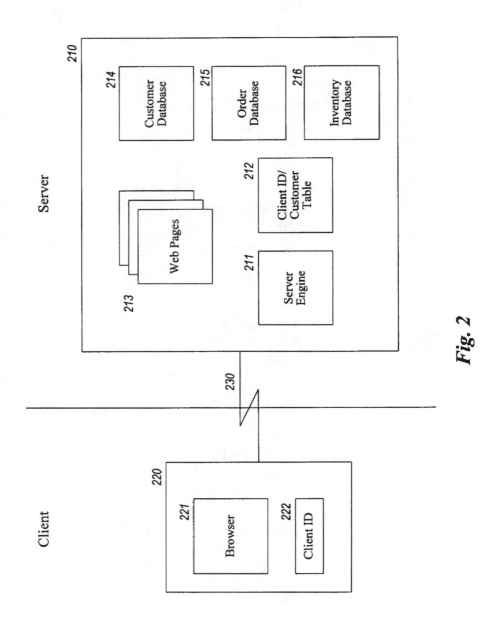

Fig. 2

FIGURE 4.1   *(Continued)*

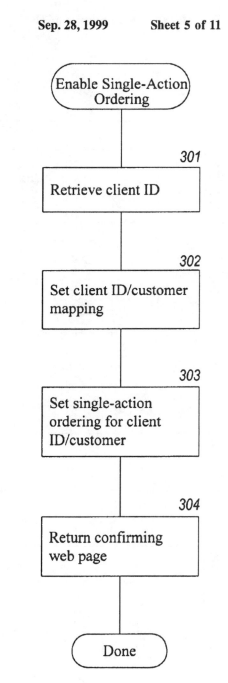

Fig. 3

FIGURE 4.1   *(Continued)*

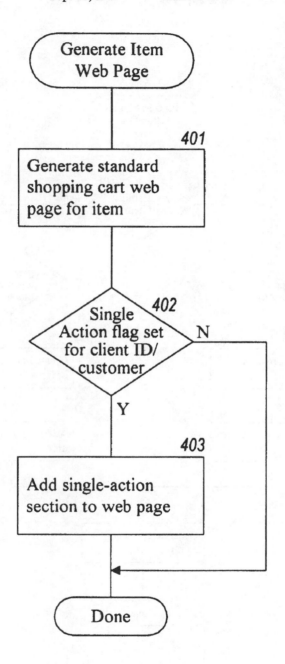

Fig. 4

FIGURE 4.1   *(Continued)*

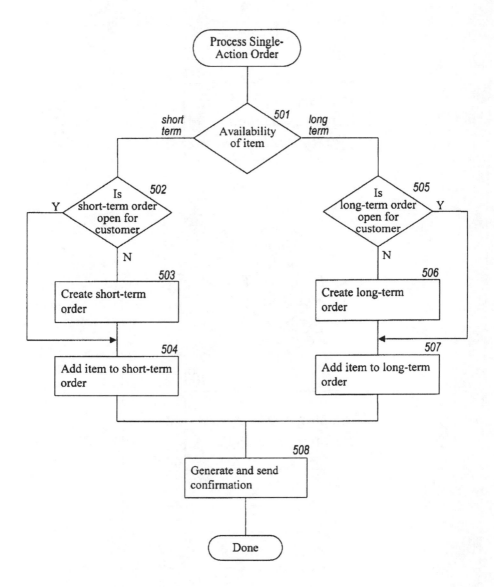

Fig. 5

FIGURE 4.1   *(Continued)*

U.S. Patent Sep. 28, 1999 Sheet 8 of 11 5,960,411

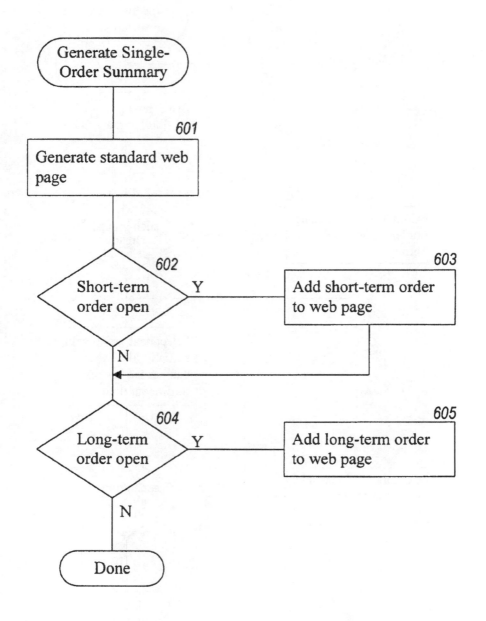

Fig. 6

FIGURE 4.1 *(Continued)*

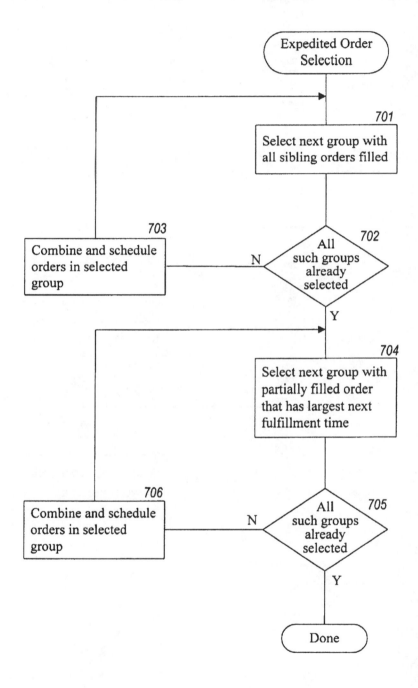

Fig. 7

FIGURE 4.1   *(Continued)*

U.S. Patent Sep. 28, 1999 Sheet 10 of 11 **5,960,411**

START

A: Customer Name & Address
B: Customer Financial Info
C: Customer Employment Info
D: Customer Education Info
.
.
.

Fig. 8A

A: First Name :
M.I. :
Last Name :
Street :
City :
State : Zip :

Next Previous

B: Customer Financial Info
C: Customer Employment Info
D: Customer Education Info
.
.
.

Fig. 8B

FIGURE 4.1 ***(Continued)***

A: Customer Name & Address

B: Net Worth:

Annual Income:

Spouse's Annual Income:

Other Income:

Next	Previous

C: Customer Employment Info

D: Customer Education Info

.

.

.

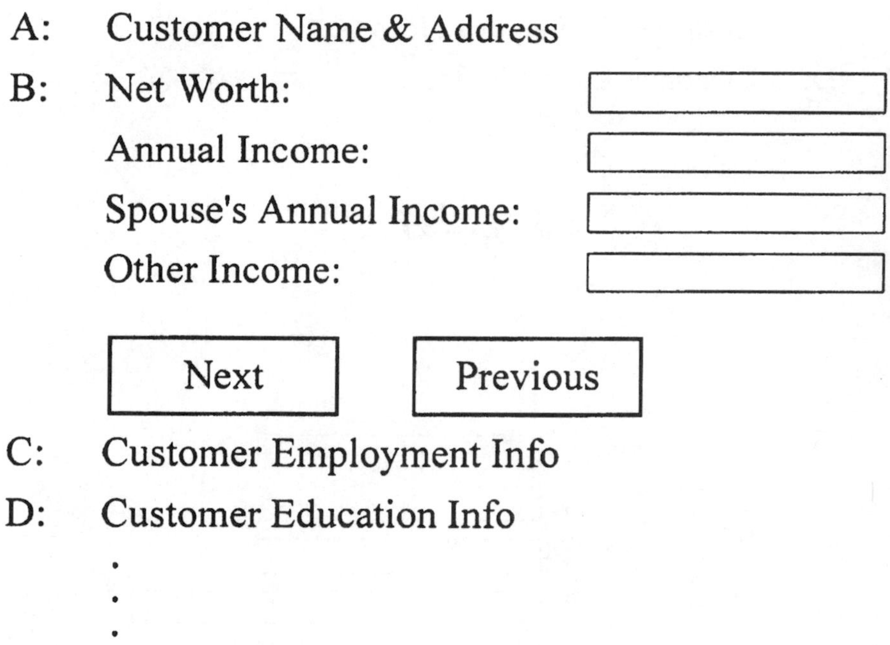

Fig. 8C

FIGURE 4.1   *(Continued)*

1

METHOD AND SYSTEM FOR PLACING A PURCHASE ORDER VIA A COMMUNICATIONS NETWORK

TECHNICAL FIELD

The present invention relates to a computer method and system for placing an order and, more particularly, to a method and system for ordering items over the Internet.

BACKGROUND OF THE INVENTION

The Internet comprises a vast number of computers and computer networks that are interconnected through communication links. The interconnected computers exchange information using various services, such as electronic mail, Gopher, and the World Wide Web ("WWW"). The WWW service allows a server computer system (i.e., Web server or Web site) to send graphical Web pages of information to a remote client computer system. The remote client computer system can then display the Web pages. Each resource (e.g., computer or Web page) of the WWW is uniquely identifiable by a Uniform Resource Locator ("URL"). To view a specific Web page, a client computer system specifies the URL for that Web page in a request (e.g., a HyperText Transfer Protocol ("HTTP") request). The request is forwarded to the Web server that supports that Web page. When that Web server receives the request, it sends that Web page to the client computer system. When the client computer system receives that Web page, it typically displays the Web page using a browser. A browser is a special-purpose application program that effects the requesting of Web pages and the displaying of Web pages.

Currently, Web pages are typically defined using Hyper-Text Markup Language ("HTML"). HTML provides a standard set of tags that define how a Web page is to be displayed. When a user indicates to the browser to display a Web page, the browser sends a request to the server computer system to transfer to the client computer system an HTML document that defines the Web page. When the requested HTML document is received by the client computer system, the browser displays the Web page as defined by the HTML document. The HTML document contains various tags that control the displaying of text, graphics, controls, and other features. The HTML document may contain URLs of other Web pages available on that server computer system or other server computer systems.

The World Wide Web is especially conducive to conducting electronic commerce. Many Web servers have been developed through which vendors can advertise and sell product. The products can include items (e.g., music) that are delivered electronically to the purchaser over the Internet and items (e.g., books) that are delivered through conventional distribution channels (e.g., a common carrier). A server computer system may provide an electronic version of a catalog that lists the items that are available. A user, who is a potential purchaser, may browse through the catalog using a browser and select various items that are to be purchased. When the user has completed selecting the items to be purchased, the server computer system then prompts the user for information to complete the ordering of the items. This purchaser-specific order information may include the purchaser's name, the purchaser's credit card number, and a shipping address for the order. The server computer system then typically confirms the order by sending a confirming Web page to the client computer system and schedules shipment of the items.

Since the purchaser-specific order information contains sensitive information (e.g., a credit card number), both

2

vendors and purchasers want to ensure the security of such information. Security is a concern because information transmitted over the Internet may pass through various intermediate computer systems on its way to its final destination. The information could be intercepted by an unscrupulous person at an intermediate system. To help ensure the security of the sensitive information, various encryption techniques are used when transmitting such information between a client computer system and a server computer system. Even though such encrypted information can be intercepted, because the information is encrypted, it is generally useless to the interceptor. Nevertheless, there is always a possibility that such sensitive information may be successfully decrypted by the interceptor. Therefore, it would be desirable to minimize the sensitive information transmitted when placing an order.

The selection of the various items from the electronic catalogs is generally based on the "shopping cart" model. When the purchaser selects an item from the electronic catalog, the server computer system metaphorically adds that item to a shopping cart. When the purchaser is done selecting items, then all the items in the shopping cart are "checked out" (i.e., ordered) when the purchaser provides billing and shipment information. In some models, when a purchaser selects any one item, then that item is "checked out" by automatically prompting the user for the billing and shipment information. Although the shopping cart model is very flexible and intuitive, it has a downside in that it requires many interactions by the purchaser. For example, the purchaser selects the various items from the electronic catalog, and then indicates that the selection is complete. The purchaser is then presented with an order Web page that prompts the purchaser for the purchaser-specific order information to complete the order. That Web page may be prefilled with information that was provided by the purchaser when placing another order. The information is then validated by the server computer system, and the order is completed. Such an ordering model can be problematic for a couple of reasons. If a purchaser is ordering only one item, then the overhead of confirming the various steps of the ordering process and waiting for, viewing, and updating the purchaser-specific order information can be much more than the overhead of selecting the item itself. This overhead makes the purchase of a single item cumbersome. Also, with such an ordering model, each time an order is placed sensitive information is transmitted over the Internet. Each time the sensitive information is transmitted over the Internet, it is susceptible to being intercepted and decrypted.

SUMMARY OF THE INVENTION

An embodiment of the present invention provides a method and system for ordering an item from a client system. The client system is provided with an identifier that identifies a customer. The client system displays information that identifies the item and displays an indication of an action (e.g., a single action such as clicking a mouse button) that a purchaser is to perform to order the identified item. In response to the indicated action being performed, the client system sends to a server system the provided identifier and a request to order the identified item. The server system uses the identifier to identify additional information needed to generate an order for the item and then generates the order.

The server system receives and stores the additional information for customers using various computer systems so that the server system can generate such orders. The server system stores the received additional information in association with an identifier of the customer and provides

FIGURE 4.1 *(Continued)*

81

the identifier to the client system. When requested by the client system, the server system provides information describing the item to the requesting client system. When the server system receives a request from a client system, the server system combines the additional information stored in association with the identifier included in the request to effect the ordering of the item.

BRIEF DESCRIPTION OF THE DRAWINGS

FIGS. 1A–1C illustrate single-action ordering in one embodiment of the present invention.

FIG. 2 is a block diagram illustrating an embodiment of the present invention.

FIG. 3 is a flow diagram of a routine that enables single-action ordering for a customer.

FIG. 4 is a flow diagram of a routine to generate a Web page in which single-action ordering is enabled.

FIG. 5 is a flow diagram of a routine which processes a single-action order.

FIG. 6 is a flow diagram of a routine for generating a single-action order summary Web page.

FIG. 7 is a flow diagram of a routine that implements an expedited order selection algorithm.

FIGS. 8A–8C illustrate a hierarchical data entry mechanism in one embodiment.

DETAILED DESCRIPTION OF THE INVENTION

The present invention provides a method and system for single-action ordering of items in a client/server environment. The single-action ordering system of the present invention reduces the number of purchaser interactions needed to place an order and reduces the amount of sensitive information that is transmitted between a client system and a server system. In one embodiment, the server system assigns a unique client identifier to each client system. The server system also stores purchaser-specific order information for various potential purchasers. The purchaser-specific order information may have been collected from a previous order placed by the purchaser. The server system maps each client identifier to a purchaser that may use that client system to place an order. The server system may map the client identifiers to the purchaser who last placed an order using that client system. When a purchaser wants to place an order, the purchaser uses a client system to send the request for information describing the item to be ordered along with its client identifier. The server system determines whether the client identifier for that client system is mapped to a purchaser. If so mapped, the server system determines whether single-action ordering is enabled for that purchaser at that client system. If enabled, the server system sends the requested information (e.g., via a Web page) to the client computer system along with an indication of the single action to perform to place the order for the item. When single-action ordering is enabled, the purchaser need only perform a single action (e.g., click a mouse button) to order the item. When the purchaser performs that single action, the client system notifies the server system. The server system then completes the order by adding the purchaser-specific order information for the purchaser that is mapped to that client identifier to the item order information (e.g., product identifier and quantity). Thus, once the description of an item is displayed, the purchaser need only take a single action to place the order to purchase that item. Also, since the client identifier identifies purchaser-specific order infor-

mation already stored at the server system, there is no need for such sensitive information to be transmitted via the Internet or other communications medium.

FIGS. 1A–1C illustrate single-action ordering in one embodiment of the present invention. FIG. 1A illustrates the display of a Web page describing an item that may be ordered. This example Web page was sent from the server system to the client system when the purchaser requested to review detailed information about the item. This example Web page contains a summary description section 101, a shopping cart section 102, a single-action ordering section 103, and a detailed description section 104. One skilled in the art would appreciate that these various sections can be omitted or rearranged or adapted in various ways. In general, the purchaser need only be aware of the item or items to be ordered by the single action and of the single action needed to place the order. The summary description and the detailed description sections provide information that identifies and describes the item(s) that may be ordered. The shopping cart section provides the conventional capability to add the described item to a shopping cart. The server system adds the summary description, the detailed description, and the shopping cart sections to each Web page for an item that may be ordered. The server system, however, only adds the single-action ordering section when single-action ordering is enabled for that purchaser at that client system. (One skilled in the art would appreciate that a single Web page on the server system may contain all these sections but the single-action ordering section can be selectively included or excluded before sending the Web page to the client system.) This example single-action ordering section allows the purchaser to specify with a single click of a mouse button to order the described item. Once the purchaser clicks the mouse button, the item is ordered, unless the purchaser then takes some action to modify the order. The single-action ordering section contains a single-action ordering button 103a, purchaser identification subsection 103b, and single-action ordering information subsections 103c and 103d. The purchaser information subsection displays enough information so that the purchaser can verify that the server system correctly recognizes the purchaser. To reduce the chances of sensitive information being intercepted, the server system sends only enough information so that the purchaser is confident that the server system correctly identified the purchaser but yet not enough information to be useful to an unscrupulous interceptor. The additional information subsections allow the purchaser to obtain various settings or obtain more information related to the single-action ordering. If the purchaser wants to verify the shipping address, the purchaser can select the "check shipping address" label. In response to this selection, the server system may require the purchaser to perform a "login" so that the identity of the purchaser can be verified before the shipping information is viewed or modified. The server system then sends a Web page to the client system for display and possible modification of the shipping address. In this way, the transmitting of the sensitive shipping address can be avoided unless requested by the verified purchaser.

When the purchaser selects the single-action ordering button, the client system sends a message to the server system requesting that the displayed item be ordered. After the server system processes the message, the server system provides to the client system a new Web page that confirms receipt of the single-action order. FIG. 1B illustrates the display of a Web page confirming a single-action order. The confirming Web page contains essentially the same information as the Web page describing the item (i.e., FIG. 1A)

FIGURE 4.1   *(Continued)*

except that an order confirmation section **105** is displayed at the top of the Web page. The order confirmation section confirms that the order has been placed and provides an opportunity for the purchaser to review and change the single-action order. Alternatively, the confirming Web page can be identical to the Web page describing the item (i.e., FIG. 1A), except that the single-action ordering button is replaced with a message confirming the order.

If a single-action ordering is not currently enabled for the client system but could be enabled, then the server system can generate a Web page like FIG. 1A, except that the single-action ordering button **103a** is replaced by a single-action ordering enable button. Such a replacement button could contain text instructing the purchaser to click on the button to enable single-action ordering. When the purchaser clicks on that button, the server system would send the Web page of FIG. 1A to be displayed. Single-action ordering can be enabled whenever the server system has stored sufficient purchaser-specific order information for that client system to complete a single-action order. If the server system does not have sufficient information, then when the purchaser selects the single-action ordering button, the server system can provide a Web page to collect the additional information that is needed. The server system may require the purchaser to "login" so that the identity of the purchaser can be verified before the single-action ordering is enabled.

To help minimize shipping costs and purchaser confusion, the server system may combine various single-action orders into a multiple-item order. For example, if a purchaser orders one item using the single-action ordering and five minutes later orders another item using the single-action ordering, then those orders may be cost effectively combined into a single order for shipping. The server system combines the single-action orders when their expected ship dates are similar. For example, if one item is immediately available and the other item will be available in one day, then the two single-action orders may be cost-effectively combined. However, if the other item will not be available for two weeks, then the two single-item orders would not be combined. FIG. 1C illustrates the display of a Web page representing four single-action orders that have been combined into two separate multiple-item orders based on the availability of the items. The order information **106** indicates that item 1 and item 2, which will be available in three or fewer days, have been combined into one order. The order information **107** indicates that items 3 and 4, which will not be available within one week, are combined into a separate order. In one embodiment, the server system may combine single-action orders that are placed within a certain time period (e.g., 90 minutes). Also, the server system may combine or divide orders when the orders are scheduled for shipment based on the then current availability of the items ordered. This delayed modification of the orders is referred to as "expedited order selection" and is described below in detail.

FIG. 2 is a block diagram illustrating an embodiment of the present invention. This embodiment supports the single-action ordering over the Internet using the World Wide Web. The server system **210** includes a server engine **211**, a client identifier/customer table **212**, various Web pages **213**, a customer database **214**, an order database **215**, and an inventory database **216**. The server engine receives HTTP requests to access Web pages identified by URLs and provides the Web pages to the various client systems. Such an HTTP request may indicate that the purchaser has performed the single action to effect single-action ordering. The customer database contains customer information for vari-

ous purchasers or potential purchasers. The customer information includes purchaser-specific order information such as the name of the customer, billing information, and shipping information. The order database **215** contains an entry for each order that has not yet been shipped to a purchaser. The inventory database **216** contains a description of the various items that may be ordered. The client identifier/customer table **212** contains a mapping from each client identifier, which is a globally unique identifier that uniquely identifies a client system, to the customer last associated with that client system. The client system **220** contains a browser and its assigned client identifier. The client identifier is stored in a file, referred to as a "cookie." In one embodiment, the server system assigns and sends the client identifier to the client system once when the client system first interacts with the server system. From then on, the client system includes its client identifier with all messages sent to the server system so that the server system can identify the source of the message. The server and client systems interact by exchanging information via communications link **230**, which may include transmission over the Internet.

One skilled in the art would appreciate that the single-action ordering techniques can be used in various environments other than the Internet. For example, single-action ordering can also be in an electronic mail environment in which an item is described in an electronic mail message along with an indication of the single action that is to be performed to effect the ordering of the item. Also, various communication channels may be used such as local area network, wide area network, or point-to-point dial up connection. Also, a server system may comprise any combination of hardware or software that can generate orders in response to the single action being performed. A client system may comprise any combination of hardware or software that can interact with the server system. These systems may include television-based systems or various other consumer products through which orders may be placed.

FIG. 3 is a flow diagram of a routine that enables single-action ordering for a customer. To enable single-action ordering, a server system needs to have information about the customer that is equivalent to the purchaser-specific order information. The server system can obtain this information in various ways. First, the server system could ask the customer if they would like to have single-action ordering enabled. If so, then the server system could prompt the customer using a Web page for the purchaser-specific order information. Second, the server system could also save the purchaser-specific order information collected when an order is placed conventionally. The server system could, either automatically or with the customer's assent, enable single-action ordering. In step **301**, the server system retrieves the client identifier that was sent by the client system. In step **302**, the server system updates the client identifier/customer table to indicate that the generated client identifier has been associated with that customer. In step **303**, the server system sets a flag indicating that single-action ordering is enabled for that client identifier and that customer combination. That flag may be stored in the client identifier/customer table. In step **304**, the server system supplies a confirming Web page to the client system. The next time a purchaser attempts to order an item, the client system will supply its client identifier to the server system. If single-action ordering is enabled for that purchaser, the server system will assume that the purchaser is the customer associated with that client identifier in the client identifier/customer table. Thus, a purchaser may not want to allow the

FIGURE 4.1 *(Continued)*

server system to enable single-action ordering if there is a possibility that someone else may use that same client system.

FIG. 4 is a flow diagram of a routine to generate a Web page in which single-action ordering is enabled. When single-action ordering is enabled, the server system generates a Web page describing an item as is conventionally done and then adds a single-action ordering section. In one embodiment, the server system adds partial purchaser-specific order information to the section. This information may include the customer's name, a shipping address moniker selected by the purchaser (e.g., "at home"), and the last five digits of a credit card number or a nickname selected by the purchaser. Such partial information should be the minimum information sufficient to indicate to the purchaser whether or not the server system is using the correct purchaser-specific order information. In step 401, the server system generates a standard shopping cart-type Web page for the item. In step 402, if the single-action ordering flag has been set for the client identifier and customer combination, then the server system continues at step 403, else the server system completes. In step 403, the server system adds the single-action section to the Web page and completes.

FIG. 5 is a flow diagram of a routine which processes a single-action order. When a purchaser performs the single action needed to place an order, the client system notifies the server system. The server system then combines the purchaser-specific order information for the customer associated with the client system with the item order information to complete the order. The single-action order may also be combined with other single-action orders and possibly with other conventionally placed orders to reduce shipping costs. In one embodiment, single-action orders can be combined if they are placed within a certain time period of each other (e.g., 90 minutes). This routine illustrates the combining of the single-action orders into a short-term order (e.g., available to be shipped in less than a week) and a long-term order (e.g., available to be shipped in more than a week). One skilled in the art would appreciate that the single-action orders can be combined in various ways based on other factors, such as size of shipment and intermediate-term availability. In step 501, if the item is expected to be shipped in the short term, then the server system continues at step 502, else the server system continues at step 505. In step 502, if a short-term order has already been opened for the purchaser, then the server system continues at step 504, else the server system continues at step 503. In step 503, the server system creates a short-term order for the purchaser. In step 504, the server system adds the item to the short-term order and continues at step 508. In step 505, if a long-term order has already been opened for the purchaser, then the server system continues at step 507, else the server system continues at step 506. In step 506, the server system creates a long-term order for the purchaser. In step 507, the server system adds the item to the long-term order. In step 508, the server system generates and sends the confirmation and completes.

FIG. 6 is a flow diagram of a routine for generating a single-action order summary Web page. This Web page (e.g., FIG. 1C) gives the user the opportunity to view and modify the short-term and long-term single-action orders. In step 601, the server system adds the standard single-action order information to the Web page. In step 602, if a short-term order is open, then the server system adds the short-term order to the Web page in step 603. In step 604, if a long-term order is open, then the server system adds the long-term order information to the Web page in step 605 and completes.

FIG. 7 is a flow diagram of a routine that implements an expedited order selection algorithm. The goal of the expedited order selection algorithm is to minimize the number of orders sent to each destination so that shipping costs are reduced. A destination may be a specific shipping address plus a specific purchaser's billing details. Orders that are sent to the same destination are known as "sibling orders." The algorithm has two stages. In the first stage, the algorithm schedules for shipment the orders for destinations for which all the sibling orders are filled. An order is filled when all its items are currently in inventory (i.e., available) and can be shipped. For each group of sibling orders, the algorithm combines those sibling orders into a single combined order so that only one order is currently scheduled for shipment to each destination. In the second stage, the algorithm combines and schedules groups of sibling orders for which some of the sibling orders are not filled or partially filled. The algorithm may split each partially filled sibling order into a filled sibling order and a completely unfilled sibling order. The algorithm then combines all the filled sibling orders into a single combined order and schedules the combined order for shipment. If any group has only one sibling order and that order is partially filled, then the algorithm in one embodiment does not split that order to avoid making an extra shipment to that destination.

During the second stage, the algorithm may select and schedule groups of sibling orders in a sequence that is based on the next fulfillment time for an item in the group. The next fulfillment time for a group of sibling orders is the minimum expected fulfillment time of the items in that group of sibling orders. For example, if a group of sibling orders has seven items that are not yet fulfilled and their expected fulfillment times range from 3 days to 14 days, then the next fulfillment time for that group is 3 days. The algorithm first schedules those groups of sibling orders with the largest next fulfillment time. For example, if 6 groups have next fulfillment times of 3, 5, 7, 10, 11, and 14 days, respectively, then the algorithm first selects and schedules the sibling orders in the group with the next fulfillment time of 14 days, followed by the group with the next fulfillment time of 11 days, and so on. By delaying the scheduling of groups with short next fulfillment times, the algorithm increases the chances of additional items becoming available (because of the shortness of the next fulfillment time) and thus combined with the scheduled order.

Steps 701–703 represent the first stage of the expedited order selection algorithm, and steps 704–706 represent the second stage of the expedited selection order algorithm. In steps 701–703, the algorithm loops selecting groups in which all sibling orders are filled and combining the orders. In step 701, the algorithm selects the next group with all sibling orders that are filled. In step 703, if all such groups have already been selected, then the algorithm continues with the second stage in step 704, else the algorithm continues at step 703. In step 703, the algorithm combines and schedules the orders in the selected group and loops to step 701. In step 704, the algorithm selects the next group of sibling orders that has the largest next fulfillment time. In step 705, if all such groups have already been selected, then the algorithm is done, else the algorithm continues at step 706. In step 706, the algorithm combines and schedules the orders in the selected group and loops to step 704. When the expedited order selection algorithm is being performed, new orders and new inventory may be received. Whenever such new orders and new inventory is received, then the algorithm restarts to schedule and combine the new orders as appropriate.

FIGURE 4.1 *(Continued)*

Although the algorithm has been described as having two stages, it could be implemented in an incremental fashion where the assessment of the first and second stages are redone after each order is scheduled. One skilled in the art would recognize that there are other possible combinations of these stages which still express the same essential algorithm.

FIGS. 8A–8C illustrate a hierarchical data entry mechanism in one embodiment. When collecting information from a user, a Web page typically consists of a long series of data entry fields that may not all fit onto the display at the same time. Thus, a user needs to scroll through the Web page to enter the information. When the data entry fields do not fit onto the display at the same time, it is difficult for the user to get an overall understanding of the type and organization of the data to be entered. The hierarchical data entry mechanism allows a user to understand the overall organization of the data to be entered even though the all data entry fields would not fit onto the display at the same time. FIG. 8A illustrates an outline format of a sample form to be filled in. The sample form contains various sections identified by letters A, B, C, and D. When the user selects the start button, then section A expands to include the data entry fields for the customer name and address. FIG. 8B illustrates the expansion of section A. Since only section A has been expanded, the user can view the data entry fields of section A and summary information of the other sections at the same time. The user then enters data in the various data entry fields that are displayed. Upon completion, the user selects either the next or previous buttons. The next button causes section A to be collapsed and section B to be expanded so that financial information may be entered. FIG. 8C illustrates the expansion of section B. If the previous button is selected, then section A would collapse and be displayed as shown in FIG. 8A. This collapsing and expanding is repeated for each section. At any time during the data entry, if an error is detected, then a Web page is generated with the error message in close proximity (e.g., on the line below) to the data entry field that contains the error. This Web page is then displayed by the client system to inform the user of the error. In addition, each of the data "entry" fields may not be editable until the user clicks on the data entry field or selects an edit button associated with the data entry field. In this way, the user is prevented from inadvertently changing the contents of an edit field. When the user clicks on a data entry field, a new Web page is presented to the user that allows for the editing of the data associated with the field. When editing is complete, the edited data is displayed in the data "entry" field. Because the fields of the form are thus not directly editable, neither "named-submit" buttons nor Java are needed. Also, the form is more compact because the various data entry options (e.g., radio button) are displayed only on the new Web page when the field is to be edited.

Although the present invention has been described in terms of various embodiments, it is not intended that the invention be limited to these embodiments. Modification within the spirit of the invention will be apparent to those skilled in the art. For example, the server system can map a client identifier to multiple customers who have recently used the client system. The server system can then allow the user to identify themselves by selecting one of the mappings based preferably on a display of partial purchaser-specific order information. Also, various different single actions can be used to effect the placement of an order. For example, a voice command may be spoken by the purchaser, a key may be depressed by the purchaser, a button on a television remote control device may be depressed by the purchaser, or

selection using any pointing device may be effected by the purchaser. Although a single action may be preceded by multiple physical movements of the purchaser (e.g., moving a mouse so that a mouse pointer is over a button), the single action generally refers to a single event received by a client system that indicates to place the order. Finally, the purchaser can be alternately identified by a unique customer identifier that is provided by the customer when the customer initiates access to the server system and sent to the server system with each message. This customer identifier could be also stored persistently on the client system so that the purchaser does not need to re-enter their customer identifier each time access is initiated. The scope of the present invention is defined by the claims that follow.

We claim:

1. A method of placing an order for an item comprising:
   under control of a client system,
      displaying information identifying the item; and
      in response to only a single action being performed, sending a request to order the item along with an identifier of a purchaser of the item to a server system;
   under control of a single-action ordering component of the server system,
      receiving the request;
      retrieving additional information previously stored for the purchaser identified by the identifier in the received request; and
      generating an order to purchase the requested item for the purchaser identified by the identifier in the received request using the retrieved additional information; and
      fulfilling the generated order to complete purchase of the item
   whereby the item is ordered without using a shopping cart ordering model.

2. The method of claim 1 wherein the displaying of information includes displaying information indicating the single action.

3. The method of claim 1 wherein the single action is clicking a button.

4. The method of claim 1 wherein the single action is speaking of a sound.

5. The method of claim 1 wherein a user of the client system does not need to explicitly identify themselves when placing an order.

6. A client system for ordering an item comprising:
   an identifier that identifies a customer;
   a display component for displaying information identifying the item;
   a single-action ordering component that in response to performance of only a single action, sends a request to a server system to order the identified item, the request including the identifier so that the server system can locate additional information needed to complete the order and so that the server system can fulfill the generated order to complete purchase of the item; and
   a shopping cart ordering component that in response to performance of an add-to-shopping-cart action, sends a request to the server system to add the item to a shopping cart.

7. The client system of claim 6 wherein the display component is a browser.

8. The client system of claim 6 wherein the predefined action is the clicking of a mouse button.

9. A server system for generating an order comprising:
   a shopping cart ordering component; and

FIGURE 4.1   *(Continued)*

5,960,411

11

a single-action ordering component including:

a data storage medium storing information for a plurality of users;

a receiving component for receiving requests to order an item, a request including an indication of one of the plurality of users, the request being sent in response to only a single action being performed; and

an order placement component that retrieves from the data storage medium information for the indicated user and that uses the retrieved information to place an order for the indicated user for the item; and

an order fulfillment component that completes a purchase of the item in accordance with the order placed by the single-action ordering component.

10. The server system of claim **9** wherein the request is sent by a client system in response to a single action being performed.

11. A method for ordering an item using a client system, the method comprising:

displaying information identifying the item and displaying an indication of a single action that is to be performed to order the identified item; and

in response to only the indicated single action being performed, sending to a server system a request to order the identified item

whereby the item is ordered independently of a shopping cart model and the order is fulfilled to complete a purchase of the item.

12. The method of claim **11** wherein the server system uses an identifier sent along with the request to identify additional information needed to generate an order for the item.

13. The method of claim **12** wherein the identifier identifies the client system and the server system provides the identifier to the client system.

12

14. The method of claim **11** wherein the client system and server system communicate via the Internet.

15. The method of claim **11** wherein the displaying includes displaying an HTML document provided by the server system.

16. The method of claim **11** including sending from the server system to the client system a confirmation that the order was generated.

17. The method of claim **11** wherein the single action is clicking a mouse button when a cursor is positioned over a predefined area of the displayed information.

18. The method of claim **11** wherein the single action is a sound generated by a user.

19. The method of claim **11** wherein the single action is selection using a television remote control.

20. The method of claim **11** wherein the single action is depressing of a key on a key pad.

21. The method of claim **11** wherein the single action is selecting using a pointing device.

22. The method of claim **11** wherein the single action is selection of a displayed indication.

23. The method of claim **11** wherein the displaying includes displaying partial information supplied by the server system as to the identity of a user of the client system.

24. The method of claim **11** wherein the displaying includes displaying partial shipping information supplied by the server system.

25. The method of claim **11** wherein the displaying includes displaying partial payment information supplied by the server system.

26. The method of claim **11** wherein the displaying includes displaying a moniker identifying a shipping address for the customer.

* * * * *

FIGURE 4.1 *(Continued)*

Functions of the United States Patent and Trademark Office

The United States Patent and Trademark Office (USPTO) is part of the Department of Commerce and is responsible for the examination and issue of patents, the registration of trademarks, and the administration of the laws that apply to those processes. The USPTO is involved in every phase of a patent's life, from initial application, to examination, to grant, and to maintenance, and it stays involved even after the patent expires by maintaining a record of it.

By maintaining and classifying records of all patents since the first was issued in 1790 and freely sharing copies of patents with anybody who asks, the USPTO supports technological progress and serves as a gatekeeper over what can, and cannot, be patented.

For those who apply for patents, the USPTO provides a complete range of services, thorough enough that even the rare individual who wants to go through the process without the aid of an attorney can do so (though, as we will see in the next section, going it alone is usually not a good idea).

The USPTO examines patents, determines whether or not a patent should be granted, publishes patents that have been applied for (after 18 months) and granted, records assignments of patents, supplies copies of records and papers, provides all necessary forms and instructions for the entire patent process, and operates an excellent web site (www.uspto.gov), which enables consumers of their services to perform an ever-increasing range of them online.

Patent examiners are broken up into groups according to their expertise. A patent you file will be assigned to a group who has the background and training necessary to evaluate it; they will make the determination as to whether a patent should be granted. The USPTO has about 6,000 employees. They receive patent applications in ever-increasing amounts, from what will probably be close to 400,000 this year and climb to 600,000 in a few more years. Currently they handle more than 5 million pieces of mail per day and an ever-increasing amount of traffic on their web site.

PRIOR TO
THE PATENT

5

BLINDED BY LOVE?

Before beginning the formal process of applying for a patent, it is important to conduct a realistic assessment of what your invention's prospects for the future are. If the patent is for an invention you simply want to keep other people from using, then all you need do is make sure there are no roadblocks (like an existing patent or prior art) and then proceed with the application. If, however, your invention is something you will be developing with the intention of making a market for it, which is an assumption the rest of this chapter will work from, there are things that you should do first.

To illustrate the process, we will use a hypothetical invention, called the Rocket Racket, a tennis racket with a unique feature in the handle that causes the racket to flex much more than normal when the ball hits the strings, then immediately spring back into position, shooting the ball off the strings with lots more force than any other racket in existence can provide, giving even the lowliest players the power of Pete Sampras.

We have recently come up with the idea and have with the skills necessary to actually get the invention to work. Before charging ahead with a patent application, in the belief that tennis players everywhere will trip all over each other to buy the racket, there are four things we should do first:

1. Seek the opinions of knowledgeable people.
2. Define the market for the invention.
3. Determine the profit potential.
4. Evaluate the path to market.

Seek Outside Opinions

A good starting place for determining the ultimate feasibility of an invention is running the idea past people with relevant knowledge and experience whose opinions you trust, and whom you also trust not to pirate your invention. It is easy for any of us to fall in love with our own ideas. Just as every parent believes their baby is the most beautiful creation in the whole world, no matter what they actually look like, so too can we become infatuated with an innovation, and our own cleverness, to the point where we lose the ability to look at it objectively.

It is important that these trusted and competent people having your ideas presented to them be honest in their evaluation. Are they forthright enough to tell you that this notion you coddle so fondly is really an ugly duckling that has no more chance of taking off in the marketplace than a dodo bird has of achieving flight? If you ask those who are merely going to be nice out of consideration, you have, at best, wasted your time and theirs; at worst you have received false encouragement that might lead to a bad decision.

You might not like hearing that your baby is ugly, but it is valuable knowledge. Bear in mind that a single opinion does not have to spell doom, so, if you have people available, do not stop at one. Maybe others will react differently; maybe you will get a range of responses, from the ugly baby opinion to a rave review that claims your baby is ready to win beauty contests everywhere.

Good, bad, or in-between, outside opinions also provide the benefit of insights you may be too close to your proposed invention to have. These insights may enable you to improve on your idea, convince you to abandon it because you missed some big problems that are obvious to an outsider, or, just maybe, let you know just how solid your concept really is.

It is not enough to seek the counsel of those evaluating your invention purely from a conceptual point of view. Knowing that your invention will work in theory is okay, but make sure it also works in the practical kinds of ways that give it appeal.

For the Rocket Racket, we should talk to people who are involved with tennis in a variety of ways. If possible, we should seek the opinions of those who have been involved in the design and manufacture of tennis rackets, people who have sold them, and tennis pros who are familiar with the game at all levels, along with anybody else whose perceptions are worth seeking.

Define the Market

Just because you have a great idea that trusted peers, friends, and experts like does not guarantee there will be a market for it. You need to calculate exactly who your invention will appeal to, why they will want it, and have an idea, roughly, of how many may actually be willing to pay for it.

In the case of the Rocket Racket, we discover that most of the top pros do not want a racket with all that power. Pete Sampras, for example, uses a racket that is around 15 years old because he hits the ball so hard that newer rackets cause it to fly out of the court. Now maybe our Rocket Racket gives pros the control necessary to contain all that power, but it's starting to sound like our market is not with the pros. It is probably not with beginners either, who have enough trouble hitting the ball that a supercharged racket would only make them dangerous.

Who then? Maybe the serious and casual amateur players whose games could benefit from having more zip on the ball. In thinking it through, it might seem that primarily older players will like it, people who have played the game for years and still are not comfortable with the new technologies that bring so much more power to the game. Our racket will be light and comfortable then, nothing too flashy looking, a friendly face that introduces players to the world of explosive power!

Determine Profit Potential

Even if your invention is something you are certain will appeal to a particular audience, it is important to determine whether any money can be made selling it to them.

In the late 1990s there were lots of dot-com firms that did terrific things on the Internet, from online cartoon series, to selling autos, to digital magazines, and the list goes on. Yet, most of these were gone, or in serious financial trouble, within a year or two.

The problem was that most had great concepts that attracted lots of traffic to their sites, but not enough paying customers to make a go of it, like having a popular road that hardly anybody will take once a toll is put on it. It was common for new dot-com firms to begin operating with a great technological application that worked just fine, but with no solid idea of how they would ever make money with it, assuming that its appeal would eventually make the path to profitability clear.

Another potential pitfall is in creating a product people are willing to buy, but not at the price you need to sell it. With Rocket Racket, we have a product with built-in appeal; almost any nonprofessional tennis player would love to have a racket that generated extra power so easily. But what if we started making them and discovered it cost $500 to put the racket into a player's hands, but that player is willing only to put $100 in our hands in exchange for it?

A market for any good or service survives only when exchanges are made that allow both sides to it to come away feeling better off than they were before. As the makers of an invention, we need to charge enough to cover our costs of production and have enough left over to compensate ourselves for all that work. The buyer of the Rocket Racket must believe that the money they are shelling out, a limited resource they could spend on other things, is well spent and brings them more valuable benefits than whatever else they might have spent their money on.

Know the Path to Market

It is possible to satisfy all of the above conditions and still fail if you are unable to get your invention to the people it is intended for. How and where is this creation going to be made? Will you sell it yourself, on the Internet, in stores, or some combination? How are you going to let consumers know about it? "Build it and they will come" might work for baseball diamonds cut out of the middle of cornfields and intended to attract the spirits of dead players, who probably do not have any money anyway, but it falls short for anything else.

For the Rocket Racket, are stores going to be willing to sell a racket that competes with their established lines? Are consumers going to believe our claims if we sell it by mail or web site? There have been lots of great ideas that worked and had plenty of potential appeal, yet failed because their intended audience never heard enough about them or had the right access.

THE TOE-IN-THE-WATER SEARCH

Once you feel reasonably confident that your invention makes sense, has a specific market, can be made and sold profitably, and can be placed in the hands of its target audience, it's time to see if it, or something very similar, already exists. Why not do this right at the beginning? You could, but in the process of going through the steps above, an invention might change and evolve, so the first search should wait until there is a clear idea of what is being searched for.

Above all, it is vital to find out if there is already a patent on the invention in question; you do not want to waste time applying for a patent somebody else already holds, or skip right to selling your invention and get sued for patent infringement. Chances are, since most original creations are made in areas the inventor is familiar with, you have a pretty good idea of what is out there already, but just because something is not on store shelves does not mean it is not patented.

The most efficient way to get a first look is to use the web site of the United States Patent and Trademark Office (www.uspto.gov), where you can search through all patents issued since 1790. In addition, most patent applications are now being published 18 months after application, so these are worth searching through also. A good commercial site is run by IBM and can be found at Delphion.com. Both sites are easy to use and provide all the directions and assistance you will need to start searching.

Bear in mind that there are more than 400 classes and 136,000 sub-classes of patents, so when you are searching, do not assume that what you are looking for does not exist just because it doesn't appear on the screen in front of you. For example, if you thought you were the inventor of a Super Soaker and did a search, it would not turn up. That is because the patent for it is found under "squirt guns."

The point here is that this is just a preliminary search; when it is time to go for the patent, have a professional do it (more on that later). At this stage, you just want to make sure there are no obvious road-blocks before you put more resources into developing your innovation.

Along with these web sites, there are other resources to check in your quest to see if you are doing as the *Star Trek* crew and boldly going where nobody has gone before. Take a look at journals and trade magazines in the area of an invention, check out manufacturers', wholesalers', and retailers' listings of goods and services being of-fered. If you have any contacts in an industry, it is also a good idea to see what you can find out about what is in the pipeline for the near fu-ture or being considered for the more distant future.

Even if nothing like our Rocket Racket is on the market now and we are sure nobody else is working on one, our first look is not over yet. Any description of what is essentially our Rocket Racket that was published in the past, any time or anywhere, is considered prior art and will prevent us from meeting the newness requirement of a patent. Search as we may, no matter how powerful the search engine or our own determination, going through all possible publications is impossible, and even going through a reasonable amount efficiently is best left to an experienced professional who knows what to look for.

For those not comfortable doing online searches on their own, the USPTO has wonderful resources anybody can make use of. In Arling-ton, Va. there is the Scientific and Technical Information Center of the Patent and Trademark Office at Crystal Plaza 3 on Jefferson Davis Highway, which has more than 120,000 volumes of scientific and tech-nical books, more than 90,000 bound volumes of periodicals, the jour-nals of around 80 foreign patent offices, and in excess of 40 million foreign patents for you to browse through.

In the same building is the Patent Search Room, where you can search through all patents granted since 1790, along with patent appli-cations not yet granted that were filed at least 18 months earlier. There are people employed in both places to provide assistance and they have excellent reputations for helpfulness.

If the distance is too great a hurdle there are patent and trademark depository libraries in cities throughout the country that, though not as complete as those at the locations above, still have an excellent array of resources. Locations of these libraries, along with hours and phone numbers, are all readily available from the USPTO.

Along with allowing you the chance to discover any obvious barriers to your prospective patent, a preliminary search can also be a great source of ideas and inspiration. Remember that, in exchange for a 20-year monopoly, acquiring a patent means that the applicant must describe how the invention works, which provides a tremendous knowledge base that anybody can draw on. It is quite possible to come across things that contribute to your own progress or even provide whole new inspirations.

In our searches for existing or expired patents, along with any other kind of prior art, let us say we come across a patented racket technology that is not exactly like ours, but is trying to accomplish something similar. By looking at what other inventors are trying to accomplish, we get a better idea of the competition, what has been attempted, how our improvement stacks up, what others have drawn on (as seen in their list of references to past patents), and a source of ideas for making our invention better. Figure 5.1 is a patent for a tennis racket that does some things similar to our Rocket Racket. As you read through it, keep in mind how valuable perusing it through the eyes of an innovator could be.

Like wandering around a bookstore, looking through other patents, and ideas from any source, can lead you to unexpected opportunities. For example, as we search for material relevant to the Rocket Racket, a patent for a racket outfitted with a portable radio catches our attention. As we glance through it (see Figure 5.2), a new idea comes to us; why not do something similar with a CD player? Back when this patent was issued, there were not CD players around that could withstand the shock of a ball and racket colliding without skipping, but what if we have a means of inserting a lightweight player that can? Even if we do not pursue it today, we now have an idea to come back to in the future, an idea inspired by what has already been accomplished.

PREVIEWING THE COMING ATTRACTION

Depending on the invention, a prototype, or at least a detailed rendering, should be created. It does not have to be fancy or cost a fortune; the idea is to have something tangible that is an embodiment of what the invention will eventually be. With things like computer software this is difficult because a working prototype might be pretty close to the finished product, but maybe you can come up with something that hits on the basics without being fully functional or

United States Patent [19]

Takatsuka

[11] **Patent Number:** **5,470,062**

[45] **Date of Patent:** **Nov. 28, 1995**

[54] **TENNIS RACKET**

[75] Inventor: **Masanori Takatsuka**, Shizuoka, Japan

[73] Assignee: **Yamaha Corporation**, Japan

[21] Appl. No.: **352,600**

[22] Filed: **Dec. 9, 1994**

[30] **Foreign Application Priority Data**

Dec. 10, 1993 [JP] Japan 5-340932

[51] Int. Cl.^{6} **A63B 49/04**
[52] U.S. Cl. .... **273/73 R; 273/73 C**
[58] Field of Search .... 273/73 R, 73 C, 273/73 G

[56] **References Cited**

U.S. PATENT DOCUMENTS

3,801,099	4/1974	Lair	273/73 C
3,913,911	10/1975	Peterson	273/73 C
4,027,881	6/1977	Hefenus .	
4,153,249	5/1979	Plagenhoef	273/73 C
4,182,512	1/1980	Kuebler	273/73 C
4,192,505	3/1980	Tabickman	273/73 C
4,196,901	4/1980	Durbin	273/73 G
4,353,551	10/1982	Arieh et al.	273/73 C
4,693,474	9/1987	Glaessgen et al. .	
5,054,780	10/1991	Chen	273/73 C X
5,083,777	1/1992	Held	273/73 C X
5,110,126	5/1992	Knebler	273/73 C

FOREIGN PATENT DOCUMENTS

2088220	6/1982	United Kingdom	273/73 C

Primary Examiner—William E. Stoll
Attorney, Agent, or Firm—Ostrolenk, Faber, Gerb & Soffen

[57] **ABSTRACT**

In construction of a tennis racket having a frame top and a yoke, balance adjusters having specific gravities larger than that of a frame are arranged at the frame top and the yoke, respectively, with a specified mass ratio between the two balance adjusters. Repulsion characteristics are much improved and vibratory impact is mitigated even at off-spot shooting whilst assuring long and speedy fly of balls with reduced physical damages on players.

9 Claims, 4 Drawing Sheets

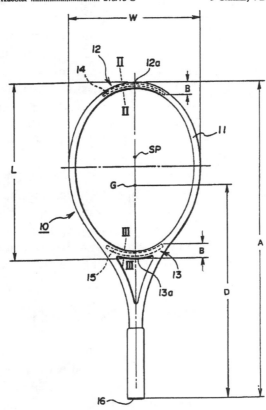

FIGURE 5.1   Tennis Racket Patent

FIG. 1

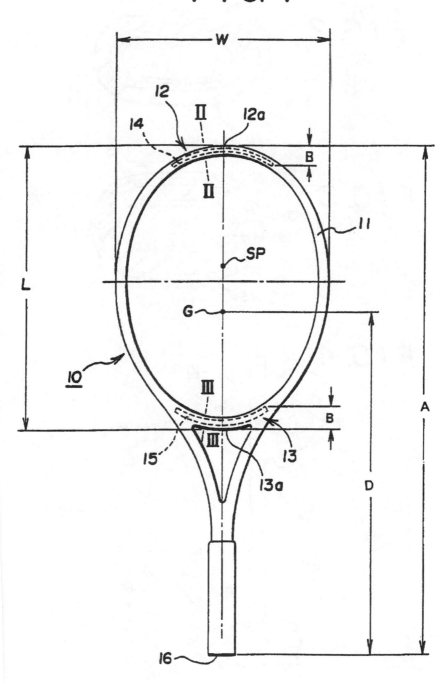

FIGURE 5.1 *(Continued)*

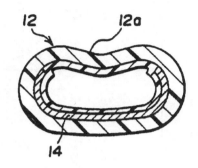

F I G. 2

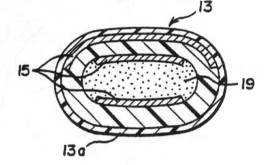

F I G. 3

F I G. 4

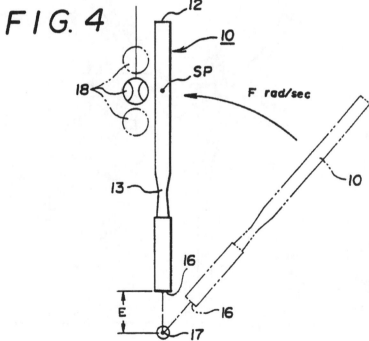

F rad/sec

FIGURE 5.1   *(Continued)*

F I G. 5

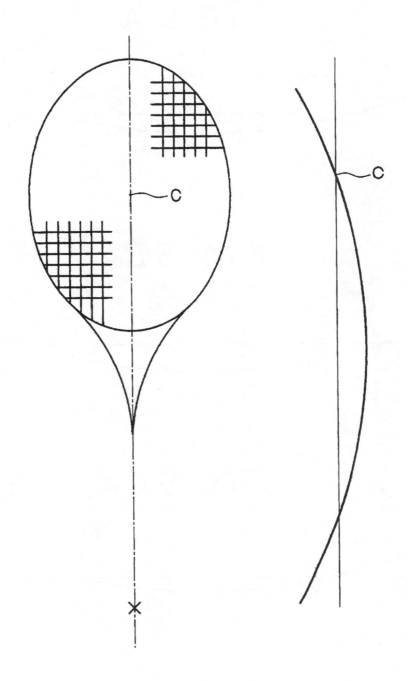

FIGURE 5.1 *(Continued)*

U.S. Patent Nov. 28, 1995 Sheet 4 of 4 5,470,062

FIG. 6A

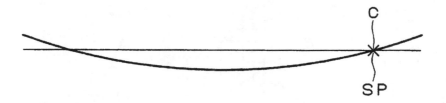

FIG. 6B

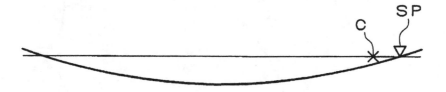

FIG. 6C

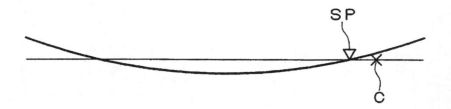

FIGURE 5.1 ***(Continued)***

1

TENNIS RACKET

BACKGROUND OF THE INVENTION

The present invention relates to a tennis racket, and more particularly relates to improvement in dynamic behaviour of a light weight tennis racket suited for use by unskilled players, in particular at off-spot shooting.

Here, the term "off-spot shooting" refers to shooting at face sections outside the sweet spot of a tennis racket.

It is already proposed to arrange a heavy mass at a section of a head corresponding to the largest width of the face of a tennis racket for higher plane stability in the case of off-spot shooting, and the mass is usually made of a material having a specific gravity larger than that of a frame of the tennis racket. For example, such a mass is made of lead or the like.

It is also proposed to arrange a heavy mass, which is made of a material of a large specific gravity such as lead, at the frame top of a tennis racket. Presence of such a heavy mass at the frame top increases the moment of inertia of area of the tennis racket and brings the center of mass near the center of the face of the tennis racket. Increased moment of inertia of area and displaced center of mass concur to assure good flight of balls even in the case of off-spot shooting.

Despite such optimization of moment of inertia and center of mass, no appreciable improvements have been attained in relation to repulsion characteristics and vibratory impact at off-spot shooting. As a result, lowering in repulsion characteristics causes low speed flight of balls and high vibratory impact tends to impose physical damages such as tennis elbow in particular on unskilled players, both in case of off-spot shooting.

In addition, presence of a heavy mass at the frame top inevitably causes undesirable displacement of the sweet spot towards the frame top. Normally, a sweet spot of a tennis racket is designed to be situated around the center area of its face. So, such displacement of the sweet spot towards the frame top reduces the effective surface area of the sweet spot because of the substantially oval shape of the face. Knowledge of this results imposes a sort of mental stress on unskilled players and makes them feel it difficult to manipulate the tennis racket as they intend.

SUMMARY OF THE INVENTION

It is the primary object of the present invention to provide a light weight tennis racket of an improved dynamic behaviour at off-spot shooting in particular suited for unskilled players.

It is another object of the present invention to maintain high repulsion characteristics at off-spot shooting, thereby assuring high speed flight of balls.

It is the other object of the present invention to mitigate vibratory impact even at off-spot shooting, thereby releasing unskilled players from the troubles of physical damages such as tennis elbow.

It is a further object of the present invention to provide a tennis racket which can be easily manipulated even by unskilled players.

In accordance with the basic aspect of the present invention, a substantially oval frame has a frame top and a yoke, the first balance adjuster is arranged at the frame top and made of the first material having the first specific gravity larger than that of the frame, the second balance adjuster is arranged at the yoke and made of the second material having

2

the second specific gravity larger than that of the frame, the mass of the second balance adjuster is 1.5 to 2.9 times larger than that of the first balance adjuster.

In one preferred embodiment of the present invention, the total mass of the tennis racket is in a range from 220 to 350 g.

In another preferred embodiment of the present invention, the first material for the first balance adjuster is same as the second material for the second balance adjuster.

In the other preferred embodiment of the present invention, the first material for the first balance adjuster is different from the second material for the second balance adjuster but the first specific gravity of the first material is same as the second specific gravity of the second material.

In the other preferred embodiment of the present invention, the first material for the first balance adjuster is different from the second material for the second balance adjuster and the first specific gravity of the first material is different from the second specific gravity of the second material.

In a further preferred embodiment of the present invention the first balance adjuster extends over a distance of 10% or less of the total racket length, i.e. the straight length of the racket along its longitudinal center axis, from the frame top end and the second balance adjuster extends over a distance of 10% or less of the total racket length from the yoke end.

BRIEF DESCRIPTION OF THE DRAWINGS

FIG. 1 is a top view of one embodiment of the tennis racket in accordance with the present invention,

FIG. 2 is a transverse sectional view taken along a line II—II in FIG. 1,

FIG. 3 is a transverse sectional view taken along a line III—III in FIG. 1,

FIG. 4 is a side view for showing operation of the tennis racket shown in FIG. 1, and

FIG. 5 is an explanatory view for showing the mode of the primary vibration of a tennis racket at shooting balls, and

FIGS. 6A to 6C are graphic views for showing the relationship between the mode of the primary vibration and the type of the mass distribution of a tennis racket.

DESCRIPTION OF THE PREFERRED EMBODIMENTS

One embodiment of the tennis racket in accordance with the present invention is shown in FIG. 1, in which a tennis racket 10 has total racket length A of 680 mm. The tennis racket 10 includes an oval head of a longitudinal diameter L equal to 360 mm and a lateral diameter W equal to 280 mm. The head has tubular constructions at least at a frame top 12 and a yoke 13 in order to accommodate first and second balance adjusters 14, 15 as shown in FIGS. 2 and 3.

The balance adjusters 4 and 5 are made of materials having a specific gravity or specific gravities by far larger than that of the frame. For example, the balance adjusters 14 and 15 are made of lead when the frame is made of carbon fibers. Glass fiber reinforced plastic can also be used for the balance adjusters. The balance adjusters 14 and 15 may be made either same or different materials. When the balance adjusters 14 and 15 are made of different materials, these materials may have either or different specific gravities.

The balance adjusters 14 and 15 are preferably given in the form of straps. In the ease of the construction shown in

---

FIGURE 5.1 *(Continued)*

FIG. 2, only one strap type balance adjuster **14** is accommodated in the frame top **12** whilst leaving the original tubular construction. Whereas in the case of the construction shown in FIG. 3, two strap type balance adjusters **15** are accommodated in the yoke **13** sandwiching a foamed polyurethane filler **19**.

Though not illustrated in FIG. 1, an additional balance adjuster of 36 g made of lead is preferably inserted into a grip within an area of 100 mm from a grip end **16** in order to adjust the position of the center of mass of the tennis racket **10**.

In one typical example, a balance adjuster **14** of 15 g is inserted into the frame top **12** whilst extending toward the yoke **13** over a distance B of 30 mm, which corresponds to about 4.4% of the total racket length (680 mm), from the frame top end **12a**. A balance adjuster **15** of 33 g is inserted into the yoke **13** whilst extending towards the frame top **12** over a distance B of 30 mm, which corresponds to about 4.4% of the total racket length, from the yoke end **13a**.

The logical basis for supporting the concept of the present invention will now be described in detail in reference to FIGS. 5 to 6C.

As stated above, it is the basic object of the present invention to enable rise in repulsion characteristics with optimal positioning of the sweet spot of a tennis racket.

In order to correctly elucidate the problems of repulsion characteristics and vibratory impact of a tennis racket at shooting balls, it is necessary to introduce the concept of vibration beyond the classical theory of rigidity. From this point of view, it is intended by the present invention to optimize participation of mass distribution in vibration characteristics in terms of the primary vibration mode in order to improve repulsion characteristics and to mitigate vibratory impact.

The relationship between the amplitude of the primary vibration and the spot of shooting is shown in FIG. 5, in which the center of the sweet spot falls on the center C of the face of a tennis racket. It is clearly observed in the illustration that the amplitude is almost equal to zero at the sweet spot center and increases gradually as the spot of shooting leaves from the sweet spot center. Roughly speaking, the node of the primary vibration falls on the sweet spot center and the antinode falls on the frame top and yoke of the tennis racket.

It is well understood that the larger the total mass of the head of a tennis racket, the higher the repulsion speed of a ball shot by such a tennis racket. Stated otherwise, the larger the total mass of a tennis racket, the better the repulsion characteristics. Despite such improvement in repulsion characteristics, too large mass of a tennis racket disenables good control on swing motion by a player. For these reasons, it is highly necessary to specify an optimal mass distribution within a given limit of the total mass which enables rise in repulsion characteristics and mitigation of vibratory impact.

The magnitude of influence of a local mass on the primary vibration mode varies depending on the location of that local mass. Such a magnitude of influence will hereinafter referred to as "percent mass participation." The mode of the primary vibration is given in the form of the kinetic energy of such a vibration as follows;

$$E = \tfrac{1}{2} \Sigma V_k^2 \cdot m_k \qquad (1)$$

V_k: velocity at a location k
m_k: local mass at the location k
A part of this formula, i.e. $\tfrac{1}{2} V_k^2$ represents the percent

mass participation.

In order to realize improvement in repulsion characteristics and mitigation of vibratory impact by effectively utilizing the total mass of a limited value, it is first reduce the mass of unrelated locations as much as the rigidity and strength requirement allows, and to next allocate collectively the excessive mass so obtained to the frame top and the yoke of a tennis racket where the percent mass participation is highest.

Next, mass allocation ratio must be fixed in consideration of optimal positioning of the sweet spot.

FIG. 6A shows the mode of the primary vibration when the tennis racket has the conventional mass allocation. Here, the sweet spot center SP falls substantially on the face center C.

FIG. 6B shows the mode of the primary vibration when the excessive mass is collectively allocated near the frame top. Here, the sweet spot center SP is displaced towards the frame top. As a consequence, the repulsion characteristics and the vibratory impact are improved on the frame top side but rather aggravated on the york side when compared with those in the FIG. 6A situation.

FIG. 6C shows the mode of the primary vibration when the excessive mass is collectively allocated near the yoke. Here, the sweet spot center SP is displaced towards the yoke. As a consequence, the repulsion characteristics and the vibratory impact are improved on the yoke side but rather aggravated on the frame top side when compared with those in the FIG. 6A situation.

From the foregoing, it will be well understood that allocation of the excessive mass has to be done with a mass allocation ratio of a limited range while take optimal positioning up the sweet spot into consideration too.

It was already confirmed by the inventor through a series of simulation tests that a high degree of cotelation exists between the yoke/frame top mass allocation ratio and the position of the sweet spot and the cotelation is given by the following formula when the sweet spot spons the area of 150 to 190 mm from the frame top;

$$R = m_y/m_f = 2.2 \pm 0.7 \qquad (2)$$

R; mass allocation ratio
m_y; mass of the yoke
m_f; mass of the frame top
It was also confirmed that the sweet spot is displaced towards the frame top when the mass allocation ratio (R) falls short of the lower limit (1.5). Whereas, the sweet spot is displaced toward the yoke when the mass allocation ratio (R) exceeds the upper limit (2.9). From this analysis, it is clear that the yoke/frame top mass allocation ratio should be in a range from 1.5 to 2.9 in order to keep the sweet spot at the optimal, central position in the face of the tennis racket.

The concrete examples for the tennis rackets shown in FIGS. A6 to 6C are as follows;

FIG. 6A (Conventional)
  m_y=219 g
  m_f=91 g
  R=2.41

FIG. 6B (Mass allocation on the frame top only)
  m_y=164 g
  m_f=156 g
  R=1.05

FIG. 6C (Mass allocation on the yoke only)
  m_y=303 g
  m_f=69 g
  R=4.39

FIGURE 5.1 *(Continued)*

5

It is clear from these data that the mass allocation ratios for the FIGS. 6B and 6C situations fall outside the above-described preferable range.

From the view point of rigidity and strength requirements, the acceptable, minimum total mass of a tennis racket is about 220 g, and more preferably 260 g. Whereas, from the viewpoint of physical load on average players, the acceptable, maximum total mass of a tennis racket is about 350 g, and more preferably 310 g. So for utmost safely in both viewpoints, a total mass in a range from 260 to 310 g is acceptable. Thus, the difference of about 50 g can be used for mass allocation.

EXAMPLES

For measurement of dynamic behaviours, a tennis racket sample of the above-described construction was subjected to various tests. The net total mass of the tennis racket was 327 g and the total mass of the tennis racket with strings in its face was 342 g. As shown in FIG. 1, the distance D between the grip end 16 and the center of mass G was 318 mm. The sweet spot SP of this tennis racket was displaced by 20 mm from the center of the head 11 towards the frame top end 12a.

For comparison purposes, a solid type conventional tennis racket with foamed urethane filler was prepared. The total mass and the position of the center of mass of this conventional sample were designed same as those of the sample of the present invention.

Each sample was set to an automatic batting machine so as to swing about a center of rotation 17 which was located at a position E of 120 mm from its grip end 16. A stationary tennis ball 18 was shot by the swinging sample at an angular velocity F of 33.7 rad/sec as shown in FIG. 4 and the resultant speed of the flying tennis ball 18 was measured.

Three shooting spots were chosen on the face of each sample. The first shooting spot fell on the sweet spot SP, the second shooting spot fell on a location of 65 mm displaced from the sweet spot SP towards the frame top end 12a, and the third shooting spot fell on a location of 65 mm displaced from the sweet spot SP towards the grip end 16. The results of measurement are given in Table 1 in which ball speeds are indicated in the form of ratios with respect to the ball speed when shot at the first shooting spot, i.e. at the sweet spot SP.

The data given in the table fairly endorse the fact that the tennis racket in accordance with the present invention is clearly excellent in repulsion characteristics, in particular in the ease of off spot shooting.

Further, for measurement of impact on the body of players at shooting balls, each sample was hung upside down via an extensible rubber string attached to its grip end 16 and subjected to an impact of the unit impulse (10^{-3}N.S). The resultant maximum displacement and maximum acceleration were measured by impulse response system. Shooting force was detected by load cells and response was detected by an acceleration meter. The results of measurement are given in Tables 2 and 3.

TABLE 1

Shooting spot	Sample of the invention	Conventional sample
First spot	1.00	1.00
Second spot	0.98	0.93
Third spot	0.82	0.78

6

TABLE 2

	Maximum displacement (m · N^{-1})	
Shooting spot	Sample of the invention	Conventional sample
Second spot	3.019×10^{-3}	3.194×10^{-3}
Third spot	2.537×10^{-3}	2.660×10^{-3}

TABLE 3

	Maximum acceleration (m · S^{-2} · N^{-1})	
Shooting spot	Sample of the invention	Conventional sample
Second spot	1.689×10^3	2.044×10^3
Third spot	1.419×10^3	1.702×10^3

It is fairly shown in the tables that the maximum displacement and the maximum acceleration in the ease of the sample of the present invention are both clearly smaller than those in the ease of the conventional sample even when off-spot shooting is committed. Stated otherwise, reduced physical damage is imposed on players.

It is clear from the foregoing that significant improvements in dynamic behaviour of a tennis racket at off-spot shooting can be expected when balance adjusters are arranged in accordance with the concept of the present invention. In addition, the sweet spot is located around the center of the face as in the case of the conventional tennis racket. Thus, comfortable feel in use much removes mental stress on unskilled players. Reduced vibratory impact at ball shooting well mitigates physical damage on players.

I claim:

1. A tennis racket comprising

a substantially oval frame including a frame top and a yoke,

a first balance adjuster arranged at said frame top and made of a first material having a first specific gravity larger than that of said frame, and

a second balance adjuster arranged at said yoke and made of a second material having a second specific gravity larger than that of said frame,

the mass of said second balance adjuster being 1.5 to 2.9 times larger than that of said first balance adjuster.

2. A tennis racket as claimed in claim 1 in which

a total mass of said tennis racket is in a range from 220 to 350.

3. A tennis racket as claimed in claim 1 in which

said first material for said first balance adjuster is same as said second material for said second balance adjuster.

4. A tennis racket as claimed in claim 3 in which

said first specific gravity of said first material is same as said second specific gravity of said second material.

5. A tennis racket as claimed in claim 3 in which

said first specific gravity of said first material is different from said second specific gravity of said second material.

6. A tennis racket as claimed in claim 5 in which

said second balance adjuster extends over a distance of

FIGURE 5.1 *(Continued)*

5,470,062

7

10% or less of the total racket length from a yoke end.

7. A tennis racket as claimed in claim 1 in which

said first material for said first balance adjuster is different from said second material for said second balance adjuster.

8. A tennis racket as claimed in claim 1 in which

said first balance adjuster extends over a distance of 10%

8

or less of the total racket length from a frame top end.

9. A tennis racket as claimed in claim 1 in which

said second balance adjuster extends over a distance of 10% or less of the total racket length from a yoke end.

* * * * *

FIGURE 5.1 *(Continued)*

United States Patent [19]

Nesbit et al.

[11] Patent Number: 4,971,320

[45] Date of Patent: Nov. 20, 1990

[54] **TENNIS RACKET EQUIPPED WITH A PORTABLE RADIO**

[76] Inventors: Charles E. Nesbit, 9206 Willard Ct., Des Moines, Iowa 50322; Mark S. Nesbit, 1248 17th, West Des Moines, Iowa 50265

[21] Appl. No.: 331,828

[22] Filed: Apr. 3, 1989

[51] Int. Cl.⁵ A63B 49/08; H05K 11/00; H04B 1/08
[52] U.S. Cl. .... 273/73 G; 273/73 R; 273/73 J; 455/344; 455/348; 455/347; 455/351
[58] Field of Search .... 273/73 R, 73 G, 73 J, 273/29 A; 455/344, 347, 348, 351

[56]   **References Cited**

U.S. PATENT DOCUMENTS

2,927,995	3/1960	Francis	455/344
4,101,132	7/1978	Conrey	273/73 R
4,257,594	3/1981	Conrey	273/29 A
4,535,986	8/1985	Richards	273/73 J

Primary Examiner—Benjamin Layno
Attorney, Agent, or Firm—Henderson & Sturm

[57]   **ABSTRACT**

A tennis racket equipped with a portable radio. The tennis racket frame has an open throat area. The housing of the portable radio is shaped for insertion within the open throat area. Bracket mounts and adjustable straps attached to the portable radio are used to secure the portable radio to tennis racket frame. The attachment of the radio to the tennis racket readily provides listening pleasure to the tennis player while he/she plays tennis.

3 Claims, 3 Drawing Sheets

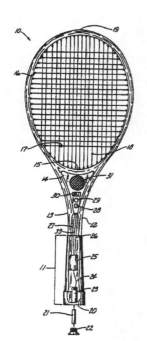

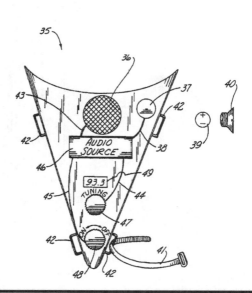

FIGURE 5.2   Radio Racket Patent

U.S. Patent   Nov. 20, 1990   Sheet 1 of 3   4,971,320

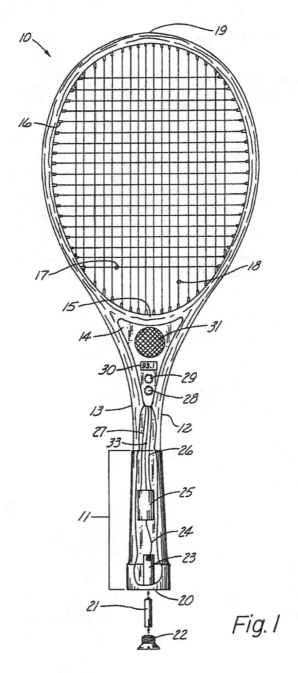

Fig. 1

FIGURE 5.2   *(Continued)*

Fig. 2

Fig. 3

FIGURE 5.2 *(Continued)*

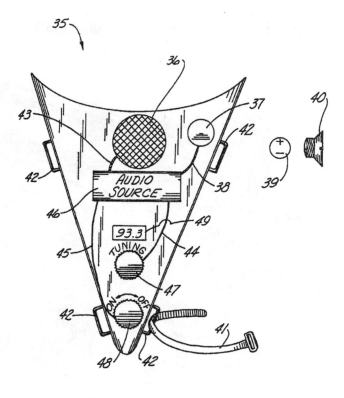

Fig. 4

FIGURE 5.2   *(Continued)*

106

1

TENNIS RACKET EQUIPPED WITH A PORTABLE RADIO

Technical Field

This invention relates to tennis rackets, and more particularly to tennis rackets housing an audio signal source with speaker assemblies secured in the throat area of the racket.

Background Art

There are many prior art devices related to the development of tennis rackets. There are also many prior art devices related to portable radio's. One problem associated with the prior art devices relating to tennis rackets is that since the game of tennis requires much body movement on the part of the player, the use of a personal portable radio mounted somewhere on the player would cause them some difficulties. Also if a tennis player were to try and use personal headphones as a source of audio enjoyment, communication between the other tennis player or players would be hampered. A problem associated with portable audio devices that are placed outside of the tennis court boundries concerns the fact that to be able to listen to the audio device the volume would have to be increased in order to reach the tennis player and thus by having the audio volume at this increased level the audio device would no longer be considered a personal audio device since the increased volume would affect others playing tennis on the same court or adjacent courts.

Those concerned with these and other problems recognize the need for an improved tennis racket with the speaker assembly contained in the throat of the tennis racket and the audio signal source attached in the shaft of the tennis racket.

Disclosure of the Invention

The present invention provides a tennis racket with a speaker or plurality of speakers attached in the throat area of a tennis racket. An audio signal source is housed inside the handle of the tennis racket and is electronically coupled to the speaker assemblies by wires that are run through the interior of the tennis racket.

An object of the present invention is the provision of an improved tennis racket for listening to an audio signal source.

Another object is to provide a tennis racket for listening to an audio signal source that leaves your hands free to hold the tennis racket.

A further object of the invention is the provision of a tennis racket that is easy to tune with just one hand, leaving the other hand free to hold the tennis racket.

Still another object is to provide a tennis racket for listening to an audio signal source that houses the speaker assemblies on the tennis racket.

A still further object of the present invention is to provide a tennis racket that houses an audio signal source that is extremely personal and portable.

Yet another embodiment of the present invention would be a portable separate audio signal source electronically coupled to a speaker assembly that would be interchangeable and fit into the open throat area of tennis rackets.

Yet still another object of the present invention is the provision of an tennis racket for listening to an audio

2

signal source that is easy to use, inexpensive to manufacture, and has a pleasing eye appeal.

Brief Description of the Drawings

These and other attributes of the invention will become more clear upon a thorough study of the following description of the best mode for carrying out the invention, particularly when reviewed in conjunction with the drawings, wherein:

FIG. 1 is a full on perspective view of the tennis racket of the present invention.

FIG. 2 is a cutaway view of the tennis racket handle showing the audio signal source integrally formed therein, showing the battery compartment in the bottom end of the handle grip, and having a portion cutaway showing the speaker wire.

FIG. 3 is a perspective view of the audio tennis racket being used in a tennis match.

FIG. 4 is a perspective view of another embodiment of the present invention which would attach by fasteners into the open throat area of the tennis racket.

Best Mode for Carrying Out the Invention

Referring now to the drawings, wherein like reference numerals designate identical or corresponding parts throughout the several views. FIG. 1 shows the tennis racket generally at 10. The tennis racket (10) comprises a handle (11) a top cap (12) a shaft (13,: the built-in throat area audio mounting system (14) the throat bridge (15) the grommet system (16) cross strings (17) main strings (18) the tip (19) the heel battery access opening (20) the battery (21) the battery access screw in cover (22) the battery compartment (23) internal wiring (24) which connects to the audio signal source (25) the audio internal wiring which connects to the on/off volume control (26) the audio internal wiring that connects to the station tuning control (27) the volume control on/off knob (28) the station tuning knob (29) the radio station viewing window (30) the attached speaker assembly (31) which connects to the audio signal source (25)' by internal speaker wiring (33).

FIG. 2 The tennis racket handle (11) has an access opening (20) which leads to the battery compartment (23) the battery access screw-in cover (22) screws into threads (32) which closes the battery access opening (20) the battery (21) electronically connects by internal wiring (24) to the audio signal source (25) the audio on/off volume internal wiring (26) and the audio internal wiring for station tuning (27) along with the internal speaker wiring (33) are shown.

FIG. 3 depicts a tennis player (34) using the radio equipped tennis racket shown at (10) the speaker assembly on/off control knob (28) and the station tuning knob (29).

FIG. 4 is an alternate embodiment of the invention shown at (35) the speaker assembly (36) electronically connects by means of internal wiring (43) to the audio signal source (46). The audio signal source (46) is supplied by power from a battery (39) the battery (39) is housed inside a battery compartment (37), the battery compartment cover (40) encloses the power supply. The power supply wiring (38) connects to the audio signal source (46) the on/off volume knob (48) connects by internal wiring (44) to the audio signal source (46). A station viewing window (49) is located on the unit. Attachment bracket mounts (42) are formed to the unit, and adjustable straps (41) would be used to secure the unit to a tennis racket frame.

FIGURE 5.2 *(Continued)*

4,971,320

3

We claim:

1. In a sports racket frame comprising a handle, a shaft, a racket head and an open throat area formed between the shaft and the racket head an improvement comprising:

an audio signal source for generating verbal and musical sounds including at least one speaker assembly; tuning and volume controls operatively associated with the audio signal source; means for electrically coupling said at least one speaker assembly to said audio signal source;

a housing dimensioned to contain all of the components associated with said audio signal source and further dimensioned to be releasably received in said open throat area in the sports racket; and,

4

means for temporarily and releasably retaining said housing within the said open throat area in the sports racket frame.

2. The improvement as in claim 1; wherein said means for temporarily and releasably retaining said housing within said open throat area comprise:

straps operatively attached to the said housing and dimensioned to secure the housing to the sports racket frame in the vicinity of the said open throat area.

3. The improvement as in claim 2; wherein said housing is further provided with brackets which are dimensioned to receive the straps for releasably securing the housing to the sports racket frame in the vicinity of the said open throat area.

* * * * *

FIGURE 5.2 *(Continued)*

108

de-bugged; even a flow chart that shows what will be accomplished, along with a description of how, could be helpful.

In addition to crystallizing your own thinking and showing how the live creation will work, a prototype also gives you a chance to try your ideas out on other people and see how they respond. If we make a sample Rocket Racket, we can observe how it works on the courts and see how people respond to its features. If things do not work as intended, we have corrections to make before going for the patent. Seeing it used may also spark additional ideas for improvements that did not come when the invention was on paper, in our heads, or a mere gleam in the eye.

The prototype also serves to provide an idea of what will really go into producing an invention and the challenges involved, which will give you a head start on solving problems instead of being ambushed when you are scrambling to ready a new product for the market.

As a guide in thinking about a prototype, remember the example of the Baby Jogger from Chapter 3. With an old stroller, some bike tires, and a few other parts, it was possible to create a prototype that both worked and provided a clear idea of what the goal for the final product was. Plenty of work remained to be done, of course, to make it marketable, but the prototype helped define the idea, provided a basis for evaluation and critique, and was instrumental in plotting the future course. Not a bad return on the investment of joining together a few simple parts.

THE NEED FOR COUNSEL

An innovation that is worth patenting is usually worth the expense of hiring a good attorney to help you navigate the process. There are simply too many aspects of the patent process where the right training, knowledge, and experience are crucial to risk going it alone, unless you are confident you already possess, or can quickly acquire, enough of those qualities.

Sure, you can apply for a patent on your own and spare the expense of hiring a lawyer, who can cost anywhere from a few hundred to many thousand dollars, depending on the extent of the services you require. All the application materials you need can easily be downloaded, or ordered by mail, from the USPTO, who do a nice job of providing clear directions and plenty of guidance. So what is the problem?

Have you ever tried something for the first time and discovered it took a lot longer, and was much more challenging, than you had imagined? Plenty of us have discovered exactly that, the night before Christmas, when we confidently approached an easy-to-assemble child's toy, a screwdriver in hand (sure that is the only tool we will need), thinking the job will take just a little while and there will be plenty of time left over to eat the cookies left out for Santa. The next morning we find ourselves struggling and frazzled, the child ready for the toy, but the toy nowhere near ready for the child. The same kind of experience may await if you attempt the patent application process alone. And even if you do get through it, you may have left land mines behind for yourself that will blow up on you months or years later, in the form of a patent that is much weaker than it could have been, or even comes to be invalidated.

The potential loss of opportunities and revenue, not to mention the experience of watching your past effort go down the drain, can be very painful. The moral here is not to be like the do-it-yourself electrician who wires his house, leaves the lights on one day, then comes home to find his home blazing away.

As the inventor of a new creation, you probably possess all the technical expertise necessary to complete a patent application. Your limitation will most likely be in the ability to word that knowledge in a way that gives you the broadest and most secure possible patent. Along with needing a lawyer's wordsmithing talents, attorneys have a familiarity with patent laws and rules and how the USPTO functions that an outsider, or even occasional insider, cannot match. These things are best acquired during a career spent specializing in the area, not picked up on the fly. Do not risk treating the patent application process like a college student who is cramming for a final exam that is being given in a class he never attended.

Also to be considered is the opportunity cost. This is the value of the next best alternative, the one not chosen. Going for a patent takes a lot of time, energy, and attention, all of which are limited resources most applicants could find more profitable things to do with, like putting them into their areas of expertise. In short, direct your energies toward the area where the most value can be added. Do not make the mistake of passing up the best available opportunity in order to focus on an endeavor your abilities do not match up with.

If you are not experienced at conducting searches for prior art, for example, you could easily miss a publication that clearly invalidates your application. Or, should you not word the claims in your patent broadly enough, somebody else could come along, make some slight changes, and patent a competing innovation that is close enough to yours to cut into the potential market for it. In other words, if you represent yourself in the process, you risk having a fool for a client.

When beginning the process of seeking an attorney, look for one who specializes in patent law. If you were a candidate for a liver transplant, a podiatrist's (foot doctor's) experience would not be appealing. Same for patents. Find somebody who has been there before and knows the ins and outs of the process, not an all-purpose lawyer who needs to read the directions along with you. The USPTO is helpful here because they have rules and regulations for the practice of attorneys seeking patents from them, including the requirements that they be of good moral character and repute, have the necessary legal and technical qualifications (some of which must be demonstrated on an examination administered by the USPTO), and possess a college degree, or the equivalent, in engineering or the physical sciences. In order to represent inventors, attorneys must be recognized by the USPTO in order to practice before them. A complete register of attorneys so recognized can be obtained from the USPTO on their web site. The USPTO also has the power to suspend and disbar attorneys for gross misconduct.

In addition to the USPTO register, it is good, when feasible, to get recommendations from others who have used an attorney to patent an innovation in your field, or one closely related. There is always that old standby, the phone book, too. Look for firms with departments that specialize in patents, or individuals and firms whose practice is solely devoted to intellectual property. Interviewing a few of them will help give you a feel for how good a fit they will be with what you are trying to accomplish.

Next, be sure to get a patent attorney who understands the area you are working in; otherwise, their lack of knowledge can be harmful in the form of a weak, or erroneous, application, which impairs the protection offered by, and value of, the patent you receive—if it is even issued. The more specialized the area, the more complicated the processes involved, or the newer the technology, the more important this is.

A related concern is the knowledge of the patent examiners. Though, as a group, they have long had an excellent reputation, we live in a time of rapidly evolving technology, where it is not unusual for only a small number of people to really understand a particular piece of it. You want to minimize the risks involved with having your patent gone over by an examiner who already has a big workload, a limited amount of time to devote to your application, and maybe a limited understanding of what it is your invention does. Very often lawyers will not have a clear understanding either, even those with a background in your area if there have been significant changes recently. The best approach in this case is to work with the attorney so that you learn from her what conditions need to be satisfied in order to secure the strongest possible patent, and she learns enough from you so that she can write up the best, most thorough, application possible.

THE SEARCH FOR PRIOR ART

Once you have covered all the bases necessary to place yourself in the position of having a workable innovation that is worth protecting as a valuable piece of intellectual property, it is time to have a serious search done. Your lawyer, or a patent agent or other professional your lawyer uses, is the one to conduct it. Your preliminary toe-in-the-water search was useful in the early stages and can also help as a guide for a professional, but make no mistake about the need to have a pro do the search.

This will be one of the few times when you hire somebody in the hope that they will search everywhere, then not find anything. Like a physician examining you for cancer, you do not want the lawyer (or hired gun) to miss anything that is really there and has the potential to come back and make life miserable in the future. At the same time, a clean bill of health, meaning that no bad news is there to be found, is the best possible result.

The cost of the search varies according to the amount of time required, but whether it be a few hundred or a few thousand dollars you are billed to conduct a thorough search, it is well worth it, especially when you consider all the time, money, and hope that will be lost if you go through the rest of the process only to have a patent examiner deny your patent.

Because the possible resources available to search through are so vast, there is always a chance that even a good patent search will miss something that turns up later. Even if your invention is not patentable, that does not have to mean your efforts are doomed. If there is an existing patent, you can contact its owner to see about buying it or arranging to pay licensing fees for its use. There are plenty of patents out there that the owner would prefer getting paid for rather than develop on their own. This is another area where a good lawyer can be of tremendous assistance in making the contacts and arrangements that give you access to the intellectual property of others.

Also bear in mind that a patent not being available does not have to equal the death of your invention and its prospects for the future. If, for example, there is an expired patent on your creation, you cannot re-patent it, but that intellectual property is now fair game so there is nothing stopping you from proceeding, unless competitors have already done something with it. The same may hold for prior art. An innovation may have been published with the express purpose of keeping others from securing a patent on it (see section on defensive publishing in Chapter 6), but not be patented itself. Again, patent protection is out of the question, but there is still plenty of room to maneuver.

As we saw in Chapter 2 with the story of Kitty Van Bortel, the key element to success is having a great idea coupled with the personal characteristics necessary to see it come to fruition. Given the right creativity and drive, you can be very successful with commonly known ideas just by implementing them better than others have, or can.

KEEPING A LID ON IT: THE STEALTH PHASE

When all the necessary preparation and steps have been made and it is time to move forward with all systems go, our first instinct might be to tell everybody in the world about the great innovation we have in the works, sort of like an advance coming out party. No matter how great the enthusiasm, though, until the patent application is filed and pending, it is best to keep things as confidential as possible.

It is a grave mistake to jeopardize the future by allowing innovations under development to become public knowledge too early. The most obvious reason for this is the desire to keep potential competitors from finding out and racing ahead on their own, with you putting all that sweat and hard work into making what you thought was an original creation patentable, only to have a patent examiner deny your application because somebody else discovered what you were doing and beat you to it.

Even without competitors lurking on the sidelines, just waiting to cut and run with your great ideas, you also have to be careful not to undermine yourself by revealing your hand too soon. By law, an inventor who starts selling the invention, or uses it publicly, or even describes it in a printed publication, must apply for a patent within a year of any of the above occurring. If an application is not made within that time period, the rights to a patent will be forfeited.

The patent application will require a description of the invention sufficient that a person with skill in the area could build it. This means that the thing must really work as claimed. Even getting an invention that has already been prototyped to that point can take a significant amount of time, more so if those doing the developing have other jobs and responsibilities.

While in stealth mode, there is no reason why you cannot keep up with new developments. It is not necessary to peek in the windows of other inventors; just keep track of new things coming out, news of research and application developments, new patents, and, what used to be kept secret, patent applications that are 18 months or more old.

As an illustration, say you have noticed that dogs are getting fatter and fatter. You believe that pet owners would appreciate a new doggie diet, so you have been working on a formula that will suppress canine appetites while still providing them adequate nutrition. One day, you happen to be scanning published patent applications and discover that somebody else is working on weight loss for dogs, too (see Figure 5.3). Their advances can help inform yours, and you still have the advantage of secrecy.

United States Patent Application
Sunvold, Gregory Dean ;   et al.

20010000786

May 3, 2001

Product for promoting *weight loss* in overweight dogs

Abstract

A process for feeding a pet food supplement or diet to an overweight canine for the purpose of promoting *weight loss,* increasing lean body mass, and enhancing the satiety of the animal is provided. The supplement or diet contains an effective amount of L-carnitine.

Inventors: **Sunvold, Gregory Dean**; *(Eaton, OH)* ; **Tetrick, Mark Alan**; *(Dayton, OH)* ;
                  Davenport, Gary Mitchell; *(Dayton, OH)*

Correspondence   Killworth, Gottman, Hagan & Schaeff, L.L.P.
Name and   One Dayton Centre, Suite 500
Address: Dayton
                     OH
                     45402-2023
                     US

Appl. No.:   **738492**
Filed: **December 15, 2000**

U.S. Current Class: **514/556**
Intern'l Class: A61K 031/205

Claims

1. A process for promoting *weight loss* in canines comprising the step of administering to a canine an effective amount of L-carnitine for a time sufficient to effect a reduction in the weight of the animal.

FIGURE 5.3   Dog Diet Patent

Description

SUMMARY OF THE INVENTION

BACKGROUND OF THE INVENTION

2. The present invention relates to a process and product for promoting *weight loss* in overweight dogs, and more particularly to a process for supplementing a canine diet with L-carnitine to promote *weight loss,* improve body composition, and enhance satiety in the animal.

3. It is estimated that 20 to 40% of the canine population is overweight or obese. This represents a very large number of animals that are in need of a means to lose weight. Obesity and being overweight are conditions associated with several health risks such as diabetes, increased blood pressure, increased blood triglycerides, impaired locomotion, skeletal stress, increased dystocia, thyroid dysfunction, etc. Consequently, ways to help treat these conditions are much needed by this population of animals. Currently, the most common form of treating obesity in dogs is through the use of diets that contain high amounts of fiber to dilute the calories of the diet.

4. While in some cases these diets can be effective, they are often associated with several side effects. These include: 1) excessive stool output, 2) decreased nutrient digestibility, 3) poor skin and haircoat, 4) decreased palatability, and 5) constipation and(or) increased frequency of defecation. As a result, alternative nutritional means to alleviate these conditions are needed.

5. Recently, it has been reported that carnitine, a vitamin-like substance, increased oxidation of octanoate in newborn pigs (van Kempen and Odle, J. Nutr. 125:238-250 (1995)), lowered fat deposition and increased fatty acid oxidation by hepatic cells in growing salmon (Ji et al, J. Nutr. 126:1937-1950 (19996), and decreased body fat accumulation in growing pigs (Owen et al, J. Anim. Sci. 74:1612-1619 (1996).

6. Accordingly, there is still a need for addressing the obesity problems of canines while still providing adequate nutrition and without the side effects associated with prior diets.

SUMMARY OF THE INVENTION

7. The present invention addresses the problem of obese and overweight canines through the use of a diet which contains supplemental L-carnitine. L-carnitine is an amino acid co-factor which is synthesized in an animal's body from the amino acids lysine and methionine. We have discovered that L-carnitine, when administered to a canine in need of treatment at extremely low supplemental amounts of 100 mg/kg of diet or less, promotes *weight loss* in the animal, improves the animal's body composition, and results in enhanced satiety in the animal. By improving the animal's body composition we mean that for a given animal ingesting a given amount of food, the percentage of body fat in the animal will be lower and the percentage of lean body mass will be higher when the animal is provided with the effective amount of supplemental L-carnitine as compared with an animal ingesting the same amount of food, but without

---

FIGURE 5.3 *(Continued)*

L-carnitine supplementation. The L-carnitine may be provided to the animal either as a supplement or contained in a diet fed to the animal. Such a supplement may be in the form of a pill or capsule, a treat or biscuit, or any other edible form. By "diet" we mean the food or drink regularly consumed by the animal.

8. In accordance with one aspect of the invention, a process for promoting *weight loss* in canines is provided and includes the step of administering to a canine an effective amount of L-carnitine for a time sufficient to effect a reduction in the weight of the animal. In one embodiment, the L-carnitine may be administered in a diet containing supplemental L-carnitine in an amount of from about 15 to about 195 mg/kg, and preferably from about 25 to about 150 mg/kg of diet. The diet preferably comprises from about 18 to 40 wt % crude protein, about 4 to 30 wt % fat, and about 2 to 20 wt % total dietary fiber, and the L-carnitine is present in the diet in a concentration of between about 15 to about 195 ppm, more preferably about 25 to about 150 ppm, and most preferably about 50 to about 100 ppm.

9. In another embodiment of the invention, the L-carnitine is administered as a supplement in an amount of from between about 1 to about 100 mg L-carnitine per day, and more preferably from between about 2.5 to about 50 mg L-carnitine per day.

10. Practice of the present invention is also useful in increasing the lean body mass of a canine as well as enhancing the satiety and decreasing voluntary food intake of a canine.

11. Accordingly, it is a feature of the invention to provide a process for feeding a pet food supplement or diet for providing *weight loss* in a canine by providing an effective amount of L-carnitine in the diet of the animal. It is also a feature of the present invention to provide a pet food supplement or diet which increases the lean body mass of the animal. It is also a feature of the present invention to provide a pet food supplement which enhances satiety and reduces voluntary food intake in a canine. These and other features and advantages of the invention will become apparent from the following detailed description, the accompanying drawings, and the appended claims.

BRIEF DESCRIPTION OF THE DRAWINGS

12. FIG. 1 is a chart illustrating comparative percent body weight change in dogs consuming an L-carnitine supplemented diet versus a non-supplemented diet;

13. FIG. 2 is a chart illustrating dietary intake in dogs consuming an L-carnitine supplemented diet;

14. FIG. 3 is a chart illustrating the body weight of dogs during ad libitum and restricted feeding of an L-carnitine supplemented diet;

15. FIG. 4 is a chart illustrating body fat in overweight dogs before and after 49 days of ad libitum feeding of an L-carnitine supplemented diet;

16. FIG. 5 is a chart illustrating the body fat of dogs during ad libitum and restricted feeding of an L-carnitine supplemented diet;

17. FIG. 6 is a chart illustrating the lean body mass of dogs during ad libitum and restricted feeding of an L-carnitine supplements diet; and

18. FIG. 7 is a chart illustrating the relationship of *weight loss* to food intake of dogs during ad libitum and restricted feeding of an L-carnitine supplemented diet.

FIGURE 5.3 *(Continued)*

CASE STUDY   Bluetie: Putting It All Together

The idea for Secure Send grew from David Koretz's frustrations at the pace doing business was slowed to when sending documents back and forth was necessary. Federal Express and its competitors could not get anything to the recipient until the next day. Couriers were faster, but more expensive, and were out of the question if the parties concerned were not in the same local area.

The Internet was an obvious choice for sending documents, but the right technology had not been worked out yet. Regular e-mail was out because it was too easy for just about anybody who desired to get into it. Though there were some services that provided software that could be installed to facilitate the transfer of files on the Internet, they seemed cumbersome and still lacking in the necessary security for David.

Before jumping into developing Secure Send, David spoke with about a half dozen people whose judgment he trusted. Like him, they shared the frustration of having the perfect vehicle (the Internet) to send documents back and forth securely, and knew the right technology existed, yet were hamstrung, too, because nobody had put the pieces together yet. David's idea made sense.

In looking at the costs involved, Secure Send made even more sense. Secure Send was to be part of a suite of Internet-based business services Bluetie would offer at a cost of around $25 per subscriber. In one brief stretch where discs and documents had to be sent back and forth quickly between his and a lawyer's office, David had spent $1,000 on courier's fees. And with Federal Express costing about $15 a package for overnight delivery, simple math told David that only a couple of documents sent by Secure Send would save more than enough to justify the subscription cost, with the added advantage of being transmitted in just seconds. And Secure Send was to be just one of a host of unique services. The market for just this one feature, let alone the rest, was anybody who needed to send more than a couple of documents per month, which covers a lot of individuals and firms.

Prior to undertaking the development of a working product, David and his coworkers took a look at the patents for existing inventions that transmitted documents over the Internet. His initial opinion proved correct; the technology employed was limited, cumbersome, and insecure. Creating something better was definitely possible, and the timing was ideal.

For David to make Secure Send a reality, he needed a group of terrific software engineers, whom he was able to attract because he was running an innovative company that allowed them opportunities to use their potential and challenge themselves in the creation of a set of unique products.

(Continued)

CASE STUDY   Bluetie: Putting It All Together *(Continued)*

Getting Secure Send to the point where the technology was patentable took 16 months. Because it required large investments of money, time, and talent, and was an invention with terrific profit potential, Bluetie protected it scrupulously during the development process. Everybody who worked on it was carefully screened and had to sign nondisclosure agreements that extended beyond their period of employment at Bluetie, should they leave. Nobody was allowed in their quarters who was not authorized, and they did not even have a sign on the front door. Nothing was published on Secure Send and those involved in its creation made sure not to even tell other people about it.

The efforts to protect Secure Send extended beyond these measures into the very wording of the patent application itself. Though their law firm was excellent, Bluetie was operating in an area new enough that few people were thoroughly familiar with it. As a result, David had to learn much of the lawyer's job. Not because he needed to step in and prepare the application, but because he needed to assist them in wording the application to afford Bluetie the greatest possible protection. Without inclusive descriptions, it would be easy for future competitors to read the patent and figure out relatively simple routes around any restrictions. Given his familiarity with the technology involved, David was able to help the lawyers choose language that did the necessary job of protecting their innovation.

Though a patent lasts for 20 years from the date of application, in the fast-moving world of high tech, firms like Bluetie do not expect a patent to provide them with effective offensive rights for more than three to five years. But in a market where so many potential clients can be reached and served quickly, that time frame provides an excellent opportunity for building both a customer base and technological lead in their market that will be difficult for competitors to match. And remember, while the competition is trying to find a way around Bluetie's patents so they can compete with them, Bluetie is already working on new ways to extend their already powerful advantage.

APPLYING FOR A PATENT

6

WHO CAN STAKE A CLAIM?

Only the inventor of an original creation is entitled to patent it. With only a few exceptions, anybody else who does so is subject to legal penalties and, even if they were to obtain a patent on somebody else's invention, it would not be valid. Should the inventor die before making an application, legal representatives, such as the executor of the estate, may make it. If the process leading up to the application is too much for the inventor and drives them insane, or if they are insane for another reason, then a legal guardian may apply for a patent in their name. Finally, if the inventor cannot be found or refuses to apply, somebody with a proprietary interest in the patent can do so, but only on the actual inventor's behalf. In the vast majority of cases, the inventor is the one who files the patent application.

Oftentimes patentable innovations are developed by two or more people who work together on it. In these cases, they will apply together as joint inventors. Just having a financial stake, no matter how big, does not qualify one to apply as a joint inventor, or as a sole inventor, either. Employees of the USPTO, for obvious reasons, cannot apply for a patent or acquire any interest in one, unless they obtain it by inheritance or bequest.

DIFFERENT KINDS OF PATENTS

Patent applications can be nonprovisional or provisional. Because the great majority are nonprovisional, we will begin by looking at the three types that make up that category: utility, design, and plant.

Utility Patents

Throughout this book we have been treating patents as a whole and utility patents as interchangeable terms most of the time. The reason is that utility patents are the kind most often sought, by far. In the year 2000, 315,015 patent applications were filed. Of these 295,926 were for utility patents, 18,292 were for design patents, and 797 were for plant patents.

A utility patent may be applied for by the creators of mechanical, electrical, and chemical inventions. These inventions may take the form of processes (including business methods), things that can be manufactured, machines, and compositions of matter. The invention does not have to be completely new (few are); improvements that are novel, as opposed to things like changes in size and color and interchangeable materials, can be patented. To be granted, a utility patent must show that the article in question is useful, which means that it has a specific purpose that can be described. It must also be nonobvious in the sense that it is unique in its own right and not readily apparent to others.

Provided it is legal, a utility patent can be had for almost anything people can come up with that can be used to accomplish something. Be it a new kind of toenail clipper or a cure for the common cold, so long as it meets the requirements, a utility patent can be granted.

Design Patents

Design patents provide protection for the external, ornamental appearance of an object. They have a shorter life than utility patents, 14 years instead of 20. If you hit on a new shape for a laptop computer and that design has purely aesthetic qualities, which means that altering the shape will not change how the computer functions, then a design patent is the way to go.

Because utility patents often change the appearance of items commonly used in practice, too, it may seem that there is plenty of room for utility and design patents to overlap. If you apply the standard of functionality, though, it becomes much easier to tell them apart. So if altering an invention's novel design aspects changes how it functions, then a utility patent is appropriate. If the design is ornamental and can be altered without altering how the invention works, then a design patent is in order.

Plant Patents

Plant patents cover the creation of unique plants that can be asexually reproduced. Asexual reproduction occurs through the use of cuttings and grafts.

PARTS TO A PATENT

There are three general components of a patent application, the specifications (includes the description and claims), drawings (when required), and the filing fee. Following is an overview of each of these categories. All the patents reprinted in this book contain these elements and can be reviewed again to see how they fit together.

Specifications

The specifications must describe the invention and how it is to be made and used. They must be written clearly and in exact, concise, yet complete enough terms that a person skilled in the particular area could make and operate it in the manner intended by the inventor.

Along with a full description, the invention must be distinguished from any others that could be considered similar, and if it is an improvement on an existing invention, the description must be limited to the particular improvement and how it interacts with the whole. In addition to complete descriptions of the invention and how it functions, the specifications must also include a short (one paragraph) abstract of technical disclosures that describe what is new and a brief summary of what the invention is and what purpose it serves.

Whatever the title of an invention, it needs to be short and to the point, so if you decide to call your latest brainstorm The Greatest Disposable Diaper in the History of Western Civilization and a Device That Will Greatly Reduce the Sufferings Endured by Parents from the Birth of a Baby until the Final Conclusion of Potty Training, the title will probably not sneak by.

At the conclusion of the specifications comes the claim(s), a vital aspect of the application. The claim points out the subject matter in a distinct fashion and serves as the foundation for the protections provided by the patent. If the day comes when legal action is necessary because your patent is being infringed on, these claims will be used by the courts in arriving at a decision, one that could prove decisive to the ongoing value of a patent.

Multiple claims can be made in the application for any patent, so long as all of them can be clearly supported by the descriptions of the invention.

Drawings

Almost every application for an invention must include drawings of it. Even patent applications for processes like business methods, which do not have a tangible product, are helped by drawings because a pictorial representation can be a great way to make the process clear in the mind of a busy patent examiner. For a good example, look again at the drawings included in the patent for Amazon. com's one-click shopping (Figure 4.1).

Each feature of an invention must be shown in a drawing, with a description of every drawing being included. Because there is a long list of requirements for drawings, and because they differ according to the item a patent is being sought for, they will not be included here. Complete lists of these requirements are readily available from the USPTO, either online or by mail.

Fees

Because they can be changed over time, specific fees are not listed in this book. They are readily available on the USPTO web site or can be ordered by mail.

The good news for independent inventors is that there are large-entity fees, usually charged to corporations, and small-entity fees, about half the dollar amount, that individual investors are charged. For utility patents you pay an application fee that is included when you apply, an issue fee after the patent is granted, and three maintenance fees, at 3, 7, and 11 years, which are necessary to keep the patent in force. Design and plant patents are pretty much the same, except maintenance fees are not required.

ELEMENTS OF A PATENT APPLICATION

To finish our discussion of the required elements of a patent application, here is a complete list in the order they are to appear in the final application.

1. Application transmittal form.
2. Fee transmittal form.
3. Title of the invention.
4. Cross-reference to related patents (if necessary).
5. Statement of federally sponsored research or development (if necessary).
6. Reference to a microfiche appendix (if necessary).
7. Background of the invention.
8. Brief summary of the invention.
9. Brief description of the drawings (if necessary).
10. Detailed description of the invention.
11. Claim or claims.
12. Abstract of the disclosure.
13. Drawings.

Though they do not do it very often, the USPTO may ask for a model, exhibit, or specimen of your invention. None of these are to be submitted unless an examiner makes a specific request. If you come up with an improvement on a greenhouse helmet, nobody at the patent office will greet the arrival of a working model with enthusiasm.

APPLICATION INSTRUCTIONS

To apply for a patent it is not necessary to fill out a specific set of forms. It is very important, however, that all the elements required of an application be present and prepared in good form. Figure 6. 1 gives the instructions provided by the USPTO for preparing and filing an application for a utility patent. Even if you have no intention of preparing the necessary documents yourself, it is worth looking at just to see what needs to be put together.

PROVISIONAL PATENTS

Beginning in 1995, patent applicants were given the option of filing provisional applications. These provide inventors a lower cost and simpler means of doing their first filing and put them on equal

UNITED STATES PATENT AND TRADEMARK OFFICE

| Home | Index | Search | System Alerts | eBusiness Center | News & Notices | Contact Us |

A Guide to Filing a Utility Patent Application

- Introduction
- Nonprovisional Utility Patent Application Requirements
- Utility Patent Application Transmittal Form Or Transmittal Letter

  Fee Transmittal Form And Appropriate Fee

  Specification
  - Title Of Invention
  - Cross-Reference To Related Applications
  - Statement Regarding Federally Sponsored Research Or Development
  - Reference To A Microfiche Appendix
  - Background Of The Invention
  - Brief Summary Of The Invention
  - Brief Description Of The Several Views Of The Drawing
  - Detailed Description Of The Invention
  - Claim Or Claims
  - Abstract Of The Disclosure

  Drawings (When Necessary)

  Oath Or Declaration

  Sequence Listing (When Necessary)

- Obtaining A Receipt For Documents Mailed To The Pto
- Drawing Requirements

  Identification Of Drawings

  Graphic Forms In Drawings

  Paper

  Views
  - Exploded Views
  - Partial Views
  - Sectional Views
  - Alternate Position
  - Modified Forms

  Arrangement Of Views

  View For The Official Gazette

  Scale

FIGURE 6.1   A Guide to Filing a Utility Patent Application

Character Of Lines, Numbers, And Letters

Shading

Symbols

Legends

Numbers, Letters, And Reference Characters

Lead Lines And Arrows

Copyright Or Mask Work Notice

Numbering Of Sheets Of Drawings And Views

Security Markings

Corrections

Holes

- Ptdl List

INTRODUCTION

The **U.S. Patent and Trademark Office** (PTO) is the government agency responsible for examining patent applications and issuing patents. A patent is a type of property right. It gives the patent holder the right, for a limited time, to exclude others from making, using, or selling the subject matter that is within the scope of protection granted by the patent. The PTO determines whether a patent should be granted in a particular case. However, it is up to the patent holder to enforce his or her own rights if the PTO does grant a patent.

The purpose of this guide is to provide you with basic information about filing a utility patent application. A patent application is a complex legal document, best prepared by one trained to prepare such documents. Thus, after reviewing this guide, you may wish to consult with a patent attorney or agent. Additional information is available:

- by calling the PTO's General Information Services at 800-PTO-9199 or 703-308-4357,
- from the PTO's Web site at **www.uspto.gov**, and
- at your nearest **Patent and Trademark Depository Library** (PTDL). You will find information regarding the nearest PTDL at the end of this guide.

There are various types of patents -- utility, design, and plant. There are also two types of utility patent application -- provisional and nonprovisional. Each year the PTO receives approximately 200,000 patent applications. Most of these are for nonprovisional utility patents.

This guide contains information to assist you in filing your nonprovisional utility patent application. It discusses the required parts of the utility patent application and includes samples of some of the forms you may use. This information is generally derived from the Patent Act, found at Title 35 of the *United States Code* (U.S.C.), and Title 37 of the *Code of Federal Regulations* (CFR). These materials are available at PTDLs and at most law libraries.

FIGURE 6.1 *(Continued)*

If you have questions about:

- other types of patent applications,
- locating a patent attorney or agent,
- obtaining the most up-to-date *Fee Schedule*, or
- obtaining copies of other PTO publications,

please contact General Information Services, the PTO Web's site, or a PTDL.

NONPROVISIONAL UTILITY PATENT APPLICATION REQUIREMENTS

A nonprovisional utility patent application must be in the English language or be accompanied by a verified translation in the English language and a fee set forth in 37 CFR §1.17(k) [Non-English Specification Fee Code 139].

All papers which are to become part of the permanent records of the PTO must be typewritten or produced by a mechanical (or computer) printer. The text must be in permanent black ink or its equivalent; on but one side of the paper; in portrait orientation; on white paper that is all of the same size, flexible, strong, smooth, nonshiny, durable, and without holes. The paper size must be either:

- 21.6 cm. by 27.9 cm. (8 1/2 by 11 inches), or
- 21.0 cm. by 29.7 cm. (DIN size A4).

There must be a left margin of at least 2.5 cm. (1 inch) and top, right, and bottom margins of at least 2.0 cm. (3/4 inch). Drawing page requirements are discussed separately below.

A nonprovisional utility patent application *must* include a specification, including a claim or claims; drawings, when necessary; an oath or declaration; and the prescribed filing fee. A complete nonprovisional utility patent application *should* contain the elements listed below, arranged in the order shown.

- Utility Patent Application Transmittal Form or Transmittal Letter
- Fee Transmittal Form and Appropriate Fee
- Specification
- Drawings (when necessary)
- Oath or Declaration
- Sequence Listing (when necessary)

These elements are further described as follows:

Utility Patent Application Transmittal Form or Transmittal Letter

A Utility Patent Application Transmittal form (Form PTO/SB/05) or a transmittal letter should be filed with every patent application to instruct the PTO on the services desired in the processing of the application. It identifies the name of the applicant, the type of application, the title of the invention, the contents of the application, and any accompanying enclosures. (Form PTO/SB/21 is to be used for all correspondance after initial filing.)

FIGURE 6.1 *(Continued)*

Fee Transmittal Form and Appropriate Fee

The Fee Transmittal form (Form PTO/SB/17) should be used to calculate the prescribed fee and indicate the method of payment.

Fees for a patent application should be submitted with the application and must be made payable to the "Commissioner of Patents and Trademarks." If an application is filed without the basic filing fee, the applicant will be notified and will be required to submit the filing fee along with a surcharge within the time period set in the notice. Fees are subject to change and the applicant should consult the current *Fee Schedule* before filing.

Please note that two sets of fees exist, one for small entities and one for other than small entities. If you qualify as a small entity for patent fee purposes, you must file the appropriate small entity statement (Form PTO/SB/09, PTO/SB/10, PTO/SB/11, or PTO/SB/12) to claim your entitlement to reduced fees.

Specification

The specification is a written description of the invention and of the manner and process of making and using the same. The specification must be in such full, clear, concise, and exact terms as to enable any person skilled in the art or science to which the invention pertains to make and use the same.

Computer program listings, when required to be submitted as part of the specification, must be direct printouts (not copies) from the computer's printer with dark, solid black letters not less than 0.21 cm. (0.08 inch) high (elite type), on white, unshaded and unlined paper; and the sheets should be submitted in a protective cover.

The pages of the specification (but not the transmittal letter sheets or other forms), including claims and abstract, should be numbered consecutively, starting with 1. The page numbers should be centrally located preferably below the text. The lines of the specification must be 1.5 or double spaced (lines of text not comprising the specification need not be 1.5 or double spaced). It is desirable to include an indentation at the beginning of each new paragraph.

It is preferable to use all of the section headings described below to represent the parts of the specification. Section headings should be in upper case without underlining or bold type. If the section contains no text, the phrase "Not Applicable" should follow the section heading.

TITLE OF INVENTION

The title of the invention (or an introductory portion stating the name, citizenship, residence of each applicant, and the title of the invention) should appear as the heading on the first page of the specification. The title should be brief but technically accurate and descriptive. It is preferred that the title not exceed 280 typewritten spaces.

CROSS-REFERENCE TO RELATED APPLICATIONS

Any nonprovisional utility patent application claiming the benefit of one or more prior filed copending nonprovisional applications (or international applications designating the United States of America) must contain in the first sentence of the specification following the title, a reference to each such prior application, identifying it by the application number (consisting of the series code and serial number) or international application number and international filing date, and indicating the relationship of the applications. Cross-references to other related patent applications may be made when appropriate.

FIGURE 6.1 *(Continued)*

STATEMENT REGARDING FEDERALLY SPONSORED RESEARCH OR DEVELOPMENT

The application should contain a statement as to rights to inventions made under federally sponsored research and development (if any).

REFERENCE TO A MICROFICHE APPENDIX

If a computer program listing printout is required and is 11 or more pages long, you must submit such listing in the form of microfiche which will not be part of the printed patent. The total number of microfiche and total number of frames should be specified.

BACKGROUND OF THE INVENTION

This section should include a statement of the field of endeavor to which the invention pertains. This section may also include a paraphrasing of the applicable U.S. patent *Classification Definitions* or the subject matter of the claimed invention. In the past, this part of this section may have been titled "Field of Invention" or "Technical Field."

This section should also contain a description of information known to you, including references to specific documents, which are related to your invention. It should contain, if applicable, references to specific problems involved in the prior art (or state of technology) which are solved by your invention. In the past, this section may have been titled "Description of the Related Art" or "Description of Prior Art."

BRIEF SUMMARY OF THE INVENTION

This section should present the substance or general idea of the claimed invention in summarized form. The summary may point out the advantages of the invention and how it solves previously existing problems, preferably those problems identified in the BACKGROUND OF THE INVENTION. A statement of the object of the invention may also be included.

BRIEF DESCRIPTION OF THE SEVERAL VIEWS OF THE DRAWING

Where there are drawings, you must include a listing of all figures by number and with corresponding statements explaining what each figure depicts.

DETAILED DESCRIPTION OF THE INVENTION

In this section, the invention must be explained along with the process of making and using the invention in full, clear, concise, and exact terms. This section should distinguish the invention from other inventions and from what is old; and describe completely the process, machine, manufacture, composition of matter, or improvement invented. In the case of an improvement, the description should be confined to the specific improvement and to the parts which necessarily cooperate with it or which are necessary to completely understand the invention.

It is required that the description be sufficient so that any person of ordinary skill in the pertinent art, science, or area could make and use the invention without extensive experimentation. The best mode contemplated by you of carrying out your invention must be set forth in the description. Each element in the drawings should be mentioned in the description. This section has often, in the past, been titled "Description of the Preferred Embodiment."

FIGURE 6.1 *(Continued)*

CLAIM or CLAIMS

The claim or claims must particularly point out and distinctly claim the subject matter which you regard as the invention. The claims define the scope of the protection of the patent. Whether a patent will be granted is determined, in large measure, by the choice of wording of the claims.

A nonprovisional application for a utility patent must contain at least one claim. The claim or claims section must begin on a separate sheet. If there are several claims, they shall be numbered consecutively in Arabic numerals, with the least restrictive claim presented as claim number 1.

The claims section must begin with a statement such as "What I claim as my invention is: . . ." or "I (We) claim: . . ." followed by the recitation of the particular matter which you regard as your invention.

One or more claims may be presented in dependent form, referring back to and further limiting another claim or claims in the same application. All dependent claims should be grouped together with the claim or claims to which they refer to the extent practicable. Any dependent claim which refers to more than one other claim ("a multiple dependent claim") shall refer to such other claims in the alternative only. Each claim should be a single sentence, and where a claim sets forth a number of elements or steps, each element or step of the claim should be separated by a line indentation.

The fee required to be submitted with a nonprovisional utility patent application is, in part, determined by the number of claims, independent claims, and dependent claims.

ABSTRACT OF THE DISCLOSURE

The purpose of the abstract is to enable the PTO and the public to determine quickly the nature of the technical disclosures of your invention. The abstract points out what is new in the art to which your invention pertains; however, it will not be used for interpreting the scope of the claim(s). It should be in narrative form and generally limited to a single paragraph, and it must begin on a separate page.

Drawings (when necessary)

A patent application is required to contain drawings if drawings are necessary for the understanding of the subject matter sought to be patented. The drawings must show every feature of the invention as specified in the claims. Omission of drawings may cause an application to be considered incomplete. Please see the detailed discussion of drawing requirements.

Oath Or Declaration

The oath or declaration (Forms PTO/SB/01, PTO/SB/02A, PTO/SB/02B, and PTO/SB/02C) must identify the application with which it is associated, and must give the name, city and either state or country of residence, country of citizenship, and post office address of each inventor. It must state whether the inventor is a sole or joint inventor of the invention claimed. Additionally, designation of a correspondence address is needed on the oath or declaration. Providing a correspondence address will help to ensure prompt delivery of all notices, official letters, and other communications.

The oath or declaration must be signed by all of the actual inventors. An oath may be administered by any person within the United States, or by a diplomatic or consular officer of a foreign country, who is authorized by the United States to administer oaths. A declaration does not require any witness or person to administer or verify its signing. Thus, use of a declaration is preferable.

FIGURE 6.1 *(Continued)*

The oath or declaration must be in a language which you understand. If you comprehend the English language, you should preferably use an English language oath or declaration. If you cannot comprehend English, any oath or declaration must be in a language which you can comprehend and shall state that you understand the content of any documents to which the oath or declaration relates. If the oath or declaration used is in a language other than English, the oath or declaration must either be (1) accompanied by a verified English translation, or (2) in a form provided or approved by the Patent and Trademark Office.

If the person making the oath or declaration is not the inventor, the oath or declaration shall state the relationship of that person to the inventor, upon information and belief, the facts which the inventor would have been required to state, and the circumstances which render the inventor unable to sign, namely death, insanity or legal incapacity or unavailability/refusal to sign. (See 37 CFR §§1.42, 1.43, and 1.47)

Sequence Listing (when necessary)

This section, for the disclosure of a nucleotide and/or amino acid sequence, should contain a listing of the sequence complying with 37 CFR §1.821 through 37 CFR §1.825.

OBTAINING A RECEIPT FOR DOCUMENTS MAILED TO THE PTO

A receipt for documents mailed to the PTO can be obtained by attaching a stamped, self-addressed postcard to the first page of the documents. The postcard should contain a detailed list that identifies each type of document and the number of pages of each document. Upon receipt at PTO, the detailed list on the postcard will be compared to the actual contents of the delivery. Any discrepancies between the detailed list and the actual contents will be noted on the postcard. The postcard will be initialed and date stamped by the person at PTO who received the delivery. The postcard will be returned by mail to the addressee whose name appears on the postcard.

The returned postcard serves as evidence of receipt in the PTO of all items listed on the postcard, unless otherwise noted by PTO on the postcard. That is, if the postcard receipt has been annotated to indicate that a particular paper was not received, the postcard receipt will not serve as evidence of receipt of that paper in the PTO. Likewise, the postcard receipt will not serve as evidence of receipt of papers which are not adequately itemized.

When preparing the detailed list of documents identified on the postcard, it is important to include the following identifying information:

- the application number (if known)
- the filing date of the application (if known)
- the title of the invention
- the name of the inventor or inventors

The postcard should also include a detailed list of every document type and the number of pages of each document that are included in the delivery. If the postcard is submitted with a patent application, the detailed listing should include the following items:

- the title and number of pages of each PTO form
- the number of pages of specification (excluding claims)

FIGURE 6.1 *(Continued)*

- the number of claims and the number of claims pages
- the number of figures of drawing and the number of sheets of drawing
- whether oath or declaration statement is included
- the type and number of other documents that are included
- the amount of payment and the method of payment (i.e., check, money order, deposit account)

It is important that the postcard itemize each component of the application. For example, a general statement such as "complete application" or "patent application" or "drawings" will not show that each of the required components of an application was included if one of the items is later found to be missing by PTO.

When the self-addressed postcard is submitted with a utility patent application, the PTO will stamp the postcard being returned to the addressee with both the receipt date and the application number before placing it in the outgoing mail.

Upon receipt of the returned postcard, the addressee should promptly review the postcard to ensure that all documents and all pages were received by PTO.

DRAWING REQUIREMENTS

Information on drawing requirements is based substantially on Title 37, Code of Federal Regulations, (CFR) §1.84. There are two acceptable categories for presenting drawings in utility patent applications: black ink (black and white) and color.

Black and white drawings are normally required. India ink, or its equivalent that secures black solid lines, must be used for drawings. Drawings made by computer printer must be originals, not photocopies.

On rare occasions, color drawings may be necessary as the only practical medium by which the subject matter sought to be patented in a utility patent application is disclosed. The PTO will accept color drawings in utility patent applications and statutory invention registrations only after granting a petition explaining why the color drawings are necessary. Any such petition must include the following:

- the appropriate fee set forth in 37 CFR §1.17(i) [or Patent Petition Fee Code 122];
- three (3) sets of color drawings; and
- the following language as the first paragraph in that portion of the specification relating to the BRIEF DESCRIPTION OF THE SEVERAL VIEWS OF THE DRAWING. If the language is not in the specification, a proposed amendment to insert the language must accompany the petition.

"The file of this patent contains at least one drawing executed in color. Copies of this patent with color drawing(s) will be provided by the Patent and Trademark Office upon request and payment of the necessary fee."

Photographs are not ordinarily permitted in utility patent applications. However, the PTO will accept black and white photographs in utility patent applications only in applications in which the invention is not capable of being illustrated in an ink drawing or where the invention is shown more clearly in a photograph. For example, photographs or photomicrographs of electrophoresis gels, blots (e.g., immunological, western, Southern, and northern), autoradiographs, cell cultures (stained and unstained), histological tissue cross sections (stained and unstained), animals, plants, in vivo imaging, thin layer chromatography plates, crystalline structures, and ornamental effects continue to be acceptable. Only

FIGURE 6.1 *(Continued)*

one set of black and white photographs is required. Furthermore, no additional processing fee is required.

Photographs must either be developed on double weight photographic paper or be permanently mounted on Bristol board. The photographs must be of sufficient quality so that all details in the drawing are reproducible in the printed patent.

Color photographs will be accepted in utility patent applications if the conditions for accepting color drawings have been satisfied.

Identification of Drawings

Identifying indicia, if provided, should include the application number or the title of the invention, your name, docket number (if any), and the name and telephone number of a person to call if the PTO is unable to match the drawings to the proper application. This information should be placed on the back of each sheet of drawings a minimum distance of 1.5 cm. ($5/8$ inch) down from the top of the page. In addition, a reference to the application number (or, if an application number has not been assigned, your name) may be included in the left hand corner of the drawing sheet, provided that reference appears within 1.5 cm. ($5/8$ inch) from the top of the sheet.

Graphic Forms in Drawings

Chemical or mathematical formulas, tables, computer program listings, and waveforms may be submitted as drawings and are subject to the same requirements as drawings. Each chemical or mathematical formula must be labeled as a separate figure, using brackets when necessary, to show that information is properly integrated. Each group of waveforms must be presented as a single figure, using a common vertical axis with time extending along the horizontal axis. Each individual waveform discussed in the specification must be identified with a separate letter designation adjacent to the vertical axis. These may be placed in a landscape orientation if they cannot be presented satisfactorily in a portrait orientation. Typewritten characters used in such formulas and tables must be chosen from a block (nonscript) type font or lettering style having capital letters which are at least 0.21 cm. (0.08 inch) high (elite type). A space at least 0.64 cm. ($1/4$ inch) high should be provided between complex formulas or tables and the text.

Paper

Drawings submitted to the PTO must be made on paper which is flexible, strong, white, smooth, nonshiny, and durable. All sheets must be free from cracks, creases, and folds. Only one side of the sheet shall be used for the drawing. Each sheet must be reasonably free from erasures and must be free from alterations, overwritings, and interlineations. Photographs must either be developed on double weight photographic paper or be permanently mounted on Bristol broad.

All drawings sheets in an application must be the same size. One of the shorter sides of the sheet is regarded as its top. The size of the sheets on which drawings are made must be:

- 21.6 cm. by 27.9 cm. ($8 1/2$ by 11 inches), or
- 21.0 cm. by 29.7 cm. (DIN size A4).

FIGURE 6.1 *(Continued)*

The sheets must not contain frames around the sight (the usable surface), but should have scan target points (cross hairs) printed on two catercorner margin corners. The following margins are required:

- On 21.6 cm. by 27.9 cm. (8½ by 11 inch) drawing sheets, each sheet must include a top margin of at least 2.5 cm. (1 inch), a left side margin of at least 2.5 cm. (1 inch), a right side margin of at least 1.5 cm. ($^5/_8$ inch), and a bottom margin of at least 1.0 cm. ($^3/_8$ inch) from the edges, thereby leaving a sight no greater than 17.6 cm. by 24.4 cm. ($6^{15}/_{16}$ by $9^5/_8$ inches).
- On 21.0 cm. by 29.7 cm. (DIN size A4) drawing sheets, each sheet must include a top margin of at least 2.5 cm. (1 inch), a left side margin of at least 2.5 cm. (1 inch), a right side margin of at least 1.5 cm ($^5/_8$ inch), and a bottom margin of at least 1.0 cm. ($^3/_8$ inch) from the edges, thereby leaving a sight no greater than 17.0 cm. by 26.2 cm.

Views

The drawing must contain as many views as necessary to show the invention. The views may be plan, elevation, section, or perspective views. Detail views of portions of elements, on a larger scale if necessary, may also be used. All views of the drawing must be grouped together and arranged on the sheet(s) without wasting space, preferably in an upright position, clearly separated from one another, and must not be included in the sheets containing the specifications, claims, or abstract. Views must not be connected by projection lines and must not contain center lines. Waveforms of electrical signals may be connected by dashed lines to show the relative timing of the waveforms.

EXPLODED VIEWS

Exploded views, with the separated parts embraced by a bracket, to show the relationship or order of assembly of various parts are permissible. When an exploded view is shown in a figure which is on the same sheet as another figure, the exploded view should be placed in brackets.

PARTIAL VIEWS

When necessary, a view of a large machine or device in its entirety may be broken into partial views on a single sheet, or extended over several sheets if there is no loss in facility of understanding the view. Partial views drawn on separate sheets must always be capable of being linked edge to edge so that no partial view contains parts of another partial view. A smaller scale view should be included showing the whole formed by the partial views and indicating the positions of the parts shown. When a portion of a view is enlarged for magnification purposes, the view and the enlarged view must each be labeled as separate views.

Where views on two or more sheets form, in effect, a single complete view, the views on the several sheets must be so arranged that the complete figure can be assembled without concealing any part of any of the views appearing on the various sheets.

A very long view may be divided into several parts placed one above the other on a single sheet. However, the relationship between the different parts must be clear and unambiguous.

SECTIONAL VIEWS

The plane upon which a sectional view is taken should be indicated on the view from which the section is cut by a broken line. The ends of the broken line should be designated by Arabic or Roman numerals corresponding to the view number of the sectional view, and should have arrows to indicate the

FIGURE 6.1 *(Continued)*

direction of sight. Hatching must be used to indicate section portions of an object, and must be made by regularly spaced oblique parallel lines spaced sufficiently apart to enable the lines to be distinguished without difficulty. Hatching should not impede the clear reading of the reference characters and lead lines. If it is not possible to place reference characters outside the hatched area, the hatching may be broken off wherever reference characters are inserted. Hatching must be at a substantial angle to the surrounding axes or principal lines, preferably 45°.

A cross section must be set out and drawn to show all of the materials as they are shown in the view from which the cross section was taken. The parts in cross section must show proper material(s) by hatching with regularly spaced parallel oblique strokes; the space between strokes being chosen on the basis of the total area to be hatched. The various parts of a cross section of the same item should be hatched in the same manner and should accurately and graphically indicate the nature of the material(s) illustrated in cross section.

The hatching of juxtaposed different elements must be angled in a different way. In the case of large areas, hatching may be confined to an edging drawn around the entire inside of the outline of the area to be hatched. Different types of hatching should have different conventional meanings as regards the nature of a material seen in cross section.

ALTERNATE POSITION

A moved position may be shown by a broken line superimposed upon a suitable view if this can be done without crowding; otherwise, a separate view must be used for this purpose.

MODIFIED FORMS

Modified forms of construction must be shown in separate views.

Arrangement of Views

One view must not be placed upon another or within the outline of another. All views on the same sheet should stand in the same direction and, if possible, stand so that they can be read with the sheet held in an upright position. If views wider than the width of the sheet are necessary for the clearest illustration of the invention, the sheet may be turned on its side so that the top of the sheet is on the right-hand side, with the appropriate top margin used as the heading space. Words must appear in a horizontal, left-to-right fashion when the page is either upright or turned so that the top becomes the right side, except for graphs utilizing standard scientific convention to denote the axis of abscissas (of X) and the axis of ordinates (of Y).

View for the Official Gazette

One of the views should be suitable for publication in the *Official Gazette* as the illustration of the invention.

Scale

The scale to which a drawing is made must be large enough to show the mechanism without crowding when the drawing is reduced in size to two-thirds in reproduction. Views of portions of the mechanism on a larger scale should be used when necessary to show details clearly. Two or more sheets may be used if one does not give sufficient room. The number of sheets should be kept to a minimum.

FIGURE 6.1 *(Continued)*

When approved by the examiner, the scale of the drawing may be graphically represented. Indications such as "actual size" or "scale $1/2$" are not permitted on the drawings since these lose their meaning with reproduction in a different format.

Elements of the same view must be in proportion to each other, unless a difference in proportion is indispensable for the clarity of the view. Instead of showing elements in different proportion, a supplementary view may be added giving a larger-scale illustration of the element of the initial view. The enlarged element shown in the second view should be surrounded by a finely drawn or "dot-dash" circle in the first view indicating its location without obscuring the view.

Character of Lines, Numbers, and Letters

All drawings must be made by a process which will give them satisfactory reproduction characteristics. Every line, number, and letter must be durable, clean, black (except for color drawings), sufficiently dense and dark, and uniformly thick and well-defined. The weight of all lines and letters must be heavy enough to permit adequate reproduction. This requirement applies to all lines however fine, to shading, and to lines representing cut surfaces in sectional views. Lines and strokes of different thicknesses may be used in the same drawing where different thicknesses have a different meaning.

Shading

The use of shading in views is encouraged if it aids in understanding the invention and if it does not reduce legibility. Shading is used to indicate the surface or shape of spherical, cylindrical, and conical elements of an object. Flat parts may also be lightly shaded. Such shading is preferred in the case of parts shown in perspective, but not for cross sections. See discussion of sectional views above. Spaced lines for shading are preferred. These lines must be thin, as few in number as practicable, and they must contrast with the rest of the drawings. As a substitute for shading, heavy lines on the shade side of objects can be used except where they superimpose on each other or obscure reference characters. Light should come from the upper left corner at an angle of 45°. Surface delineations should preferably be shown by proper shading. Solid black shading areas are not permitted, except when used to represent bar graphs or color.

Symbols

Graphical drawing symbols may be used for conventional elements when appropriate. The elements for which such symbols and labeled representations are used must be adequately identified in the specification. Known devices should be illustrated by symbols which have a universally recognized conventional meaning and are generally accepted in the art. Other symbols which are not universally recognized may be used, subject to approval by the PTO, if they are not likely to be confused with existing conventional symbols, and if they are readily identifiable.

Legends

Suitable descriptive legends may be used, or may be required by the examiner, where necessary for understanding of the drawing, subject to approval by the PTO. They should contain as few words as possible.

FIGURE 6.1   *(Continued)*

Numbers, Letters, and Reference Characters

The English alphabet must be used for letters, except where another alphabet is customarily used, such as the Greek alphabet to indicate angles, wavelengths, and mathematical formulas.

Reference characters (numerals are preferred), sheet numbers, and view numbers must be plain and legible, and must not be used in association with brackets or inverted commas, or enclosed within outlines (encircled). They must be oriented in the same direction as the view so as to avoid having to rotate the sheet. Reference characters should be arranged to follow the profile of the object depicted.

Numbers, letters, and reference characters must measure at least 0.32 cm. ($1/_8$ inch) in height. They should not be placed in the drawing so as to interfere with its comprehension. Therefore, they should not cross or mingle with the lines. They should not be placed upon hatched or shaded surfaces. When necessary, such as indicating a surface or cross section, a reference character may be underlined and a blank space may be left in the hatching or shading where the character occurs so that it appears distinct.

The same part of an invention appearing in more than one view of the drawing must always be designated by the same reference character, and the same reference character must never be used to designate different parts.

Reference characters not mentioned in the description shall not appear in the drawings. Reference characters mentioned in the description must appear in the drawings.

Numbers, Letters, and Reference Characters

The English alphabet must be used for letters, except where another alphabet is customarily used, such

proximity of the reference character and extend to the feature indicated. Lead lines must not cross each other. Lead lines are required for each reference character except for those which indicate the surface or cross section on which they are placed. Such a reference character must be underlined to make it clear that a lead line has not been left out by mistake. Lead lines must be executed in the same way as lines in the drawing.

Arrows may be used at the ends of lines, provided that their meaning is clear, as follows:

- on a lead line, a freestanding arrow to indicate the entire section towards which it points;
- on a lead line, an arrow touching a line to indicate the surface shown by the line looking along the direction of the arrow; or
- to show the direction of movement.

Copyright or Mask Work Notice

A copyright or mask work notice may appear in the drawing, but must be placed within the sight of the drawing immediately below the figure representing the copyright or mask work material and be limited to letters having a print size of 0.32 cm. to 0.64 cm. ($1/_8$ to $1/_4$ inches) high. The content of the notice must be limited to only those elements provided for by law. For example, "©1983 John Doe" (17 U.S.C. 401) and "*M* John Doe" (17 U.S.C. 909) would be properly limited and, under current statutes, legally sufficient notices of copyright and mask work, respectively. Inclusion of a copyright or mask work notice will be permitted only if the authorization language set forth in 37 CFR §1.71(e) is included at the beginning (preferably as the first paragraph) of the specification.

FIGURE 6.1   *(Continued)*

Numbering of Sheets of Drawings and Views

The sheets of drawings should be numbered in consecutive Arabic numerals, starting with 1, within the sight (the usable surface). These numbers, if present, must be placed in the middle of the top of the sheet, but not in the margin. The numbers can be placed on the right-hand side if the drawing extends too close to the middle of the top edge of the usable surface. The drawing sheet numbering must be clear and larger than the numbers used as reference characters to avoid confusion. The number of each sheet should be shown by two Arabic numerals placed on either side of an oblique line, with the first being the sheet number and the second being the total number of sheets of drawings, with no other marking.

The different views must be numbered in consecutive Arabic numerals, starting with 1, independent of the numbering of the sheets and, if possible, in the order in which they appear on the drawing sheet(s). Partial views intended to form one complete view, on one or several sheets, must be identified by the same number followed by a capital letter. View numbers must be preceded by the abbreviation **FIG.** Where only a single view is used in an application to illustrate the claimed invention, it must not be numbered and the abbreviation **FIG.** must not appear.

Numbers and letters identifying the views must be simple and clear and must not be used in association with brackets, circles, or inverted commas. The view numbers must be larger than the numbers used for reference characters.

Security Markings

Authorized security markings may be placed on the drawings provided they are outside the sight, preferably centered in the top margin.

Corrections

Any corrections on drawings submitted to the PTO must be durable and permanent.

Holes

No holes should be made by the applicant in the drawing sheets.

Patent and Trademark Depository Library (PTDL) LIST

The **Patent and Trademark Depository Library Program** is comprised of a network of Patent and Trademark Depository Libraries (PTDLs) located in the 50 states, the District of Columbia, and Puerto Rico which provide access to many of the same products and services offered at the PTO search facilities in Arlington, VA. The scope of PTDL collections, hours of operation, services, and fees (where applicable) vary depending on PTDL location. Users are advised to call ahead to determine products and services available at a particular PTDL. PTDLs also offer automated access to patent and trademark information. All PTDLs offer free access to the *Cassis* CD-ROM series search tools to assist patrons in the use of patent and trademark collections.

FIGURE 6.1 *(Continued)*

footing with applicants for foreign patents, which are often filed earlier in the process than U.S. patents because most other countries do not give inventors the full year grace period between the initial publication of an invention and the time when an application must be filed.

Along with providing an earlier initial filing date for a patent, a provisional application allows inventors to use the term "patent pending." This term does not have the same legal force of the final patent, but it does warn others by letting them know one is in the works and that the invention will probably be off limits soon.

The requirements for a provisional application are much less stringent that for a nonprovisional. Instead of including all the elements listed above, a completed provisional application needs to include a written description of the invention, drawings as needed, the name of the inventor, a cover sheet, and the filing fee. Provisional applications are not examined on their merits, as nonprovisionals are, so the bar is not set nearly as high for getting the USPTO to accept one.

A provisional patent lasts for one year. The applicant has that time period to file a regular application; otherwise the provisional status expires and it is too late for any further filing.

The best reasons for seeking a provisional patent are to document an invention you feel has value and establish a date in case of later disputes. If your invention is workable, the pending status allows you to write about, market, and sell your creation with a year's breathing room until the formal application is filed. If your invention has been disclosed within the past year and you will run out of time before a nonprovisional application can be prepared, a provisional application will provide a filing date and extend the drop-dead date. A provisional application is also a good idea if you fear somebody else is going to document the same invention and you want to establish a prior claim. It must be remembered, though, that a provisional application provides no guarantee that the nonprovisional application will be accepted.

THE EXAMINATION PROCESS

USPTO patent examiners are grouped together according to their training and expertise. Once a patent has been filed and is determined to be complete, it is assigned to a group according to the area of technology it is in. Generally, patents are examined in the order received, a process that takes about 18 months.

During the examination a search is conducted of available patent documents and other relevant literature to determine if the invention described in the patent is new, legal, and nonobvious. Based on this search and an evaluation of the results, the examiner makes the decision to grant, or not grant, the patent.

After the decision has been made, the applicant or their attorney or agent of record is mailed a written decision. Any objections, additional requirements, or adverse actions will be detailed in the decision. If the examiner has discovered prior art, or decides the invention is not of a patentable nature or lacks novelty, it will be rejected. Most patent applications contain a number of claims, and it is common for some claims to be accepted while others are rejected, or more information is required of the applicant before a decision is reached. Bear in mind that most patent applications do not sail through the whole process unscathed, but about 72% of them do go on to be approved.

WHAT IF THE PATENT IS REJECTED?

If a patent or any claims within it are rejected, the applicant can request a reconsideration. This response must be in writing and be specific about any errors the examiner is thought to have made; it must address all grounds for rejections and objections and be a real effort to move the matter to finality. A letter just expressing the opinion that the conclusions of the examination were wrong is not enough. There are time limits for applicants to respond to a rejection, ranging from 30 days to 6 months. If no response is made within the period, the USPTO will assume that the patent has been abandoned. If more time to respond is needed, a continuation application can be filed that effectively extends the deadline.

This is another instance where a good attorney can be a huge help. They have been through it before and know how to handle a response, along with having good insight into whether or not pursuing the matter is worthwhile. An experienced attorney knows how to interact with the USPTO. The danger an individual on unfamiliar ground faces is losing the opportunity to change a decision, not because their reasons are lacking, but because they failed to communicate in the ways that would have received the best reception.

After the applicant, or applicant's representative, has responded, the response will be considered. A second office action will be issued in a format similar to the first. Whether the action is favorable to the applicant, it is usually the final decision. The second action can be appealed to the Board of Patent Appeals and Interferences of the USPTO, but the chances for success at this point are usually very limited, unless a clear error was made by the examiner. Very rarely, an adverse decision on appeal will be taken to the next level, a federal appeals court.

PROTECTING YOUR PATENT AT HOME AND ABROAD

7

THE NATURE OF PATENTS

After the application, examination, and approval processes are successfully completed, a patent, with the seal of the USPTO, is issued to its owner in the name of the United States. Considering all the time, energy, and anxiety that usually goes into securing a patent, it almost seems unfair that the power it grants you is limited to "the right to exclude others from making, using, offering for sale or selling the invention throughout the United States or importing the invention in the United States," and that this power lasts only 20 years from the date of application, with a minimum duration of 17 years, after which anybody who wants to can use it, instead of continuing until the end of time.

From the time a patent is granted until it expires, it is solely up to the owner to make something of it. The USPTO's involvement during the life of a patent is limited, usually confined to collecting maintenance fees and making corrections to the patent if necessary.

One thing to be aware of is that any person can request that the USPTO conduct a reexamination of the patent if prior art, in the form of existing patents or documents, is found to exist. The result can range from a clean bill of health for the patent to its being invalidated based on the same conditions, but now with additional materials, which were applied during the examination phase. Given the power of search engines available today, it is more important than ever to have a thorough search conducted prior to applying for a patent, lest you run the risk of losing the patent because you missed prior art that somebody else was able to find. There are even some commercial online services where rewards are offered to those who can find prior art references that successfully invalidate particular patents.

So maybe a good way to motivate yourself, and anybody you hire, to search thoroughly is to envision somebody eagerly pecking away at their computer, with nothing better to do than earn a few dollars by blowing up your patent.

FOREIGN PATENTS

The offensive rights granted to the holder of a United States patent have power only within the boundaries of the United States. Inventors who believe their products can be sold profitably abroad and desire the protection of a patent will have to apply for one in the regional offices of the desired countries. If possible, it is wise to assess early in the process if your invention will be sold outside the United States so you can start right off with an attorney who has experience with foreign patent offices, in addition to the USPTO.

There is nothing unusual about inventors seeking patents outside their home countries. In fact, with the Internet making it so much easier to promote awareness of new goods almost anywhere people have computer access to it, it is increasingly common to come right out of the gate with an eye toward an international market. In the United States, approximately 46% of the utility patents granted last year were to individuals and firms from outside the country, up from 27% in 1970. Japan is consistently the country receiving the most U.S. patents, at an annual rate of 2–3 times greater than the next closest country, Germany.

Fortunately, there are some agreements in force to facilitate the acquisition of foreign patents. The Paris Convention for the Protection of Industrial Property is followed by 140 countries, the United States among them. The terms of this treaty stipulate that every member guarantees citizens of other member countries the identical rights in patents and trademarks available to its own citizens. It also stipulates that by filing in one member country a patent holder has the right of priority in the other countries, so that, within a given period of time, that patent's application date in the first foreign country becomes the filing date in all subsequent countries where patent protection is sought. Another treaty is the Patent Cooperation Treaty. This agreement is adhered to by 90 countries, including the United States, and its purpose is to provide a standardized format for application and centralized filing procedures.

Before you go to seek patents throughout the world, be aware that filing in key locations globally can make an application that cost $12,000 or $15,000 in the United States have a final filing cost of four or five times those amounts.

PATENT INFRINGEMENT

When a patented invention of any kind is being sold, it is very important to mark it with the word "patent" and the patent number. This way, if legal action is pursued it cannot be claimed that the patented status of an item was unknown because of a lack of marking, which could jeopardize the action. The terms "patent pending" and "patent applied for" can be used for inventions an application has been applied for, but not yet granted. Though these do not carry the weight of a complete patent, they do inform others that a claim has been made and a patent with offensive rights is likely to be forthcoming.

A patent is infringed when another party runs afoul of the exclusive rights granted to its owner by making, using, offering for sale, or importing, any patented item in the United States without permission. If infringement occurs, the USPTO does not get involved; the body with the necessary authority to negotiate the dispute is the federal court system.

A patent holder who feels their patent is being infringed can initiate legal action with the goals of stopping the offending party, collecting royalties on the unauthorized sale of the patented invention, or collecting damages. The key to the success of legal action lies in the original wording of the patent claims, for if it cannot be shown that the actions in question are covered by the claims, then there is no literal infringement. Once again, this highlights just how important it is to have good counsel during the application process. Most individuals are perfectly capable of performing the steps necessary to obtain a patent, but in saving legal fees early on there is the risk of not including the kind of language that will give their claims enforceable power during a legal struggle.

Even if it is shown that infringement has occurred, the infringer may question the validity of the patent, possibly because they have found what they consider to be prior art. This is another case where inventors need to protect themselves in advance. For if a thorough search is not done prior to the granting of a patent, the risk will remain, throughout the life of the patent, that documents exist that can be used to negate it.

A particularly daunting aspect to legal action, no matter how solid one's grounds for it are, is the expense. Depending on the nature and extent of the proceedings, pursuing a patent infringement case can cost from a few thousand to a few million dollars, with the average cost of a suit weighing in at $1.2 million according to an industry survey. Patent attorneys charge between $100 and $300, so it does not take long for the cost to add up. For individuals with limited resources who are considering taking on large firms, the struggle can quickly become very unequal, with an infringer with deep pockets willing to run the risk of a lawsuit because the patent holder does not appear to have the teeth necessary to do much about it.

The infringement of patents, trademarks, copyrights, and trade secrets has become a growing problem in foreign countries, particularly those with no patent treaties or agreements with the United States. Anything that can be easily copied, in the form of a direct duplication or a process that can be readily imitated, is at risk if there is an economic market for it. Recalling the example from Chapter 1, consider the antifungal medication that costs $10 a pill in the United States and is sold for $.25 in India, a country that does not have a patent treaty with the United States, or the billions of dollars in copyright and patent fees that are lost each year in the illegal copying and sale of software.

The best defense against infringement is to remain aware of goods similar to yours and keep an eye out for those that cross the line from similarity to duplication. Maybe the infringer is honestly unaware of your patent and willing to stop, or negotiate an agreement to pay for the use of your intellectual property. If an infringer is not willing to stop or make other agreements that are suitable, legal action can be taken, but be aware of the potential costs and benefits before pursuing it.

It must also be remembered that no matter how inventive your ideas and how well worded the patent language that defines their expression in practice, innovative competitors, if your creation has a profitable market, will work hard to produce similar items that skirt the infringement issue by being just different enough, or claiming just enough of an improvement, that they can target your market without running afoul of your offensive rights. A case that illustrates this point was reported in the December 21, 2000 issue of *The Wall Street Journal*.

Juanita Donica and Dianne Syme, a mother/daughter team, created a Christmas light display, called Icicle Lights, in the early 1990s, which quickly became very popular, with $5 million in orders the first year they were marketed nationally. The inventors had a patent, but it covered only the strip the lights were hung from. Larger, wealthier competitors were able to devise other ways of hanging the lights and used their superior resources to market products similar enough to catch the eye of consumers attracted to Icicle Lights. In 1997, the second year of national marketing for Icicle Lights, the women's sales increased substantially, but in the 2000 Christmas season their sales had dropped below the $5 million mark, while one competitor with a similar display, who claimed they had made the lights easier to install, sold $80 million of their lights.

The form of infringement that could well prove to be the biggest threat might not be in the form of directly stealing your invention, an event you can make legal responses to. It can be in the form of legally infringing on the market you have targeted by producing a good or service with similar enough features, while still being legal, to compete. Anytime you are showing off new wares at a trade show, or start advertising or talking them up, there is the possibility that somebody is taking a close look at what you are doing with an eye toward preempting it.

DEFENSIVE PUBLISHING

What can be done to keep competitors from making improvements on your inventions and cutting into the market for them? The best strategy is to quickly establish your product in its market and establish it as a brand name (which can be trademarked) customers will develop a positive association with. Easier said than done, of course. Another strategy is to anticipate the kinds of incremental improvements that can be made on your invention and then block competitors from patenting them, which could have the effect of hampering your own growth or allowing them to invade the territory you have worked hard to carve out for yourself.

One way to block competitors is to apply for additional patents that cover variations, developments of, and improvements on your invention. With patents running between $3,000 and $20,000 apiece (assuming you use an attorney) this can be an expensive approach, but if you foresee a large market for an invention, it could prove to be an excellent investment.

Another approach is to keep patenting core innovations, then publish incremental improvements on your invention in the public domain. This will not prevent others from making use of them, but it can be used to prevent patents from issuing that would get in the way of the evolution of your product. Why do this instead of patenting everything? The dollar cost to put your material in the public domain is very small compared to financing a patent, and it can be done much faster and is far easier. As a strategic device, defensive publishing is used not only to keep competitors from heading off the evolution of an invention, but it can also be used to keep patents from issuing on innovations you are considering developing in the future. If you can get prior art out into the public domain and, most important of all, make it easily accessible to a patent examiner, you can keep a host of options open at a low cost.

The key here is in making your publication easy to find. Just publishing on your own web site is not the best way to do it because, with so many millions—and growing—of web sites around, it would be a mistake to assume yours will pop right up when a search is done. The work load of patent examiners has grown by an estimated 75% since 1992, so do not expect them to have time for surfing personal home pages. Popular journals and trade publications that are in common use are good, but, like any print publication or Internet resource whose submissions must be refereed or evaluated first, there can be a time lag between your submission and publication. Why leave an opening like that?

The best source at present for defensive publishing is IP. com, an Internet-based intellectual property company that will publish your documents on the Internet quickly for a reasonable fee. Their data base is widely employed in prior art searches and is very user friendly.

THE KING OF PATENTS

8

. . . all progress, all success, springs from thinking.
—Thomas Edison

Hell, there are no rules here—we're trying to accomplish something.
—Thomas Edison

AN ADDLED STUDENT

Born as the last of seven children to Samuel and Nancy Edison in 1847, Thomas Edison began attending school in Port Huron, Michigan, at the age of seven. It did not go well. As with many a teacher since, the Reverend G.B. Engle did not like being asked a lot of questions, which young Thomas quickly got into the habit of doing. Reverend Engle decided that Thomas was a dull, addled student with little capacity for learning. When he shared his opinion of Thomas' inability to learn with Mrs. Nancy Edison, Thomas' mother, she became angry at Engle's inflexibility and took Thomas out of school. The unhappy experience had lasted three months.

His parents tried him in a couple of other schools at different times, but Thomas' attendance was poor and neither attempt lasted long. Though there are some today who look back at Thomas Edison's school experience and claim he had a learning disability or was afflicted with attention deficit disorder, the truth is more likely that he had an exceptionally active and inquisitive mind that did not take well to the restrictions imposed by a school environment that must have been insufferably dull to him.

Fortunately for him, Edison's parents were great readers and they passed their love of reading on to him, with Shakespeare and histories of the Roman Empire examples of the works Thomas had read by the age of 12. His parents were strong believers in educating their children and, at the same time, were willing to let them follow their natural inclinations. With Nancy Edison being a former school teacher and Samuel Edison a man with the capacity to quickly pick up the skills necessary to perform a variety of jobs, from selling real estate to operating a grocery store, Thomas' home environment was the ideal place for the development and nurturing of his tremendous curiosity.

When Thomas was nine his mother gave him an elementary science book and he quickly did every experiment in it, then asked for more. Before long, he became particularly fond of chemistry and used all the money he could get his hands on to buy chemicals and equipment to further his experiments and learning. At age 10 he built his first laboratory in the basement of the family home. Not bad for an addled kid who went on to invent so many transforming technologies that he is sometimes considered also to have "invented the twentieth century."

It is not at all unusual for people who clashed with educators at school, received poor grades, and were regarded as problem children to go on and become successful inventors, patent holders, entrepreneurs, and CEOs. The willingness to test rules, push the limits, and ignore boring input in favor of paying closer attention to one's own thoughts and creative impulses as a child can pay dividends later on. Plenty of people with bad report cards have gone on to get great patents.

INTO THE WORKING WORLD

Thomas Edison got his first job at 12, working for the Grand Trunk Railway where he sold newspapers and candy to passengers. Whatever he earned was immediately used to finance the acquisition of more books, chemicals, and equipment for his laboratory. At 13 he wrangled permission to set up his laboratory in the baggage car, where he could do experiments during layovers. Unfortunately, the life of his lab was a short one, ending when the train lurched and a fire resulted from chemicals that spilled. Both Thomas and his lab were banned from the train. After that he sold his newspapers at train stations.

In addition to his experiments, Thomas continued to be a voracious reader, consuming everything worthwhile he could get his hands on in areas like electricity, manufacturing, mechanics, and anything else having to do with science and technology. In addition, as an early member of the Detroit Free Library (card number 33), he continued to read widely in many other subjects.

At 16 Edison developed his first invention, a device that could transmit and receive telegraph signals automatically. It was motivated by one of the requirements of his job at the time, as a telegraph assistant. He was supposed to send a signal every hour to the office in Toronto. Doing this by hand seemed inefficient to him, so he came up with the means of having it done independently, even when he was asleep.

At 21 Thomas was working as a night telegraph operator in Boston while he continued to do his experiments, particularly with electrical currents, during the day. He decided to devote himself entirely to inventing and, with a loan from a friend, was able to quit his job and throw himself into it. The first invention he patented was an electronic vote recorder (see Figure 8.1). Though it made voting a much more efficient process, he was unable to sell the vote recorder at the time. Eventually it was a success, however, and is still being used in some states as a means of recording legislative votes.

When Thomas Edison moved to New York in 1869, where a friend let him sleep in a basement office on Wall Street, he was broke, but not for long. He became interested in the stock market ticker, which was similar in its workings to the telegraphs he had experience with. After being hired to repair a broken stock market ticker, he was hired by the impressed owners to build a new one that incorporated his improvements on the existing technology. About a year later the Edison Universal Stock Printer (see Figure 8.2) was ready for action and he sold the rights to it for $40,000, a terrific sum of money at the time.

He used that money to set himself up in business in Newark, New Jersey. There he manufactured high-speed telegraphs and his stock tickers and contributed new innovations to the typewriter that enabled users to produce more words, more efficiently.

THE FIRST INVENTION FACTORY

Edison remained in Newark for six very creative years, a period that saw him obtain patents for a telegraph recording instrument, galvanic batteries, an electrical printing machine, and an electromotor escapement, among other things. Then, in March 1876, he and his two partners moved into a new facility they had built in Menlo Park, N.J.

They employed about 60 people here who came with all sorts of backgrounds. For Edison, their pedigrees did not matter. His success was due to talent and hard work and those were the same qualities he looked for in the people who worked for him. His 10 years at Menlo Park were Edison's most productive period, with his applying for around 400 patents during a couple of them.

It was at Menlo Park that Edison created what he regarded as his favorite invention, the phonograph, or "talking machine." While most of his other patents were for improvements on existing inventions, as are most other patents, this was something new. Interestingly, it was not something he set out to invent: he came across it by accident while

UNITED STATES PATENT OFFICE.

THOMAS A. EDISON, OF BOSTON, MASSACHUSETTS, ASSIGNOR TO HIMSELF AND DEWITT C. ROBERTS, OF SAME PLACE.

IMPROVEMENT IN ELECTROGRAPHIC VOTE-RECORDER.

Specification forming part of Letters Patent No. 90,646, dated June 1, 1869.

To all whom it may concern:

Be it known that I, THOMAS A. EDISON, of Boston, in the county of Suffolk and State of Massachusetts, have invented a new and useful apparatus named "Electrographic Vote-Recorder and Register," of which the following is a full, clear, and exact description, reference being had to the accompanying drawing, which represents a plan view of the apparatus, and to the letters of reference thereon.

The object of my invention is to produce an apparatus which records and registers in an instant, and with great accuracy, the votes of legislative bodies, thus avoiding loss of valuable time consumed in counting and registering the votes and names, as done in the usual manner; and my invention consists in applying an electrographic apparatus in such a manner that each member, by moving a switch to either of two points, representing an affirmative and opposing vote, has his name imprinted, by means of electricity, under the desired head, on a previously-prepared paper, and at the same time the number of votes is indicated on a dial-plate by the operation.

Referring to the drawings, in the central portion of the plate a a is secured a block, k, upon which are set, in metallic types, two columns of names, n n', the one being headed by the word "no," the other by "yes," each column containing the name of every voter, and the like names standing opposite each other, as Mann under head "no" opposite to Mann under head "yes," &c. The types are separated by intervening spaces.

Along two sides of the block k, and parallel with the two columns n n', are two rails, j j', composed of any good insulating material, as hard rubber.

Opposite the intervening spaces between two names the upper faces of the rails j j' are intersected by metallic strips o o o o' o' o'.

On the rails j j' are mounted two rollers, q q', insulated from one another, and insulated from and surrounded by the cylinder p, in such a manner that the rollers q q' project beyond said cylinder p and rest immediately upon the rails. These rollers are metallic, and the larger one, p, is of such a size as to come in contact with a chemically-prepared paper placed upon the types, and is, furthermore, in communication with battery b by means of conducting-wire r r, or in any other suitable manner.

The rollers q q' communicate with the two magnets v v'' by the wires s s', and through them operate the armatures v' v''', the escapements w w' and the pointers x x', which latter show the numbers of votes on the dial-plates marked with as many figures as there are voters.

The battery b, with the two poles c and d, is connected with and operates the apparatus in the following manner: The pole c is in constant communication with the metallic types l m, representing, respectively, "no" and "yes," by means of the conducting-wires y z; but the pole c is connected by the wires c' c'' c'', with as many switches e e' as there are voters.

From the points f f' g g' the conducting-wires i i' h h' pass to the metallic strips o o o' o', and from thence to the nearest metallic type, or they may pass first to the types and then branch back to the respective strips, as seen in the column to the left.

From the pole d of battery b communication is established with the cylinder p by the wire r r, and from the same pole by the wire u u t to the two magnets, where the aforesaid conducting-wires s s' lead to the two insulated rollers q q'.

The apparatus is placed before the recording clerk's desk, and a paper, which is previously chemically prepared for printing by electricity by saturating it in any known solution for that purpose, is placed upon the types, and covering the two columns and their heading.

Every voter is also provided with a switch, e, and moves the same *ad libitum*, as the occasion may require, on the point f or g. Thus an electric current is established between the pole c of the battery, the switch e e', and the types l m, and the clerk then rolls the rollers q q' with cylinder p on the paper upon the types. As soon as the cylinder p comes on the type of the headings the circuit becomes completed through the paper, (as the wires y y connect the pole c with the types, and the wire r the pole d with the cylinder p,) and de-

---

FIGURE 8.1   Voting Machine Patent

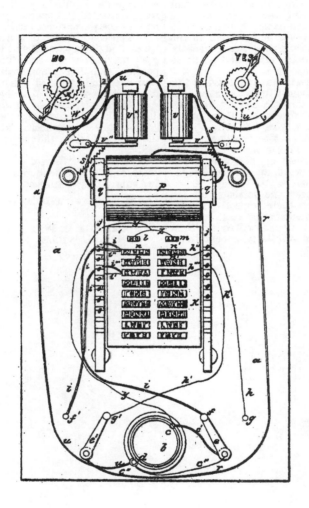

Witnesses.

Carroll D. Wright

DeWitt C. Roberts

Inventor.

Thomas A. Edison.

FIGURE 8.1 *(Continued)*

composes the chemicals, thereby discoloring the paper in contact with the types, and thus produces the printing.

When the cylinder p comes over the two names—Mann, Mann—the current from pole c through switch e and wire i to the types bearing the name on the left becomes completed through the paper, with cylinder p, wire r, and pole d, and, discoloring the paper, produces the name Mann on the paper; but there is no connection of the other name Mann to the right with the switch and pole c; consequently no decomposition takes place, and no name shown.

The roller p passing on and leaving the types the circuit becomes broken; but as soon as the rollers q q' come in contact with the metallic strips o o' the circuit from pole c through the switch e, wire i i'', strip o', and through roller q', magnet v'', wire t and u to pole d, becomes closed, the armature v''' attracted the escapement w', and with it the pointer x' moved forward, and here one negative vote recorded, &c.

Thus, it will be seen, the names of all the voters are printed on their respective heads, and also the whole number of votes counted in an instant, or as long as it will require time to roll the cylinder p over the types containing the list of all the names in metallic types, with more dispatch and accuracy than it can possibly be done in any other way.

Having thus fully described my invention, what I claim as new, and desire to secure by Letters Patent, is—

1. The combination of a switch or switches e e', types and cylinder p, with an electric battery, connected and operating substantially as and for the purpose set forth.

2. The combination of switch e, strips o o', types, and the separated and insulated rollers q q'; magnets v v'', armature, escapement, pointer, and dial-plate, with the battery b, connected and operated substantially as and for the purpose above described.

3. The combination of switch, types, cylinder p, rollers q q', strips o o', and insulators j j', magnets v v'', armature, &c., constructed in the manner and for the purpose above specified.

In testimony whereof I have signed my name to this specification in the presence of two subscribing witnesses.

THOMAS A. EDISON.

Witnesses:
CARROLL D. WRIGHT,
M. S. G. WILDE.

FIGURE 8.1 *(Continued)*

UNITED STATES PATENT OFFICE.

THOMAS A. EDISON, OF NEW YORK, N. Y., ASSIGNOR TO SAMUEL S. LAWS, OF SAME PLACE.

IMPROVEMENT IN PRINTING-TELEGRAPH APPARATUS.

Specification forming part of Letters Patent No. **96,567,** dated November 9, 1869.

To all whom it may concern:

Be it known that I, THOMAS A. EDISON, of the city, county, and State of New York, have invented a new and useful Improvement in Electrical Printing Instruments; and I do hereby declare the following to be a full, clear, and exact description thereof, which will enable those skilled in the art to make and use the same, reference being had to the accompanying drawings, forming part of this specification, in which drawings—

Figure 1 represents a side elevation of this invention, showing the printing mechanism. Fig. 2 is a front view of the unison mechanism detached. Fig. 3 is a side elevation of my instrument, showing the mechanism for imparting to the type-wheel a step-by-step movement in either direction. Fig. 4 is a plan of the paper-feed mechanism detached. Fig. 5 is a front view of the same.

Similar letters indicate corresponding parts.

This invention relates to certain improvements in that class of instruments for which Letters Patent were granted to S. S. Laws December 31, 1867, and March 24, 1868, and also described in an application for a patent filed by said S. S. Laws in the Patent Office January 4, 1869.

My present improvements consist in the arrangement of two dogs, pawls, or clicks pivoted to two armature-levers and acting on a star-shaped or double ratchet-wheel, in combination with stationary pins which are not connected with the ratchet or pawls and which act on the pawls in such a manner that by one set of pins the pawls are thrown out of gear with the ratchet, and by the other set of pins said pawls are locked in gear with the ratchet, and that by the action of the two pawls a uniform step-by-step movement can be imparted to the ratchet in either direction with ease and facility, the mechanism required for this purpose being exceedingly simple and not liable to get out of repair, and the type-wheel or ratchet is held in position, when at rest, by means of a graduated or adjustable friction instead of holding-pawls.

The invention consists, also, in the arrangement of a separate magnet in combination with the unison-lever in such a manner that the operator has absolute control over the unison-stops of all the instruments in the line without danger of disturbing the power of any of the other magnets.

In the drawings, the letter A designates a bed-plate, from which rises an arm, B, which may be cast solid with or otherwise rigidly attached to said bed-plate. The outer end of this arm B is bored out to form a bearing for a shaft, a, on one end of which is mounted the type-wheel C, while on its other end is mounted the ratchet-wheel D, said shaft being fitted in its bearings, so that it turns freely therein; but sufficient friction is secured by adjusting the position of the type-wheel to retain it in any position into which it may be brought. This friction may be obtained and regulated by the pressure of an adjustable spring upon the ratchet-shaft or some part carried around thereby.

The ratchet-wheel D is star-shaped or double-acting, and it is acted upon by two pawls or clicks, b c, which are pivoted to levers E F, extending from the armatures G H of two electro-magnets, I J. Said levers have a common fulcrum on the pivot or stud d, which is rigidly secured in the arm B, and their armatures and electro-magnets are arranged in such relation to said levers and to the ratchet-wheel that by alternately closing and opening the circuits through said electro-magnets the levers E F are caused to oscillate in opposite directions, and that by the action of one of the clicks the ratchet-wheel assumes a step-by-step movement in one direction, while the other click produces a step-by-step movement of the ratchet-wheel in the opposite direction. The position of the clicks, in relation to the teeth of the ratchet-wheel, is governed by two sets of pins,. e f, g h, which are secured in a disk, K, that is rigidly attached to the end of the arm B. The pins e and f act on projections on the inner edges of the clicks b and c, and if the levers E and F are forced back, by the action of their springs i and j, said pins lift and hold the points of the clicks out of the path of the ratchet-teeth, and if either of the armatures is attracted and its lever caused to move, the pawls, being released of the pins e and f, are thrown in gear with the ratchet-teeth by the action of their springs, and the stop-pin g or h acts against the outside edge of the corresponding click and

---

FIGURE 8.2   Printing Machine Patent

holds it in gear and locks it with the ratchet-wheel, causing the same to stop at the distance of one tooth. The stop-pins g and h might be combined into one pin, serving the same purpose for each of the pawls. By this arrangement a step-by-step movement can be imparted to the ratchet-wheel, governed by the action of the stationary pins $e\,f\,g\,h$ on the projections on the edges of said clicks, the friction of the type-wheel arbor being made sufficient to prevent the ratchet from moving when the lever-pawls are drawn back from the teeth.

It is obvious that the effect of the two clicks will be the same if they are made to engage with two ratchet-wheels on the same arbor, with teeth facing in opposite directions, such ratchets being a mechanical equivalent of the star-shaped ratchet shown in the drawings.

The electro-magnets I and J are fastened to the arm B, so that they straddle said arm, and easy access can be had to them and to their connections.

In order to throw all the instruments on a line in unison, a "unison-lever," L, is used, such as described in the application of S. S. Laws for a patent on printing-telegraph, filed in the Patent Office January 4, 1869. This unison-lever is hinged to a bracket, R, which is firmly secured to the main arm B, and to said lever is attached the armature l of a separate electro-magnet M, which is secured to the bracket R. The lower end of the unison-lever L forms a hook, (see Fig. 1,) and if the circuit through the electro-magnet M is closed, this hook is thrown in the path of a pin, m, which projects from the shaft a, (see Figs. 1 and 2,) so that the motion of said shaft is stopped as soon as the pin m comes in contact with the unison-lever. The pins m on the several instruments in a line are made to correspond in position to a certain type or character on the several type-wheels, and consequently by working all the instruments round in either direction until the several pins m are brought in contact with the several unison-levers, all the type-wheels are arrested in the same position and all the instruments are thrown into unison.

The object of working the unison-lever by a separate magnet is to enable the operator to control the position of said unison-lever without disturbing any other part of the mechanism, and particularly without diminishing the power of the main magnets, as when the unison-lever is operated by secondary armatures from either or both of the main magnets.

The strip of paper Z is carried through between the platen N and the type-wheel by the feed mechanism O. A roller, r, presses the strip of paper against one of the serrated rims or flanges o of the feed-wheel, and as the platen-lever oscillates, by the combined action of its electro-magnet and its detaching-spring the ratchet of the feed-drum acts against the click g and receives an intermittent rotary motion, so that for each oscillation of the platen-lever the strip of paper is moved a sufficient distance to make room for a subsequent impression. The pressing-roller r is situated on the inside of the feed-drum, and consequently the letters and characters printed on the strip of paper are not at all concealed by it while the strip passes through the feed mechanism, and said characters remain open to view from the time when they have been printed.

Having thus described my invention, what I claim as new, and desire to secure by Letters Patent, is—

1. The stationary pins $e\,f\,g\,h$, in combination with the clicks $b\,c$, actuated by the armature-levers E F, and acting on the ratchet D, substantially as and for the purpose described.

2. The combination of a separate electro-magnet with the unison-lever L, substantially as set forth.

THOMAS A. EDISON.

Witnesses:
W. HAUFF,
E. F. KASTENHUBER.

FIGURE 8.2 *(Continued)*

T. A. EDISON.

Electrical Printing Instrument.

No. 96.567.   Patented Nov. 9, 1869.

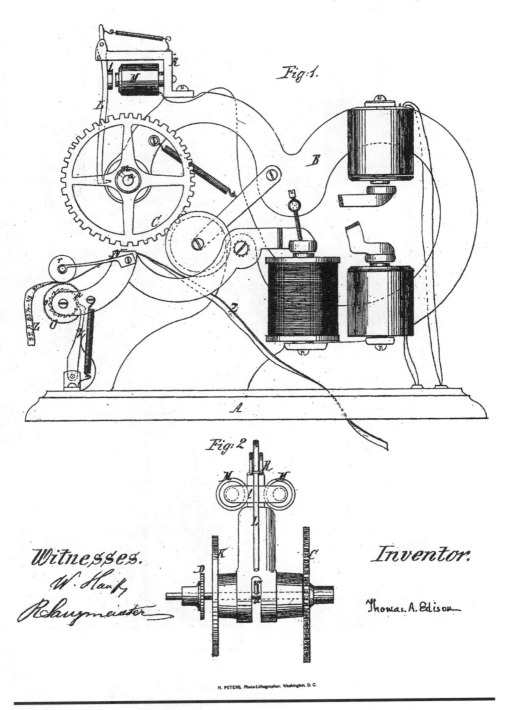

Fig. 1.

Fig. 2.

Witnesses.   Inventor:

W. Hauf,   Thomas. A. Edison

R Laupmeister

FIGURE 8.2 *(Continued)*

T. A. EDISON.

Electrical Printing Instrument.

No. 96,567.

Patented Nov. 9, 1869.

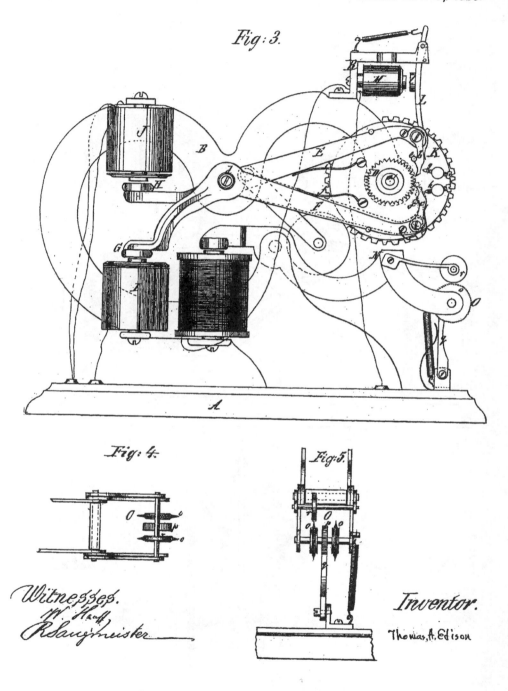

Fig: 3.

Fig: 4.

Fig: 5.

Witnesses.

W. Hauff

R. Langmeister

Inventor.

Thomas A. Edison

FIGURE 8.2 *(Continued)*

working on additional advances for telegraphs and telephones (see Figure 8.3). Possessed of a very flexible mind and the ability to spot new opportunities, even when unexpected, Edison immediately ran with it. From working on a way to record messages on a cylinder, he jumped into developing the means to record and play sounds, with musical recordings quickly becoming popular with the public when the invention began being sold in 1878.

This was an invention Edison was to keep working on and improving for the rest of his life, still applying for new patents on advances in the technology even in the 1920s (Figure 8.4). As this demonstrates, Edison was a master not only of invention, but of continuing to make the most of his innovations.

Another feature of Edison's that is crucial to all successful inventors and patent applicants was his tenacity, as he demonstrated spectacularly in his efforts to develop electric light (the patent is Figure 8.5). In his search for the right filament for bulbs, he tested more than 6,000 materials from plants and trees he had sent people all over the world to gather. Finally, after about 1,200 experiments and spending many thousands of dollars to finance them, Edison developed a bulb that could burn for two days. First lighting his factory, Edison went on to apply his lighting technology in Manhattan, which was the first place on the planet where electricity was sent to people's homes and provided them an efficient source of light, which was an enormous improvement over the candles and gas lights that had been used up until then. No surprise that his nickname was The Wizard of Menlo Park.

A WIZARD AT WORK

More than any innate wizardness he possessed, Edison's never-ending quest to keep learning enabled him to spot opportunities that others either did not spot or were not able to take advantage of. For example, his dedication to reading everything he could on photographic optics gave him a big boost in patenting a series of inventions for movie cameras. In addition, a lot of learning occurred just in the process of Edison's experimentation and development, where his experience enabled him to become increasingly better at the process of innovation. This experience also enabled him to apply his gift for innovation to a wide range of areas, and sometimes those where few would have expected Edison to show interest. For example, look at Figure 8.6, for Edison's method of preserving fruit. It seems awfully far afield from the kinds of things he was normally involved in, but when curiosity is boundless, nothing is off limits.

UNITED STATES PATENT OFFICE.

THOMAS A. EDISON, OF MENLO PARK, NEW JERSEY.

IMPROVEMENT IN PHONOGRAPH OR SPEAKING MACHINES.

Specification forming part of Letters Patent No. **200,521**, dated February 19, 1878; application filed December 24, 1877.

To all whom it may concern:

Be it known that I, THOMAS A. EDISON, of Menlo Park, in the county of Middlesex and State of New Jersey, have invented an Improvement in Phonograph or Speaking Machines, of which the following is a specification:

The object of this invention is to record in permanent characters the human voice and other sounds, from which characters such sounds may be reproduced and rendered audible again at a future time.

The invention consists in arranging a plate, diaphragm, or other flexible body capable of being vibrated by the human voice or other sounds, in conjunction with a material capable of registering the movements of such vibrating body by embossing or indenting or altering such material, in such a manner that such register-marks will be sufficient to cause a second vibrating plate or body to be set in motion by them, and thus reproduce the motions of the first vibrating body.

The invention further consists in the various combinations of mechanism to carry out my invention.

I have discovered, after a long series of experiments, that a diaphragm or other body capable of being set in motion by the human voice does not give, except in rare instances, superimposed vibrations, as has heretofore been supposed, but that each vibration is separate and distinct, and therefore it becomes possible to record and reproduce the sounds of the human voice.

In the drawings, Figure 1 is a vertical section, illustrating my invention, and Fig. 2 is a plan of the same.

A is a cylinder having a helical indenting-groove cut from end to end—say, ten grooves to the inch. Upon this is placed the material to be indented, preferably metallic foil. This drum or cylinder is secured to a shaft, X, having at one end a thread cut with ten threads to the inch, the bearing P also having a thread cut in it.

L is a tube, provided with a longitudinal slot, and it is rotated by the clock-work at M, or other source of power.

The shaft X passes into the tube L, and it is rotated by a pin, 2, secured to the shaft, and passing through the slot on the tube L, the object of the long slot being to allow the shaft X to pass endwise through the center or support P by the action of the screw on X. At the same time that the cylinder is rotated it passes toward the support O.

B is the speaking-tube or mouth-piece, which may be of any desired character, so long as proper slots or holes are provided to re-enforce the hissing consonants. Devices to effect this object are shown in my application, No. 143, filed August 28, 1877. Hence they are not shown or further described herein.

Upon the end of the tube or mouth-piece is a diaphragm, having an indenting-point of hard material secured to its center, and so arranged in relation to the cylinder A that the point will be exactly opposite the groove in the cylinder at any position the cylinder may occupy in its forward rotary movement.

The speaking-tube is arranged upon a standard, which, in practice, I provide with devices for causing the tube to approach and recede from the cylinder.

The operation of recording is as follows: The cylinder is, by the action of the screw in X, placed adjacent to the pillar P, which brings the indenting-point of the diaphragm G opposite the first groove on the cylinder, over which is placed a sheet of thick metallic foil, paper, or other yielding material. The tube B is then adjusted toward the cylinder until the indenting-point touches the material and indents it slightly. The clock-work is then set running, and words spoken in the tube B will cause the diaphragm to take up every vibration, and these movements will be recorded with surprising accuracy by indentations in the foil.

After the foil on the cylinder has received the required indentations, or passed to its full limit toward O, it is made to return to P by proper means, and the indented material is brought to a position for reproducing and rendering audible the sounds that had been made by the person speaking into the tube B.

O is a tube similar to B, except that the diaphragm is somewhat lighter and more sensitive, although this is not actually necessary. In front of this diaphragm is a light spring, D, having a small point shorter and finer than

---

FIGURE 8.3 Speaking Machine Patent

the indenting-point on the diaphragm of B. This spring and point are so arranged as to fall exactly into the path of all the indentations. This spring is connected to the diaphragm F of C by a thread or other substance capable of conveying the movements of D. Now, when the cylinder is allowed to rotate, the spring D is set in motion by each indentation corresponding to its depth and length. This motion is conveyed to the diaphragm either by vibrations through a thread or directly by connecting the spring to the diaphragm F_2, and these motions being due to the indentations, which are an exact record of every movement of the first diaphragm, the voice of the speaker is reproduced exactly and clearly, and with sufficient volume to be heard at some distance.

The indented material may be detached from the machine and preserved for any length of time, and by replacing the foil in a proper manner the original speaker's voice can be reproduced, and the same may be repeated frequently, as the foil is not changed in shape if the apparatus is properly adjusted.

The record, if it be upon tin-foil, may be stereotyped by means of the plaster-of-paris process, and from the stereotype multiple copies may be made expeditiously and cheaply by casting or by pressing tin-foil or other material upon it. This is valuable when musical compositions are required for numerous machines.

It is obvious that many forms of mechanism may be used to give motion to the material to be indented. For instance, a revolving plate may have a volute spiral cut both on its upper and lower surfaces, on the top of which the foil or indenting material is laid and secured in a proper manner. A two-part arm is used with this disk, the portion beneath the disk having a point in the lower groove, and the portion above the disk carrying the speaking and receiving diaphragmic devices, which arm is caused, by the volute spiral groove upon the lower surface, to swing gradually from near the center to the outer circumference of the plate as it is revolved, or vice versa.

An apparatus of this general character adapted to a magnet that indents the paper is shown in my application for a patent, No. 128, filed March 26, 1877; hence no claim is made herein to such apparatus, and further description of the same is unnecessary.

A wide continuous roll of material may be used, the diaphragmic devices being reciprocated by proper mechanical devices backward and forward over the roll as it passes forward; or a narrow strip like that in a Morse register may be moved in contact with the indenting-point, and from this the sounds may be reproduced. The material employed for this purpose may be soft paper saturated or coated with paraffine or similar material, with a sheet of metal foil on the surface thereof to receive the impression from the indenting-point.

I do not wish to confine myself to reproducing sound by indentations only, as the transmitting or recording device may be in a sinuous form, resulting from the use of a thread passing with paper beneath the pressure-rollers t, (see Fig. 3,) such thread being moved laterally by a fork or eye adjacent to the roller t, and receiving its motion from the diaphragm G, with which such fork or eye is connected, and thus record the movement of the diaphragm by the impression of the thread in the paper to the right and left of a straight line, from which indentation the receiving-diaphragm may receive its motion and the sound be reproduced, substantially in the manner I have already shown; or the diaphragm may, by its motion, give more or less pressure to an inking-pen, u, Fig. 4, the point of which rests upon paper or other material moved along regularly beneath the point of the pen, thus causing more or less ink to be deposited upon the material, according to the greater or lesser movement of the diaphragm. These ink-marks serve to give motion to a second diaphragm when the paper containing such marks is drawn along beneath the end of a lever resting upon them and connected to such diaphragm, the lever and diaphragm being moved by the friction between the point being greatest, or the thickness of the ink being greater where there is a large quantity of ink than where there is a small quantity. Thus the original sound-vibrations are reproduced upon the second diaphragm.

I claim as my invention—

1. The method herein specified of reproducing the human voice or other sounds by causing the sound-vibrations to be recorded, substantially as specified, and obtaining motion from that record, substantially as set forth, for the reproduction of the sound-vibrations.

2. The combination, with a diaphragm exposed to sound-vibrations, of a moving surface of yielding material—such as metallic foil—upon which marks are made corresponding to the sound-vibrations, and of a character adapted to use in the reproduction of the sound, substantially as set forth.

3. The combination, with a surface having marks thereon corresponding to sound-vibrations, of a point receiving motion from such marks, and a diaphragm connected to said point, and responding to the motion of the point, substantially as set forth.

4. In an instrument for making a record of sound-vibrations, the combination, with the diaphragm and point, of a cylinder having a helical groove and means for revolving the cylinder and communicating an end movement corresponding to the inclination of the helical groove, substantially as set forth.

Signed by me this 15th day of December, A. D. 1877.

THOS. A. EDISON.

Witnesses:
  GEO. T. PINCKNEY,
  CHAS. H. SMITH.

FIGURE 8.3 *(Continued)*

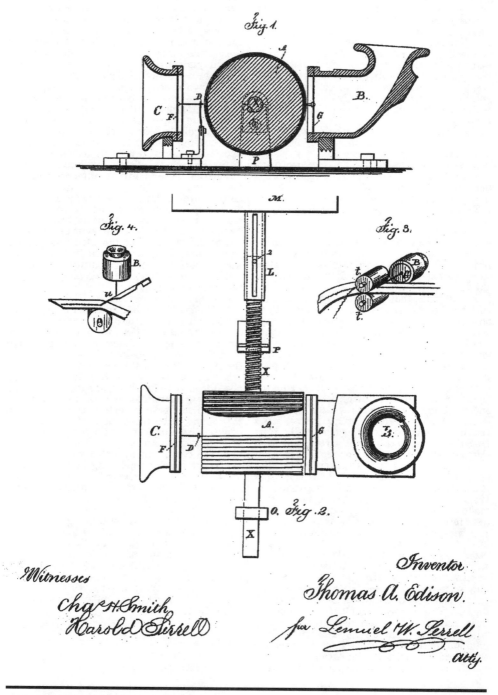

FIGURE 8.3   *(Continued)*

Patented Apr. 9, 1929.   1,708,692

UNITED STATES PATENT OFFICE.

THOMAS A. EDISON, OF LLEWELLYN PARK, WEST ORANGE, NEW JERSEY, ASSIGNOR TO THOMAS A. EDISON, INCORPORATED, OF WEST ORANGE, NEW JERSEY, A CORPORATION OF NEW JERSEY.

PHONOGRAPH.

Application filed February 13, 1926. Serial No. 88,049.

My invention relates to phonographs, and more particularly though not exclusively, to disc phonographs, wherein means are provided for automatically moving or feeding the reproducer across the record support or turntable at a rate in conformity with the pitch of the threads of the record being reproduced or operated upon.

The principal object of my invention is to provide a phonograph of the character described with an improved and simple arrangement and construction of the means for automatically feeding or moving the sound box or reproducer across the record support, whereby for a given speed at which the said support is rotated, the sound box may be fed across the support at either of two rates of speed, one of which, for example, may be suitable for operating upon a record having 150 threads per inch and the other for operating upon a record having 450 threads per inch.

Another object of my invention is to provide a compact and simple device which may be made in the form of an attachment capable of being readily substituted for parts of the feeding mechanism with which disc phonographs of the type referred to above have heretofore been generally equipped, to convert said feeding mechanism into a change-speed feeding mechanism such as described.

Other objects and features of my invention will be hereinafter more fully described and claimed.

In order that my invention may be more clearly understood, attention is directed to the drawings accompanying and forming a part of this specification, and in which:

Fig. 1 is a view in side elevation, with the cabinet partly broken away, of a disc phonograph equipped with a preferred form of my invention;

Fig. 2 is an enlarged detailed view in front elevation, partly in section, of the phonograph shown in Fig. 1, showing the construction of the change-speed automatic feed mechanism and the manner in which the same is applied to the phonograph; and

Fig. 3 is a plan view of the means for controlling the change-speed feed mechanism and the arrangement for securing such means to the top-plate or other part of the frame of the phonograph mechanism.

Referring to the drawing, and especially to Fig. 1, the stylus 1 of the reproducer 2 is adapted to track a record 3 carried by the turntable or record support 4. The reproducer shown is of a well-known type employed for playing hill and dale records and comprises a sound box 5 in which the diaphragm (not shown) is mounted, a floating weight 6 supported from the sound box for up and down and lateral movements with respect thereto, and a lever 7 pivotally mounted on the floating weight 6 carrying the stylus 1 at one end thereof and connected at its other end to the diaphragm. The floating weight 6 is provided at its forward end with the usual limit pin 8 extending within the limit loop 9 depending from the sound box. Reference character 10 designates the bed or top-plate of the frame of the phonograph mechanism, said top-plate being mounted on brackets 12 secured to the side walls of the cabinet 11. The turntable 4 is mounted on the upper end of a rotating spindle 13 which extends through the top plate 10 and is supported at its lower end in a bracket 14 depending from the top-plate 10, this spindle being provided with a worm 15 whereby it may be driven by a gear 16 which engages said worm and is secured to the rotating spring-barrel 17 forming a part of the spring motor. The reproducer 2 is supported by the horn or sound amplifier A, the neck of the reproducer extending rearwardly from the sound box and being connected to the small end of the horn by any suitable connection 18, which may comprise a sleeve-like member rotatably mounted on the amplifier and connected to the neck of the reproducer by a bayonet-joint, as shown. The amplifier or horn extends from the connection 18 rearwardly, as shown at 19, then downwardly past the record support and motor, as shown at 20, and terminates in a forwardly directed exit portion 21.

The horn or amplifier A and the reproducer 2 carried thereby are supported for pivotal movement about a vertical axis so that the sound box may be moved to traverse a record carried by the turntable 4, and for rectilinear vertical movement so that the reproducing stylus may be moved to and from operative relation with respect to the record, as follows: Secured to the horn at the top of the exit end thereof is a bracket 22, a similar bracket, (not shown) being secured to the exit end of the horn at the bottom thereof.

FIGURE 8.4   Phonograph Patent

April 9, 1929.   T. A. EDISON   1,708,692

PHONOGRAPH

Filed Feb. 13, 1926   2 Sheets—Sheet 1

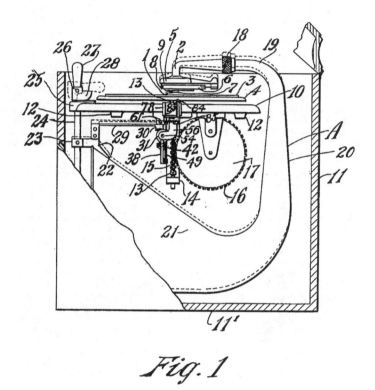

Fig. 1

INVENTOR
Thomas A. Edison
BY
Henry Lanaham
ATTORNEY

FIGURE 8.4 *(Continued)*

April 9, 1929.   T. A. EDISON   1,708,692
                                  PHONOGRAPH
                          Filed Feb. 13, 1926   2 Sheets—Sheet 2

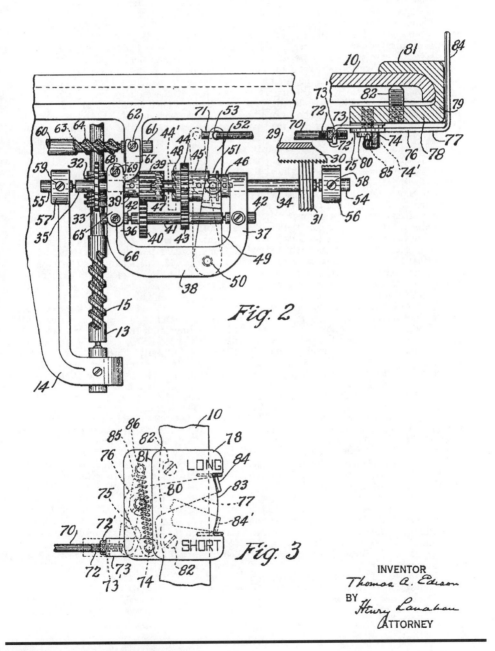

Fig. 2

Fig. 3

INVENTOR
Thomas A. Edison
BY
Henry Lanahan
ATTORNEY

FIGURE 8.4   (Continued)

163

Each of the said brackets is provided with a collar, only one of which is shown at 23, these collars being provided with vertically aligned openings therethrough, in which is disposed a cylindrical rod 24. The rod 24 is suitably secured to the said collars and is mounted for pivotal and vertical movements in two spaced bearings, one of these bearings being provided in the top plate 10, as shown at 25, and the other bearing (not shown) being carried by the bottom wall 11′ of the cabinet 11. The rod 24 extends through the bearing 25 a short distance above the top-plate 10 and has pivotally secured to the upper end thereof at 26, a member provided with a handle 27 at one side and with a cam 28 at the other side of said pivot. The cam 28 is adapted to co-act with the upper flat surface of the portion of the top plate 10 in which the bearing 25 is provided, when the handle 27 is moved to the horizontal dotted-line position shown in Fig. 1, to lift the rod 24 and thereby raise the horn A and the reproducer 2 to inoperative position as indicated in dotted lines. When the handle 27 is moved from such horizontal position to a vertical position, the weight of the horn and the parts carried thereby cause the rod 24 to move downwardly in its bearings and return the horn and the parts connected thereto to their operative positions, as shown in full lines. It will be apparent that the horn A and the reproducer 2 are thus mounted for swinging movement about the axis of the vertical rod 24 and that they are also mounted for rectilinear vertical movement in the direction of said axis so as to control the movement of the reproducer to and from operative position with respect to a record carried by the turntable 4.

The feeding means employed for causing the reproducer to traverse the record during the operation of the phonograph preferably comprises an arm 29 secured at one end to the bracket 22 and extending rearwardly therefrom, the rear end of said arm being provided with a sector having a downwardly extending toothed portion or rack 30 curved on the arc of a circle coaxial with the rod 24. The rack 30 will therefore partake of the movements of the horn A, and the arrangement is such that when the horn and reproducer are in their lowered operative positions, the rack 30 will engage a worm gear 31 driven from the spindle 13 to thereby effect swinging movement of the horn about the axis of rod 24 and movement of the reproducer 2 transversely of the record 3, and when the horn and reproducer are raised, by movement of the handle 27 to a horizontal position, the rack 30 will also be raised from engagement with the worm gear 31.

The worm gear 31 is arranged to be driven from the spindle 13 by means comprising a worm 32 provided on the spindle just above the worm 15, a worm wheel 33 engaging the worm 32, and suitable change-speed gearing between the worm wheel 33 and the worm gear 31, whereby for a given or predetermined and substantially constant speed of the spindle 13 and turntable 4 the worm gear 31 may be driven at either of one of two speeds, preferably bearing a ratio of one to three and preferably respectively adapted to cause the reproducer 2 to traverse the turntable 4 at speeds proper to operate on records having the usual number of grooves to the inch, namely 150 grooves to the inch, and on records having 450 record grooves per inch. The worm gear 31 is secured to a shaft 34, and the worm wheel 33 is secured to a similar shaft 35, these shafts being disposed in alignment and being respectively rotatably mounted intermediate their ends, in bearings provided at the ends of the legs 36 and 37 of a U-shaped bracket 38. The worm gear 31 and the worm wheel 33 are respectively mounted on those portions of the shafts 34 and 35 which extend outwardly beyond the bracket 38. The shaft 35 extends from the leg 36 of bracket 38 a short distance toward the leg 37 and has secured to such extending portion a gear 39, this gear preferably being secured to the shaft 35 by having its hub 39′ pinned to the shaft. The gear 39 meshes with a second and larger gear 40 secured to a counter-shaft 41 which is mounted on adjustable pivot pins 42, carried by the legs of the bracket 38, in a position parallel to the shafts 34 and 35. A gear 43, smaller in diameter than the gear 40, is also rigidly secured to the counter-shaft 41 and is adapted to engage and drive a larger gear 44 which is fixed to a sleeve 45 intermediate the ends of the latter; the sleeve 45 being splined to that portion of the shaft 34 extending from the leg 37 of bracket 38 towards the leg 36, so that it is slidable on the shaft but will rotate therewith. The shaft 34 extends through the sleeve 45 and into the axial opening in the gear 39 to a position in which the end thereof substantially abuts the adjacent end of the shaft 35; and as the gear 39 is fixed to the shaft 35 with its hub 39′ closely adjacent the leg 36 of the bracket 38, and as the shaft 34 has a collar 46 pinned thereto and located in a position closely adjacent the leg 37 of said bracket, any substantial endwise movement of either of the shafts 34 and 35 with reference to the bracket 38 is prevented. The adjacent ends of the gear 39 and the sleeve 45 are respectively provided with toothed clutch sections 47 and 48, the teeth of which sections, when the sleeve 45 is moved on the shaft 34 from the position shown, to the left, will be brought into engagement to effect a direct drive connection between the shafts 35 and 34, under which conditions the worm gear 31 will be turned or rotated at the same speed at which the worm wheel 33 is rotated by the spindle 13, while the gears 40 and 43 and the

FIGURE 8.4   *(Continued)*

countershaft 41, though they will be rotated by reason of the engagement of gear 40 with gear 39, will merely idle as the gear 44 will then be out of engagement with the gear 43 and in the dotted-line position indicated at 44'. When the sleeve 45 is in the position shown in Fig. 2, however, the gear 44 will be in engagement with gear 43 and the clutch sections 47 and 48 will be disengaged; and under these conditions the shaft 34 and the worm gear 31 will be rotated from the shaft 35, through the reducing gearing consisting of the gears 39, 40, 43 and 44, at a reduced speed as compared with the rotation of the shaft 35 and the worm wheel 33, the speed reduction thus effected preferably being 3 to 1. The means for shifting sleeve 45 on shaft 34 to effect either a direct drive connection between the shafts 35 and 34 or a drive connection through the speed reducing gearing, as described, comprises an arm 49 pivotally mounted at one end on a horizontal pin 50 carried by the base of the U-shaped bracket 38, and provided at its other end with a yoke, the arms of this yoke carrying pins extending into an annular recess or groove 51 with which the sleeve 45 is provided. The rear arm of the said yoke is provided with an extension 52 having an opening 53 at its upper end whereby such arm is adapted for connection with the device, hereinafter described, for controlling said shifting means.

The bracket 38 and the parts mounted thereon are supported on the frame of the phonograph mechanism in proper position by pivot pins 54 and 55 adjustably mounted in brackets 56 and 57, carried by said frame, and respectively engaging recesses in the outer ends of the shafts 34 and 35. The pivot pins 54 and 55 are secured in proper position in the brackets 56 and 57 to support the shafts 34 and 35, the bracket 38 and all the parts carried by the latter, by means of set screws 58 and 59. Reference character 60 designates the shaft of the speed governor of the phonograph, this shaft being supported at its ends on pivot pins (one of which is shown at 61) adjustably secured in brackets provided on the frame of the phonograph mechanism. The pivot pins supporting the governor shaft 60 are preferably adjustably held in position by means of set screws, the set screw for holding the pivot pin 61 in position being shown at 62. The governor shaft 60 is driven from the spindle 13 by means comprising a worm wheel 63 mounted on the spindle and a worm 64 provided on the shaft and engaging said worm wheel.

In a well-known make of disc phonograph adapted for playing hill and dale records, the feed mechanism for moving the sound reproducer across the record, as compared with the feed mechanism described above, comprises but a single shaft, in place of the two shafts 34 and 35, carrying only a worm gear

and a worm wheel respectively corresponding to the worm gear 31 and the worm wheel 33; the said single shaft having a length equal to the combined length of the two shafts 34 and 35 and being supported at its ends on pivot pins, exactly corresponding in location with the pivot pins 54 and 55, so that the worm gear thereon is adapted to co-act with a feed rack carried by the horn and corresponding to the rack 30 and the worm wheel thereon engages a worm corresponding to the worm 32 and carried by the vertical driving spindle of the phonograph mechanism.

From the foregoing it will be apparent that the bracket 38 together with the shafts, gears and other elements carried thereby, comprise an attachment which may be readily substituted for the said single shaft and the worm gear and worm wheel carried thereby, in the feed mechanism in a disc phonograph of the construction described below, to convert such feed mechanism into a change-speed feed mechanism. Reference character 65 designates an arm which is pivotally mounted on the leg 36 of the bracket 38 as by means of a screw 66, this arm being provided with an extension 67 having a forked end which is engaged beneath the head of the set screw 62 for holding the pivot pin 61 in place, so as to prevent the bracket 38 and the countershaft 41, gears 40 and 43, and arm 49 carried by said bracket, from partaking of any appreciable rotary movement about the shafts 34 and 35 when the attachment is embodied in a phonograph mechanism as shown. The frames of the mechanisms of disc phonographs of the type referred to herein consist of castings which are subject to slight variations; and to compensate for any such variation so as to permit the fork at the end of the extension 67 of arm 65 to be engaged beneath the head of the set screw corresponding to the screw 62 illustrated, means are provided whereby the said arm 65 may be secured in various positions of adjustment about the screw 66, this means preferably comprising a slot 68 formed in the arm 65 and a screw 69 extending through said slot and threaded into the leg 36 of the bracket 38.

The device for controlling the means for shifting the change-speed gearing of the feeding mechanism is also preferably so constructed that it may be readily attached to a disc phonograph of the type referred to herein as usually constructed, and, indeed, may be considered as a part of the attachment which includes the bracket 38, and the shafts, gears and other elements carried by such bracket. This controlling device comprises a cylindrical rod 70 having one end portion 71 in the form of an off-set which is removably connected to the shifting lever 49 by engagement with the opening 53 in the latter (this connection being in the nature of a button-hole connection) and having its

---

FIGURE 8.4 *(Continued)*

4   1,708,692

other end portion 72 adjustably connected to a bell-crank control lever 76. The connection between the rod 70 and the lever 76 comprises a flat bar or link 73 having an angular end portion or extension 73′ threaded on the end portion 72 of said rod; the said threaded end portion 72 of the rod carrying a lock-nut 72′ for securing the member 73 in any position to which it may be adjusted on the rod. The link or member 73 is provided at the end thereof opposite the extension 73′ with an opening which is removably engaged by the upper end of a pin 74 secured to and extending through the end portion of the arm 75 of the bell-crank lever. The bell-crank lever 76 is removably and pivotally mounted, at the junction of its arms 75 and 77, on one arm 78 of a channelled bracket 79 by means of a shouldered screw 80. The bracket 79 is mounted on the top-plate 10 of the frame of the phonograph mechanism, with its arm 78 disposed beneath said top-plate, and with the base and arm 81 thereof respectively engaging the rim and top surface of said top-plate; the bracket being removably and rigidly secured in this position by two screws 82 which are threaded through openings provided in the arm 78 and are turned up into tight engagement with the under surface of the top-plate 10. The outer side of the base of the bracket 79 is recessed as indicated at 83, the bottom of the recess being formed on an arc concentric with the screw 80 on which the bell-crank lever 76 is pivotally mounted; and the arm 77 of the bell-crank lever is provided with an upstanding end portion 84 disposed in the said recess 83 and extending above the bracket. The upstanding end portion 84 of the lever arm 77 comprises a convenient handle whereby the lever 76 may be actuated to effect, through link 73, rod 70 and lever 49, the shifting of sleeve 45 so as to provide either a direct drive connection between the shafts 35 and 34 or a drive between these shafts through the speed-reducing gearing as described above. The arrangement is such that when the sleeve 45 is in a position to effect the driving of the shaft 34 from the shaft 35 through the speed reducing gearing 39, 40, 43 and 44, the upstanding end portion 84 of the lever arm 77 will be in engagement with that end of the recess 83 in the bracket 79 designated "Long", and when the sleeve 45 is shifted to a position in which a direct drive connection is effected between said shafts by the engagement of the clutch sections 47 and 48, the said end portion 84 of the lever arm 77 will be in engagement with the end of the recess 83 designated "Short", as indicated in dotted lines at 84′ in Fig. 3. A coiled spring 85 is connected at one end to the lower end portion 74′ of the pin 74 and at its other end to a pin 86 which is secured to and extends downwardly from the arm 78

of bracket 79. The arrangement is such that in the movement of the bell-crank lever 76 between the limits defined by the ends of the recess 83 in the bracket 79, the spring 85 will be moved about the pin 86 from a position at one side of the pivot screw 81 to a position at the other side thereof, as clearly indicated in Fig. 3. Accordingly this spring not only assists in moving the bell-crank lever 76 in either direction after the lever arm 75 passes the dead center position, as determined by the pins 74 and 86 and the pivot screw 81, but also acts to yieldingly hold or lock the bell-crank lever at either end of its movement with the end portion 84 of the lever arm 77 in engagement with the respective end of the recess 83 and to yieldingly hold or lock the change-speed gearing of the feeding mechanism in the respective position of adjustment to which it has been shifted by the bell-crank lever. The link or member 73 connecting the rod 70 and the lever 76 may be readily adjusted to and locked in such position on the rod as to insure the proper adjustment of the change-speed gearing when the lever arm 77 is at either limit of its movement.

It is to be understood that the construction specifically shown and described herein is merely illustrative of my invention and that such construction is subject to various changes and modifications without departure from the spirit of the invention and the scope of the appended claims.

Having now described my invention, what I claim as new and desire to protect by Letters Patent is as follows:

1. In a phonograph, the combination of a record support, actuating means adapted to drive said support at a predetermined and substantially constant speed, a reproducer, a sound conveyer carrying said reproducer, and means operated from said actuating means for moving said conveyer to thereby feed said reproducer across said support, said feeding means including a change-speed device which is shiftable to effect the feeding of said reproducer across said support at any of a plurality of different speeds while said record support is driven by said actuating means at such predetermined and substantially constant speed, substantially as described.

2. In a phonograph, the combination of a record support, actuating means adapted to drive said support at a predetermined and substantially constant speed, a reproducer, a sound conveyer carrying said reproducer, and means operated from said actuating means for moving said conveyer to thereby feed said reproducer across said support, said feeding means including change-speed gearing which is shiftable to effect the feeding of said reproducer across said support at either of two speeds while said record support is

FIGURE 8.4   (Continued)

driven by said actuating means at such predetermined and substantially constant speed, substantially as described.

3. In a phonograph, the combination of a turntable, motive means adapted to rotate said turntable at a predetermined and substantially constant speed, a reproducer, a sound conveyer supporting said reproducer from one end thereof and mounted for swinging movement about a given axis, means actuated from said motive means for swinging said conveyer about said axis to thereby feed the reproducer transversely of said turntable, said feeding means including a change-speed device shiftable to effect the feeding of said reproducer across said turntable at either of two speeds while said turntable is rotated by said motive means at such predetermined and substantially constant speed, substantially as described.

4. In a phonograph, the combination of a turntable, motive means adapted to rotate said turntable at a predetermined and substantially constant speed, a reproducer, a horn supporting said reproducer from its small end and mounted for swinging movement about a vertical axis, means actuated from said motive means for swinging said horn about said axis to thereby feed the reproducer transversely of said turntable, said feeding means including a change-speed device shiftable to effect the feeding of said reproducer across said turntable at either of two speeds while said turntable is rotated by said motive means at such predetermined and substantially constant speed, substantially as described.

5. In a phonograph, the combination of a record support, means for actuating said support, a reproducer, a sound conveyer carrying said reproducer, means operated from said actuating means for moving said conveyer to thereby feed said reproducer across said support, said feeding means including change-speed gearing which is shiftable to effect the feeding of said reproducer across said support at either of two speeds for a given speed of actuation of said record support, and means for effecting and controlling the shifting of said change-speed gearing and for yieldingly locking the same in either of the operative positions to which it is shifted, substantially as described.

6. In a phonograph, the combination of a record support, means for actuating said support, a reproducer, a sound conveyer carrying said reproducer, means operated from said actuating means for moving said conveyer to thereby feed said reproducer across said support, said feeding means including change-speed gearing which is shiftable to effect the feeding of said reproducer across said support at either of two speeds for a given speed of actuation of said record support, and means comprising a lever and a spring coacting therewith for effecting and

controlling the shifting of said change-speed gearing and for yieldingly locking the same in either of the operative positions to which it is shifted, substantially as described.

7. In a phonograph, the combination of a record support, means for actuating said support, a reproducer, a sound conveyer carrying said reproducer, means operated from said actuating means for moving said conveyer to thereby feed said reproducer across said support, said feeding means including change-speed gearing which is shiftable to effect the feeding of said reproducer across said support at either of two speeds for a given speed of actuation of said record support, and means for effecting and controlling the shifting of said change-speed gearing comprising a manually operable member and an adjustable connection between said member and gearing, substantially as described.

8. In a phonograph, the combination of a rotatable record support, motive means for operating said record support, a reproducer, a movably mounted sound conveyer carrying said reproducer, and feeding mechanism for moving said conveyer to thereby cause said reproducer to traverse said support, said feeding mechanism comprising a feeding member connected with said conveyer and change-speed connecting means between said motive means and said feeding member comprising two shafts and a shiftable member movable to effect either a direct connection or a speed reducing connection between said shafts, substantially as described.

9. In a phonograph, the combination of a rotatable record support, motive means adapted to drive said record support at a predetermined and substantially constant speed, a reproducer, a movably mounted sound conveyer carrying said reproducer, a member adapted to be driven by said motive means independently of said record support, a feeding element connected with said conveyer, and change-speed connecting means between said member and element comprising a shaft carrying said driven member, a second shaft carrying a member adapted to actuate said feeding element, clutch elements respectively mounted on said shafts, and reduction gearing between said shafts, the clutch element on one of said shafts being movable to a position in which it engages the other clutch element to form a direct drive connection between said shafts and in which said reduction gearing is rendered inoperative, and to another position in which it is out of engagement with the other clutch element and in which said reduction gearing is rendered operative, substantially as described.

10. An attachment for disc phonographs of the type provided with means for automatically feeding the sound box across the record support, comprising a bracket having

FIGURE 8.4 *(Continued)*

6
1,708,692

two shafts rotatably mounted thereon, one of said shafts having secured thereto a member adapted to be driven by the motive means of the phonograph and the other of said
5 shafts having secured thereto a member adapted when such shaft is rotated to effect feeding movement of the sound box, and a change-speed device connecting said shafts and mounted on said bracket, said change-
10 speed device being shiftable to effect the driving of one of said shafts from the other at either of two speeds, substantially as described.

11. An attachment for disc phonographs
15 of the type provided with means for automatically feeding the sound box across the record support, comprising a bracket having two shafts rotatably mounted thereon and speed reducing gearing carried thereby

and connecting said shafts, said gearing in- 20 cluding a member slidably but non-rotatably mounted on one of said shafts, said member being adapted when moved to one position on its shaft to render said gearing operative to drive one shaft from the other at a re- 25 duced speed and when moved to another position on its shaft to render said gearing inoperative and to effect a direct drive connection between said shafts; and means comprising a manually operable member and a 30 spring connected therewith for controlling the movement of said slidably mounted member on its shaft and for yieldingly locking such slidably mounted member in either of its said positions, substantially as described. 35

This specification signed this 1st day of February, 1926.

THOS. A. EDISON.

FIGURE 8.4 *(Continued)*

UNITED STATES PATENT OFFICE.

THOMAS A. EDISON, OF MENLO PARK, NEW JERSEY

IMPROVEMENT IN ELECTRIC LIGHTS.

Specification forming part of Letters Patent No. **214,636,** dated April 22, 1879; application filed October 14, 1878.

CASE 156.

To all whom it may concern:

Be it known that I, THOMAS A. EDISON, of Menlo Park, in the State of New Jersey, have invented an Improvement in Electric Lights, of which the following is a specification.

Electric lights have been produced by a coil or strip of platina or other metal that requires a high temperature to melt, the electric current rendering the same incandescent. In all such lights there is danger of the metal melting and destroying the apparatus, and breaking the continuity of the circuit.

My improvement is made for regulating the electric current passing through such incandescent conductor automatically, and preventing its temperature rising to the melting-point, thus producing a reliable electric light by rendering conducting substances incandescent by passing an electric current through them.

In my apparatus the heat evolved or developed is made to regulate the electric current, so that the heat cannot become too intense, because the current is lessened by the effect of the heat when certain temperatures are reached, thereby preventing injury to the incandescent substance, by keeping the heat at all times below the melting-point of the incandescent substance.

Various devices for carrying my improvement into practice may be employed, and I have tested a large number. I however have shown in the drawings my improvement in a convenient form, and contemplate obtaining separate patents hereafter for other and various details of construction, and I state my present invention to relate, broadly, to the combination, with an electric light produced by incandescence, of an automatic thermal regulator for the electric current.

Figure 1 represents the electric-light apparatus in the form in which the thermal regulator acts by the heating effect of the current itself, and Fig. 2 illustrates the same invention when the radiated heat from the incandescent conductor operates the thermal regulator.

The incandescent metal is to be platinum, rhodium, iridium, titanium, or any other suitable conductor having a high fusing-point, and the same is used in the form of a wire or thin plate or leaf.

I have shown the platinum wire a as a double spiral, the two ends terminating upon the posts b c, to which the conductors d e are connected. The double spiral a is free to expand or contract by the heat, as both ends are below the spiral.

A circuit-closing lever, f, is introduced in the electric circuit, the points of contact being at i, and there is a platinum or similar wire, k, connected from the lever f to the head-piece or other support l.

The current from a magneto-electric machine, a battery, or any other source of electric energy, is connected to the binding-posts n o, and when contact at i is broken the current passes from o through lever f, wire k, support l, wire e, post c, platina coil a, post b, and wire d, or metallic connection, to binding-screw n. In this instance the wire k, being small, is acted upon by the electric current and heated, and by its expansion the lever f is allowed to close upon i and short-circuit the current.

The contact-point i is movable, and it is adjusted so that the shunt will not be closed until the temperature of the apparatus arrives at the desired height, and, by diverting a portion or the whole of the current, the temperature of the incandescent conductor is maintained in such a manner that there will be no risk of the apparatus being injured by excessive heat or the conductor fused.

If the wire k is small, so as to be heated by the electricity itself, it may be placed in any convenient position relatively to the light; but if such wire is heated by radiation from the electric light, then it should be adjacent to the incandescent material.

In all instances, the expansion or contraction of a suitable material under changes of temperature forms a thermostatic current-regulator that operates automatically, to prevent injury to the apparatus and to the body heated by the current.

In Fig. 2 the current does not pass through the wire k, and the short-circuiting lever is

FIGURE 8.5   Light Patent

169

T. A. EDISON.
Electric-Lights

No. 214,636. Patented April 22, 1879.

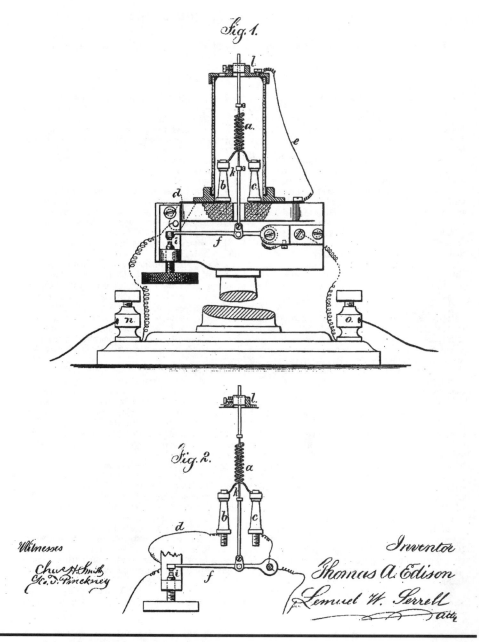

FIGURE 8.5 *(Continued)*

2   214,636

operated by the radiated heat expanding the wire *k*. This in practice does not operate as rapidly as the device shown in Fig. 1.

The electric light may be surrounded by a glass tube or any other suitable device, such as two concentric glass tubes with the intervening space filled with alum-water or other bad conductor of heat, the object being to retain the heat of the incandescent metal and prevent loss by radiation, thus requiring less current to supply the loss by radiation.

I am aware that the electric current has been used to produce heat, and that such heat has been employed to vary the relative position of the light-giving electrodes and the length of the intervening arc. In my light there is no electric arc.

I claim as my invention—

1. In combination with an electric light having a continuous incandescent conductor, a thermostatic circuit-regulator, substantially as set forth.

2. In combination with an electric light, a thermostatically - operated shunt, substantially as set forth.

Signed by me this 5th day of October, A.D. 1878.

THOMAS A. EDISON.

Witnesses:
ALFRID SWANSON,
STOCKTON L. GRIFFIN.

FIGURE 8.5 *(Continued)*

UNITED STATES PATENT OFFICE.

THOMAS A. EDISON, OF MENLO PARK, NEW JERSEY.

PRESERVING FRUIT.

SPECIFICATION forming part of Letters Patent No. 248,431, dated October 18, 1881.

Application filed December 14, 1880. (No model.)

To all whom it may concern:

Be it known that I, THOMAS A. EDISON, of Menlo Park, in the county of Middlesex and State of New Jersey, have invented a new and
5 useful Improvement in Preserving Fruit; and I do hereby declare that the following is a full and exact description of the same, reference being had to the accompanying drawings, and to the letters of reference marked thereon.
10 The object I have in view is to produce an economical method of putting up fruits, vegetables, and other organic substances in their natural condition without cooking, for preservation in high vacuo, which method will in-
15 sure the maintenance of such high vacuo, and consequently the preservation of the articles; and the articles will be surrounded by an envelope which cannot affect them injuriously. This I accomplish by placing the articles to be
20 preserved, or one of them, in a properly-constructed glass vessel, which is shaped up and connected with a glass tube leading to or connected with apparatus for producing in the vessel a high degree of exhaustion; or the open-
25 ing of the vessel through which the articles are placed therein may be closed by fusion, and the glass exhaust-tube attached at any other suitable point. When the desired high vacuum is obtained the glass tube is "sealed
30 off"—that is to say, the tube is fused by the flame of a blow-pipe—at a point near the vessel, and the vessel is drawn away from the tube at the point of fusion, the result being to hermetically close the vessel and at the same
35 time disconnect it from the glass tube. The articles are then inclosed in an envelope which is essentially a homogeneous piece of glass, and which will maintain for any length of time the high vacuum. The envelope being entirely of
40 glass, the articles cannot be affected injuriously thereby.

My invention consists, first, in the peculiar method of putting up organic substances for preservation and transportation; and, second,
45 in the complete vessel as a new article of manufacture, having the articles sealed in high vacuum therein by the fusion of the glass, the articles being surrounded by an envelope composed essentially of one piece of glass.
50 In the drawings, Figure 1 is an elevation of the apparatus employed by me for producing

high vacuo, a vessel being shown as connected therewith; and Fig. 2, a view of the complete vessel.

A is the vessel, made of glass and filled, or 55 partly filled, with the fruit, vegetables, or other organic substances to be preserved; or it may be made of proper size for holding a single article. The glass vessel is shaped up and joined with a glass tube, a, connected with the air- 60 exhausting apparatus. This junction may be formed in several ways. The neck of the vessel may be fused to the glass tube, as shown in Fig. 1; or the neck of the vessel can be formed with a socket, into which a stopple on 65 the tube a can be forced and the joint made light by a mercury seal above the stopple; or this arrangement can be reversed and the mercury seal dispensed with. The glass tube a is a branch from or is connected with a pipe, d' m, 70 the portion m of which is connected with an air-pump, B, by means of a joint, b. This joint b is of the usual construction of joints in apparatus of similar character to this, and is composed of a stopple on the tube m, setting into 75 a cup. A mercury seal may be used above the stopple.

The branch m is provided with cock c, for cutting off or turning on the connection between the pump and vessel A, and a gage, C, 80 may be provided to indicate the degree of exhaustion produced by the pump.

The branch d' is connected with a mercury drop or Sprengel pump, of ordinary construction. This is shown as composed of the mer- 85 cury-trough G, the receiver F, from which the mercury is raised to G, drop-tube D, tube e, branch d, tube E H, and gage f.

The air-pump is used as an auxiliary to commence the exhaustion, in order to save time; 90 but if the vessel A is of small capacity and nearly filled with some substance, the mercury-drop can alone be used. The vessel A, containing the articles or article, being connected with glass tube a—as for example, by fusing 95 the tube to the neck of said vessel—the cock c is opened and a partial vacuum produced by the air-pump. The cock c is then closed and the exhaustion continued by means of the Sprengel pump. When the desired high vac- 100 uum has been reached the connection with the air-pump, preferably at the juncture of the

---

FIGURE 8.6 Preserving Fruit Patent

2   **248,131**

tube *a* and neck of vessel A, is fused by a blow-pipe, and the vessel A is gradually drawn away from the tube *a*, the separation taking place at the point of fusion, and the vessel be-ing twisted or turned around so as to hermetically close the neck of the vessel. The seal can then be made more perfect, if desired, by the further fusion and working the glass, the complete vessel having the appearance shown in Fig. 2. Another vessel A is then connected with tube *a*—for example, by the fusion of the glass tube to the neck of the vessel—and the operation just explained is repeated.

What I claim is—

1. The method of putting up organic substances for preservation and transportation, consisting in placing them in a glass vessel, producing a high vacuum therein, and then hermetically closing the vessel by sealing off the channel to the air-pump, the envelope produced being essentially a homogeneous piece of glass.

2. As a new article of manufacture, a highly-exhausted glass vessel containing an organic substance sealed therein by the fusion of the glass, the enveloping-vessel being essentially a homogeneous piece of glass, substantially as set forth.

This specification signed and witnessed this 11th day of December, 1880.

THOS. A. EDISON.

Witnesses:
    H. W. SEELY,
    WM. CARMAN.

FIGURE 8.6   *(Continued)*

T. A. EDISON.
PRESERVING FRUIT..

No. 248,431.   Patented Oct. 18, 1881.

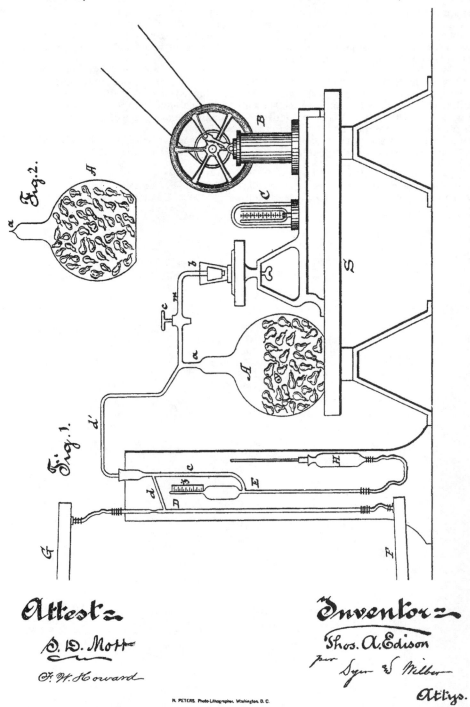

FIGURE 8.6   *(Continued)*

Another important aspect to Edison's success was that he did not regard failure as a bad thing; rather, it provided new opportunities. A lot of this probably came from his father. Samuel Edison took risks on a variety of business ventures and did not get discouraged if one did not work out as he wanted it to. Instead, he learned from the experience and went on to something new. When this kind of persistence exists, failure is not really a failing because it only adds to an innovator's capacities. There is an Edison story about when he conducted 10,000 experiments, in the effort to develop storage batteries, which failed. Where many people would have quit after a few tries, he is reported to have said, "Why, I have not failed. I've just found 10,000 ways that won't work." Another example is when Edison tried to develop an underseas telegraph but was unable to make it workable. What he learned in the process, however, enabled him to make further improvements in telephone technology. Edison knew that good things happened if you refused to give up and that that ability to stick with it was at least as important as any other personal resource.

Thomas Edison was known as a workaholic, justifying the endless hours he spent toiling away on research, invention, and development with his famous saying that "Genius is one percent inspiration and ninety-nine percent perspiration." In his work habits he gave us a preview of the kinds of schedules today's high tech entrepreneurs have become famous for. The 40-hour work week was a foreign concept to Edison, who thought nothing of putting in more than 100 hours per week on a regular basis. His second wife had a cot put in his lab to at least provide him a small measure of comfort when he worked late and decided to grab a nap at work rather than come home. It had to have been better than napping while Edison was slumped over a work bench.

As with other successful entrepreneurs, his creativity, dedication, and hard work inspired those around him. Not only did Edison generate a seemingly endless stream of ideas, he also encouraged others to do the same. Another important habit of his was to hire people who knew more about a subject than he did. Rather than be threatened by somebody with superior knowledge, he made that person a member of his team and encouraged them to make the most of their talents. His practice of assembling flexible teams that worked out of a facility where he and his partners invented, developed, and produced their inventions was revolutionary at the time, though today it is a common practice.

Thomas Edison, either himself or in partnership with others, received 1,093 patents during his long, productive working life. Though it is probably not realistic for any of us to expect ourselves to perform at anything close to that level, anybody interested in the

UNITED STATES PATENT OFFICE.

THOMAS A. EDISON, OF MENLO PARK, NEW JERSEY, AND PATRICK KENNY, OF NEW YORK, N. Y.

FAC-SIMILE TELEGRAPH.

SPECIFICATION forming part of Letters Patent No. 479,184, dated July 19, 1892.

Application filed December 6, 1881. Serial No. 47,216. (No model.) Patented in England July 19, 1881, No. 3,140; in Belgium September 15, 1881, No. 55,623; in Canada October 19, 1881, No. 13,577, and in France November 3, 1881, No, 144,646.

To all whom it may concern:

Be it known that we, THOMAS A. EDISON, of Menlo Park, in the county of Middlesex and State of New Jersey, and PATRICK KENNY, of 5 New York, in the county of New York and State of New York, have invented a new and useful Improvement in Fac-Simile Telegraphs, (for which we have obtained Letters Patent in Great Britain, No. 3,140, dated July 10 19, 1881; in France, No. 144,646, dated November 3, 1881; in Belgium, No. 55,623, dated September 15, 1881, and in Canada, No. 13,577, dated October 19, 1881;) and we do hereby declare that the following is a full and exact 15 description of the same, reference being had to the accompanying drawings and to the letters of reference marked thereon.

The object we have in view is to produce telegraphic apparatus for recording at the 20 receiving-station a fac-simile of the original dispatch, which apparatus will be simple in the arrangement and construction of its parts, will be commercially efficient and economical in operation, and will require no spe- 25 cial preparation of the original dispatch or particular skill on the part of the operator.

In carrying out our invention we make use of the depressions produced upon the surface of paper or other suitable material by mark- 30 ing, writing, or sketching thereon with a hard lead-pencil or other suitable instrument. For this purpose only slightly more than the ordinary pressure is required upon paper or other suitable material having sufficient body 35 to retain the impressions. A slip or sheet having the message written thereon in this manner is mounted upon a cylinder of insulating material, (preferably of wood,) its ends being secured close together in a groove or 40 grooves of the cylinder. The receiving-sheet used in the instrument at the other end of the line may be of about the same size as the transmitting-sheet, and is soaked in any of the well-known solutions heretofore used in 45 electro-chemical telegraphs. This slip or sheet is secured upon a metal cylinder, being removably fastened thereto in any suitable manner. These insulating and conducting cylinders are mounted upon the revolving spindles of the machines at the ends of the 50 line, which spindles are preferably arranged in vertical positions and turn through metal base-plates resting on insulating-supports. The spindles are revolved by electric motors of the Pacinotti or other pattern. Each motor 55 is arranged with its ring armature in a horizontal position centrally below the cylinder-carrying spindle of the machine. The axle of the motor-armature has a crank-arm on its upper end, to which is secured a slotted curved 60 plate. An inclined rod carrying a centrifugal ball has a box on its lower end, which slides in and is held by the slot of this curved plate. The inclined rod passes up into the collar of a universal rocking joint located centrally be- 65 low the cylinder-spindle. From this universal rocking joint the inclined rod projects a short distance upwardly into a small box held by a curved slotted crank-arm on the lower end of the cylinder-spindle. The electric motor 70 is run by the current from a battery or other source of electrical energy, the speed of the motor being regulated in any well-known way. Click-springs are struck by a pin on the upper end of the inclined rod when the motor 75 has more or less than its normal speed.

In the operation of the apparatus it is essential that the movements of the two machines should be synchronous, or such parts thereof as affect directly the transmitting and 80 receiving of the message, so that an exact copy of the original can be produced. This is accomplished in the following manner: On the cylinder-spindle of one of the machines, which we will term the "synchronistic ma- 85 chine," is a sleeve, which is held in frictional contact therewith by spring-pressure, the sleeve having a faced disk which rests upon a disk secured to the spindle, the disks being forced together by nuts on the upper end of 90 the spindle, which press on a spiral spring bearing on the end of the sleeve. This sleeve carries the cylinder of the machine, instead of the spindle itself, as in the other machine, which is hereinafter designated the "simple 95 machine."

Since each machine is adapted by changing the form of style and character of cylinder,

---

FIGURE 8.7   Fac-Simile Telegraph Patent

2   479,184

which are removable parts, to be used either for transmitting or receiving, it is evident that it makes no difference which machine is provided with the cylinder-carrying sleeve.

5   The spindle of one machine and sleeve of the other are provided near the base-plates with similar cams, each having a smooth concentric surface and a single stepped depression. On each base-plate is pivoted a horizontal T-shaped lever, the central stem of which has a projection working on the cam. The projection on the stem of this lever is thrown into the depression of the cam by a spring, which spring is connected with the line through a switch, which we will designate for clearness the "line-switch."

To the head of each T-lever is secured a metal plate, which is insulated from all parts of the lever except the spring just referred to. This plate carried by the T-lever plays at one end between two adjustable contacts, being kept closed against the inner contact by the concentric surface of the cam and thrown against the outer contact by the spring when the projection on the stem of the T-lever enters the depression of the cam.

The outer contact of each machine is connected with the coils of an electro-magnet having suitable armature, and from thence on one machine the wire runs through a battery to the ground, while on the other machine it passes from the electro-magnet directly to the ground. When the outer contacts of the machines are made at the same time, a circuit will be completed through the electro-magnets. On the simple machine the armature of the magnet is used simply as a sounder, while on the synchronistic machine it has the additional function of making and breaking the circuit of a local battery. This local circuit energizes an electro-magnet supported by the base-plate of the machine, the armature of which when attracted tips a latch engaging with a catch-arm on the cylinder-carrying sleeve before described, the latch engaging the catch and stopping the further revolution of the sleeve until tripped at the same moment the T-lever enters the cam depression, and the relay-magnet is thrown in connection with the line by the making of the outer contact.

The motor of the synchronistic machine is regulated to run with a slightly-greater speed than that of the simple machine, so that its T-lever will make the outer contact and the catch-arm of the sleeve will be locked by the latch just in advance of the making of the outer contact by the simple machine. When the outer contact is made, however, by the T-lever of the simple machine, the line-circuit will be completed through the relay-magnets, and the local circuit of the synchronistic machine will be closed, attracting the latch-armature and releasing the catch-arm of the sleeve, allowing the cylinder to continue its revolving movement. In this manner the two cylinders will be made to start exactly together at each revolution by checking one of them.

In starting the machines the latch is withdrawn by a lever until the synchronistic machine overtakes the simple machine and the two outer contacts are made simultaneously. This will be indicated by the click of the relay-magnet armatures. The latch is then released immediately and checks the cylinder on the next revolution. The slightly-increased speed given one cylinder does not affect the record produced sufficiently to injure its practical value as a fac-simile, but for producing an exact copy in every respect the cylinders used on the synchronistic machine may be made slightly smaller than those of the simple machine.

For giving the necessary signals in starting the machine a Morse key is placed in circuit between a contact of the line-switch and the electro-magnet of each machine. By swinging the line-switch onto the second contact each machine will be cut out of circuit and the Morse key thrown in. After signals are exchanged the line-switches are shifted, throwing in the machines and cutting out the Morse keys.

The cylinders being revolved synchronously, as described, the message is transmitted and received by the following mechanism: Each machine is provided with a weighted carriage traveling vertically and supported by a rack and pinion. The downward drop of each carriage is regulated by an escapement operated by a continuation of the depression in the revolving cam, into which depression takes a projection on the end of the escapement-lever. The carriage is connected electrically with the base-plate, while a vertical guide near the carriage has connection with the inner contact of the T-lever through a switch, which we will term the "style-switch." The base-plate of each machine is connected with a switch, (the battery-switch,) one contact of which switch is connected through a battery to the ground, while the other has a direct ground connection. The transmitting-style carries two contacts, one connected with the carriage when the style is placed in position thereon and through it the base-plate and "battery-switch" and the other by a spring with the vertical guide and through it with the style-switch. One of these contacts is carried by a spring having a point pressing upon the surface of the paper on the insulating-cylinder. The smooth surface of the paper keeps the contacts separated; but when they point into the depression made by a line the contacts come together, completing the circuit through the style-switch and the contact of the T-lever. The receiving-style is insulated from its carriage and has a spring connecting with the vertical guide. This style carries a point bearing upon the surface of the paper, and when the style-switch is closed the current passes through the receiving-style, the recording-paper, and the metal cylinder

FIGURE 8.7 *(Continued)*

479,184   3

to the base-plate, from whence it passes to ground through the battery-switch. When the message is completed, the operator at the transmitting-station throws the style off of the cylinder by a lever. This allows the contacts of the style to close and a continuous line is recorded at the receiving-station. This may be used as a signal that the message has been completed. The style-switches are then thrown open and a new set of cylinders put in position. A latch is arranged to lock the escapement when each carriage reaches its lowest position, such latch being released by the movement of the carriage.

In order to neutralize the effect of the static charge in working long lines and produce clear sharp lines at the receiving-instrument, the plate on the head of the T-lever is extended in the form of a spring to the other end of the lever-head, where it strikes a contact connected to the ground through a resistance or its equivalent. This ground-contact is made when the inner contact at the other end of the lever is also made and the ground is further retained for an instant after the inner contact is broken, so that the static charge will pass off into the ground after the battery-circuit is opened by the T-lever and will not operate the relay. This ground-contact, however, is broken before the outer or relay contact is made by the further movement of the T-lever.

The foregoing will be better understood from the drawings, in which—

Figure is a diagrammatic view of the circuits and connections; Fig. 2, a vertical section through the motor-case, showing the motor in elevation; Fig. 3, a top view of the synchronistic machine; Fig. 4, an elevation of the upper part of the synchronistic machine, the T-lever being removed for clearness, and the cylinder and sleeve being in vertical section; Fig. 5, a rear elevation of the pen-carriage and the mechanism for regulating its drop; Fig. 6, a top view of the magnet of the synchronistic machine and the lever for controlling its armature; Figs. 7 and 8, top views, respectively, of the transmitting and receiving styles; Fig. 9, an end view of one of the cylinders, showing the means for securing the paper thereto; Fig. 10, a view of a telegram-blank with a message written thereon, and Fig. 11 a sectional view of the transmitting-cylinder with the message-blank secured thereon and the transmitting-stylus in operation.

Like letters and numerals denote corresponding parts in all the figures.

A and B are respectively the simple and synchronistic machine. Each has a base-plate C, mounted on insulating-supports above another plate C', which is supported upon the case C², inclosing the motor. Through the center of plates C C' passes the vertical spindle D.

E is the electric motor situated in the bottom of case C² and preferably of the Pacinotti or Gramme pattern. It is arranged horizontally and has a slotted curved crank-arm a on the upper end of its vertical spindle. The spindle D also has a slotted curved crank-arm b on its lower end, and in the slots of the arms a and b move collars on the ends of a rod F, having a centrifugal regulating-ball F' near its lower end. Near arm b the rod F is carried by a universal rocking joint F². The motor-circuit and the adjustable resistance placed therein are not shown.

The click-springs for indicating when the motor is running at a higher or lower rate of speed than desirable are shown at $c\,c'$.

G is the sleeve of the synchronistic machine, held in frictional contact upon the spindle D by a spring d and nut d'. This sleeve and the spindle of the simple machine have the cam depression e (shown in dotted lines) and are provided above the same with an arm e', having a pin which holds and locates correctly either the transmitting or receiving cylinder H.

I is the T-shaped lever, pivoted on base-plate C. Its central stem f has a projection which is thrown into the depression e by a spring g, which spring is connected to the line through the line-switch S'. The metal plate f' on the head of the lever I has electrical connection with g and plays at one end between the adjustable outer and inner contacts $h\,i$, while at the other end it springs outwardly and makes contact with j. The outer contacts of the two machines are connected with the coils of electro-magnets K K'. From K the wire passes through a battery B' to the ground, which battery may be the main battery at that end of the line. From K' the wire passes directly to ground. The armature k acts simply as a sounder. k', besides performing that function, makes and breaks the circuit of the local battery B³ at the synchronistic machine.

L is the electro-magnet in the circuit of the local battery B³. The pivoted lever l, carrying the armature of this magnet, forces back a spring-latch l', which engages a catch-arm $l²$, carried by the sleeve G. The spring of l' keeps it forward in the path of $l²$, but the closing of the local circuit forces l' back, allowing the point of $l²$ to swing clear. The lever for withdrawing the latch l' is shown at m, Fig. 6. It is worked by a push-rod m' and forces the armature against the magnet L', holding it there whether such magnet is energized or not.

M M' are the Morse keys for signaling, placed between contacts of S' and the electro-magnets K K'.

The weighted carriage of each machine is designated by N. It slides vertically in ways rising from plate C, as shown, and has a horizontally-pivoted spring-block n, upon which either style is placed; the spring throwing the style inwardly against the cylinder. This

FIGURE 8.7 *(Continued)*

4   479,184

carriage has a rack O, projecting downwardly therefrom and engaging a pinion o just above plate C.

On the same spindle with pinion O is an 5 escape-wheel O′, with which engage the pallets of an anchor O². This anchor has an arm $o′$ pivoted with a head, which is thrown into the depression e by the anchor-spring allowing the anchor to swing in that direction, 10 while it is thrown in the opposite direction by the forcing of the head of arm $o′$ out of the depression e as the spindle revolves. Thus at every revolution of the cylinder the escapewheel will move two teeth. The pinion o and 15 escape-wheel O′ are supported by a pivoted lever Q, by moving which the pinion can be thrown out of gear with the rack, so that the carriage can be raised independent of the escapement. The carriage has a finger p, which 20 when it reaches its lowest position pushes a pin $p′$ and forces a hook-lever Q′ from under a sustaining-lug $p²$, allowing such lever to drop and engage the arm $o′$ of the anchor O², so as to prevent the head of such arm from again 25 entering the depression e and stopping the further operation of the escapement. The carriage is connected electrically with the base-plate C by its ways, while the vertical guide q has connection with the inner con- 30 tact i through the style-switch S². The baseplate of each machine is connected with the battery-switch S³, one contact of which connects with main battery B′ or B², and the other contact has a direct ground connection.

35 T is the transmitting-style, having two contacts, one carried by spring r, which is connected by $r′$ with the guide q, when the style is in position on the carriage, and the other by arm s, connected by spring $s′$ with the carriage. 40 The spring r has a point $r²$, which traverses the surface of the paper and separates the contacts against the pressure of spring r, except when it drops into a depression.

The contacts are shown, for clearness, in 45 Fig. 7 as forced apart, the normal position when the style is removed from the carriage being the reverse.

The receiving-style U, Fig. 8, has its point t connected by a spring $t′$ only with the guide 50 q, the current being carried off through the cylinder to base-plate and thence to ground. A pivoted lever u is used to throw either pen off of the cylinder when the message is complete.

55 V represents the electro-magnet or resistance, or both, through which the contact j of each machine is connected with the ground.

In Fig. 9 is shown means for securing the paper upon the cylinder. This consists of a 60 spring-plate v, which is forced under the projecting edge of a slot in the cylinder; but any other efficient device can be used.

The binding-posts numbered on the diagram Fig. 1 are for the following circuits: 1, 65 the base-plate circuit; 2, the sounder and relay circuit; 3, the compensation-circuit; 4, the line-circuit; 5 and 6, the style-circuit, and 7 and 8 the local circuit.

The operation of the apparatus is as follows: When no messages are being sent, the 70 switch S′ of the machine is thrown to the right, the position of the other switches being immaterial. The throwing of both switches S′ to the right establishes a regular Morse line from the ground at the machine A through 75 the battery B′ to the relay K, to the key M of the machine A, through switch S′ at the machine A to the line, through switch S′ at the machine B to the key M′ at the machine B, and through the relay K′ to the 80 ground. Assume, now, that a message is to be sent from A to B. The operator at A calls the operator at B on the Morse line and makes the predetermined signal which means "receive," and the operator at B answers "ready." 85 Each operator then starts his machine revolving (if not already running) by closing the circuit to the motor E and pushing the pendulum with his hand. The operator at A 90 then puts on his machine a transmitting cylinder and pen, while the operator at B puts on his machine a receiving cylinder and pen, the switches S′ being opened or placed in a central position as soon as the Morse signals are understood. Now the operator at A 95 throws his switch S³ to the left, connecting the positive pole of the battery B′ with the base of the machine A, while the operator at B throws his switch S³ to the right, connecting the base of the machine B directly with 100 the ground. The switches S′ are kept open during this time, so that each operator can keep the line open until he is entirely ready to proceed. As each operator gets ready he connects his machine with the line by mov- 105 ing his switch S′ to the left. The line being kept open at each machine, except at one point in the revolution of the cylinder when the plate $f′$ is thrown against the contact h, the relays K K′ do not close until the con- 110 tacts h at the two machines are made simultaneously, which, since the machine B has a slightly-greater speed than the machine A, must occur in the course of a few revolutions. The moment the operator at B hears the click 115 of the relay K′ he pulls out the rod $m′$, permitting the armature-lever l to drop away from the magnet L and allowing the springlatch $l′$ to come forward into the path of the catch-arm $l²$ on the sleeve G, this bringing 120 the latch $l′$ under the control of the magnet L. Now the latch $l′$ will check the cylinder of the machine B at each revolution, as before explained, so that the machines will run synchronously. Now the operators count the clicks 125 of the relays until the predetermined number has been reached—say ten—and then each operator closes the pen-switch S², bringing the pens at the same moment into circuit. The pens, which have up to this time been held off of 130 the cylinders by the levers u, are allowed to drop onto the cylinders by moving such levers u, and

FIGURE 8.7 *(Continued)*

479,184   5

the carriage-escapements are released by depressing the outer ends of the levers Q', these movements being made before or after closing the pen-switch S², but preferably just
5 before. Now the message will be transmitted, as has been explained, the pen starting at the tops of the cylinders and moving downwardly by a step-by-step movement. When the operator A finds that the transmitting-
10 pen of his machine has passed over all the writing, he lifts the pen off of the cylinder by moving the lever u. This allows the transmitting-pen to close the circuit, making a line at the receiving-instrument B. Now
15 both the operators open the pen-switches S² and put on fresh cylinders, raising the pen-carriages to bring the pens to the tops of the cylinders. This is all done while the operators are counting the clicks of the relays,
20 and when ten clicks have been heard the operators are expected to be ready to drop the pens upon the cylinders and close the pen-switches. A small difference in the time when this is done is immaterial in practice,
25 since the transmitting-operator starts the pen far enough above the writing on the blank to allow for any error which might occur. This operation is continued until the operator at A has disposed of all the messages he has to
30 send, when he opens the line at the switch S', stopping the clicking of the relays, when both operators throw their switches S' to the right, putting the apparatus into position to receive a call on the Morse line. If, by rea-
35 son of any accident to or improper adjustment of the mechanisms—say, for illustration, an improper adjustment of the transmitting-pen—the writing at the receiving-instrument is imperfect, the operator at B opens the
40 line-circuit by opening the switch S' and the relays stop clicking. This indicates to the operator at A that something is wrong, and both operators then close the Morse line, as before explained, by throwing the switches
45 S' to the right and the operators communicate with each other and remedy the difficulty, and then proceed again.

When the operator at B desires to transmit to A, he signals A on the Morse lines, and the
50 operators then put the appropriate cylinders and pens upon their machines and proceed the same as when sending from A to B, as already explained, with the exception that the battery-switches are thrown to the opposite
55 sides, so that the battery B² will supply the current for writing instead of the battery B'.

What we claim as our invention is—

1. A fac-simile telegraph having transmitting and receiving instruments, the transmit-
60 ting-circuit being controlled by the depressions produced by marking autographically upon paper or other material, substantially as set forth.

2. In fac-simile telegraphs, the combination
65 of the transmitting and receiving instruments with a transmitting-style having circuit con-

nections and contacts in circuit controlled by the depressions in the surface of the prepared message caused by marking autographically thereon, substantially as set forth.   70

3. In fac-simile telegraphs, the synchronously-revolving cylinders, one carrying the message prepared by marking autographically upon the transmitting-sheet and the other a chemically-prepared recording-paper, in com- 75 bination with the transmitting and receiving styles having a movement at right angles to the cylinders, the said transmitting-style having contacts in circuit controlled by the depressions in the surface of the message, sub- 80 stantially as set forth.

4. In fac-simile telegraphs, the combination of the synchronously-revolving cylinders with movable contacts operated by the machines for breaking the circuit when the styles are 85 passing the secured edges of the paper, substantially as set forth.

5. In fac-simile telegraphs, the combination of the two machines having cylinders revolving at slightly-different speeds with a device 90 for checking the faster cylinder and contacts made simultaneously by the two machines for operating the checking device by completing the circuit through the same, substantially as set forth.   95

6. In fac-simile telegraphs, the combination of two machines having cylinders revolving at slightly-different speeds with a checking device for the faster cylinder, operated by an electro-magnet in the circuit of a local bat- 100 tery, and contacts made simultaneously by the two machines and completing the main circuit through an electro-magnet controlling said local circuit, substantially as set forth.

7. In fac-simile telegraphs, the combination 105 of the cylinders and the electro-magnetic checking device with sounders for indicating the synchronism of the cylinders, signaling-keys placed in shunts around the machines, and switches for throwing in and out the ma- 110 chines and keys alternately, whereby the sounders will be operated by the machines or the keys, according to the position of the switches, substantially as set forth.

8. In fac-simile telegraphs, the combination 115 of the two machines having cylinders and motors revolving the said cylinders at different speeds and an electro-magnetic checking device for one of them with a pivoted lever on each machine connected to line and two con- 120 tacts between which said lever plays, one connected through the style-circuit to battery or ground and the other through the relay and sounder circuit, such lever being moved once during each revolution of each cylinder to 125 break the style-circuit and make the relay and sounder circuit, substantially as set forth.

9. In fac-simile telegraphs, the combination, with the synchronously-revolving cylinders and motors and the transmitting and receiv- 130 ing styles, of cams revolving with the cylinders, pivoted levers worked by said cams and

FIGURE 8.7 *(Continued)*

6   479,184

connected to line, and making contacts for completing the style, the sounder, and the "compensation" circuits, substantially as set forth.

5   10. In fac-simile telegraphs, the combination, with the revolving cylinders and the motors working such cylinders, of the revolving cams and the style-carriages controlled by escapements worked by said cams and having 10 a step-by-step movement, substantially as set forth.

11. In fac-simile telegraphs, the combination of the electric motors with weighted centrifugal arms arranged oblique to the motor-15 shafts, said arms being carried by universal rocking joints and connecting the motors with the driven mechanisms, substantially as set forth.

12. In fac-simile telegraphs, the combination of the horizontal electric motors with the 20 weighted centrifugal arms arranged oblique to the motor-shafts, said arms being carried by universal rocking joints and the slotted cranks, substantially as set forth.

This specification signed and witnessed this 25 26th day of July, 1881.

                       THOS. A. EDISON.
                       PATRICK KENNY.

Witnesses:
   RICHD. N. DYER,
   H. W. SEELY.

FIGURE 8.7 *(Continued)*

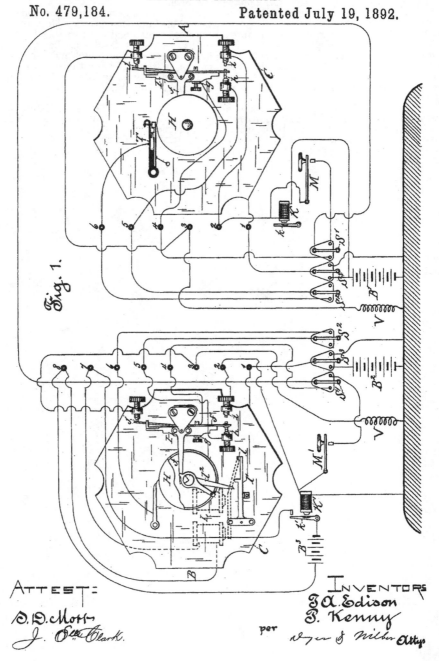

(No Model.)   5 Sheets—Sheet 1.

T. A. EDISON & P. KENNY.
FACSIMILE TELEGRAPH.

No. 479,184.   Patented July 19, 1892.

Fig. 1.

ATTEST:

INVENTORS
J. A. Edison
P. Kenny
per
Dyer & Wilber Attys

FIGURE 8.7 *(Continued)*

182

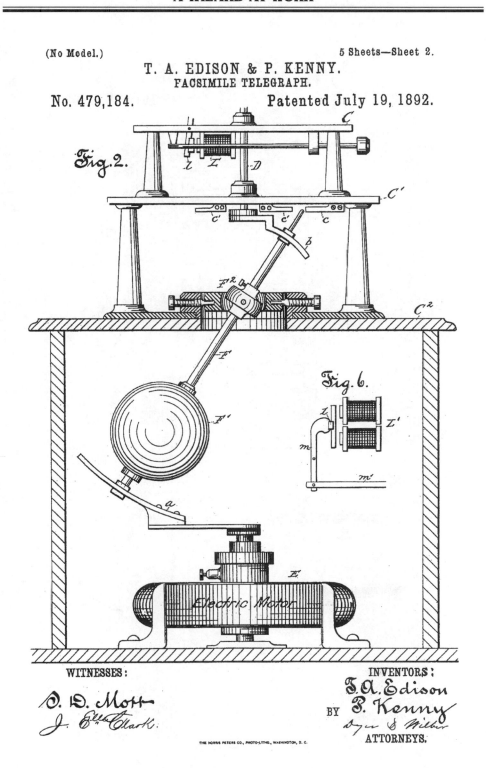

FIGURE 8.7 *(Continued)*

(No Model.)   5 Sheets—Sheet 3.

T. A. EDISON & P. KENNY.
FACSIMILE TELEGRAPH.

No. 479,184.   Patented July 19, 1892.

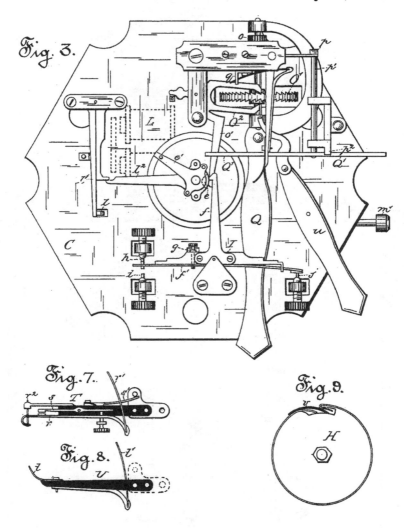

WITNESSES:
Ð. Ð. Mott
J. Ella Clark.

INVENTORS
T. A. Edison
BY P. Kenny
Dyer & Wilber
ATTORNEYS.

FIGURE 8.7 *(Continued)*

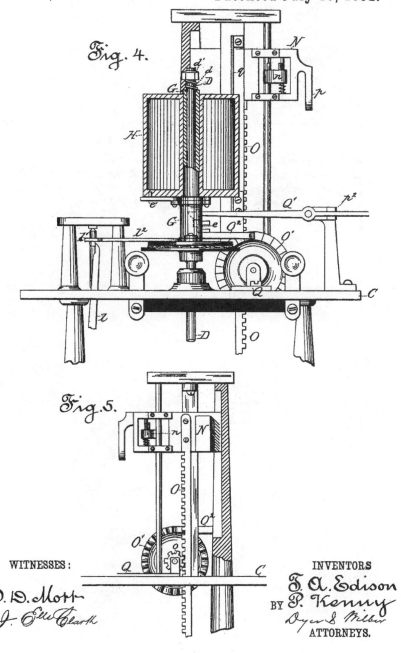

5 Sheets—Sheet 4.

T. A. EDISON & P. KENNY.
FACSIMILE TELEGRAPH.

No. 479,184.

Patented July 19, 1892.

Fig. 4.

Fig. 5.

WITNESSES:

D. D. Mott

J. Ellis Clark

INVENTORS

T. A. Edison

BY P. Kenny

Dyer & Miller

ATTORNEYS.

THE NORRIS PETERS CO., PHOTO-LITHO., WASHINGTON, D. C.

FIGURE 8.7 *(Continued)*

(No Model.) 5 Sheets—Sheet 5.

T. A. EDISON & P. KENNY.

FACSIMILE TELEGRAPH.

No. 479,184. Patented July 19, 1892.

Fig. 10.

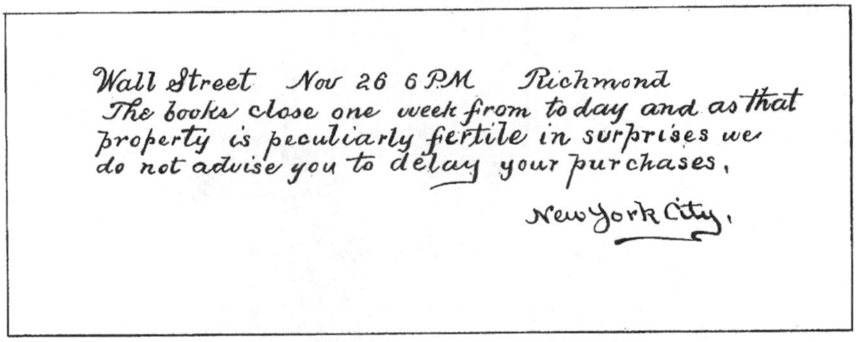

Wall Street Nov 26 6 P.M. Richmond
The books close one week from to day and as that
property is peculiarly fertile in surprises we
do not advise you to delay your purchases.
New York City.

Fig. 11.

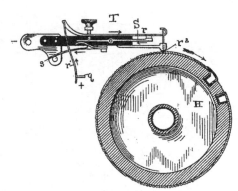

T
S
r
r²
s
r
q
+
H

WITNESSES:
R. Rowland,
W. Pelzer

INVENTORS:
Thomas A. Edison,
Patrick Kenny
BY
Rich. N. Dyer
ATTORNEY

THE NORRIS PETERS CO., PHOTO-LITHO., WASHINGTON, D. C.

FIGURE 8.7 ***(Continued)***

process of invention and patenting can learn quite a bit from Edison. Though he died back in 1931, still inventing and experimenting right up to the end, there is no better example of an innovator and inventor to learn from. What makes this especially so was his ability to develop new inventions with a sense of their significance for the future, not just the immediate present. As a final example of one of Edison's inventions, to make the point, look at his patent for a Fac-Simile Telegraph from 1881 (Figure 8.7), a creation that, in today's form, is a staple of office technology. Who but Edison would have thought it possible 120 years ago?

THE FINANCING, LICENSING, AND SALE OF PATENTS

9

RAISING MONEY

Though patents provide their owners with the right to protect their intellectual property, producing an invention and bringing it to the right market for consumers to purchase is entirely up to the patent holders. If you are one of the fortunate few, money to pay for all of this is no problem. Most patent owners, though, need financial resources in addition to their own if they intend to develop and market their innovations.

Raising money when your most valuable assets are in the form of intellectual property can be very difficult. Obtaining a loan from a bank is tough unless you have tangible assets that can be clearly valued and used as collateral. Intellectual property, unless you already have a solid track record of turning it into successful ventures, in which case raising money is a much easier task, may not cut it as an asset that can be used to secure a loan simply because of the difficulties inherent in predicting how it will pan out in the future.

At the same time, if a startup is pinning its future on the development of intellectual property, investors must be able to see that these assets are safely in place (patented, trademarked, copyrighted in good form, with trade secrets securely kept) and those in charge of developing them have the means to turn intangible ones into ones that can be verified and counted, like money. Since intellectual property may be the only assets of significant value, it is vital that potential investors be shown the future cash flows this property can be used to generate and how to translate them into their equivalent value in today's dollars, which can be a tall order.

No matter whom you are seeking money from, be it a bank, individual investors, the Small Business Administration, a group of venture capitalists, or maybe even your mother, you have to demonstrate to investors that you have a clear plan, the means to pull it off, and the kind of demand in your market that will assure them of being compensated for taking on the risk of investing in you. Since the primary focus of this book is intellectual property, patents in particular, we will not spend much time distinguishing between the possible sources of financing. Rather, the focus will be on the common requirements and challenges. Having a working knowledge of these can be used to greatly increase your chances of obtaining financing.

Following is a case study where the insights of a man whose firm raises venture capital for small businesses, whose financing needs range from $2 million to $20 million, highlight issues of crucial importance in the search for funding.

Because business plans are so important, great care should go into preparing them. If you prepare it yourself, be sure you are doing it right. There are plenty of books, organizations (like the Small Business Administration) and Internet resources to help you, which are easy to find. It is also a good idea to have experienced people read through your plan and provide input. Another option is to hire somebody whose expertise you trust to prepare the plan for you.

On the following pages (Figure 9.1) is a copy of an outline for preparing a business plan that is freely available from the Small Business Administration, an excellent resource in a range of areas. They, along with the training module this outline comes from, can be accessed at sba.gov.

PATENT LICENSING

Instead of seeking out the money necessary to finance an invention on your own, another option is to license the technology to somebody else, let them take care of the production and marketing, and you collect a portion of their revenues in the form of royalties. A licensing agreement is a promise by the patent owner not to assert their offensive rights against the licensor who makes or sells the invention. Usually the promise is made in exchange for royalties, but there is no requirement that anything be given in return. There is no format that a license agreement must follow; it is a contract whose terms are up to the parties involved. If you decide to license your invention, be sure to have a competent attorney draw up the agreement.

Revenue from patent licensing has grown steadily, from $15 billion in 1990 to more than $100 billion in the year 2000. IBM, earning

CASE STUDY   Mark Palazzo, President of Pittsford Capital Group

Mark's group constantly receives calls from people seeking financing for their ventures. Out of every 1,000 inquiries Pittsford Capital receives, maybe 1 of those will go on to have money raised for them. That does not have to mean your own chances are one-tenth of a percent, however, because you can significantly improve your individual odds by being properly prepared from the onset. Most people are not.

When approached, Mark looks at three things in order to decide if the group should proceed to the next step.

1. The quality of the idea.
2. The management team.
3. The likelihood of raising money.

1. The idea has to be for something that will actually work, and make money, in the real world. An idea that sounds good in theory but cannot be connected to successful practice does not have a chance. During the salad days of dot-com firms when money seemed to be thrown at anybody with an idea and a web site, professionals at Mark's firm would hear these sorts of proposals, scratch their heads, and ask themselves "How can anybody make money at this?" In retrospect, a lot more head scratching should have been going on. Pittsford Capital has to believe in the product and know it will work in the market; they have to able to support the idea as clearly viable themselves before they will consider raising money for it.

2. Usually the people with ideas have the necessary technical skills, but the question is one of whether or not they possess the management skills necessary to use the money they are seeking to take the company to the next level. As Mark wants to know, "Once you have the money, what are you going to do with it?" The skills necessary to come up with a patentable, marketable innovation are different from those required to oversee the operations of a functioning enterprise. If those with the ideas do not have these skills, whom are they going to get who does? And even if they are capable of running a firm, Mark might be concerned about the opportunity costs involved; if the great innovator leaves the lab for the board room, who is going to be doing the innovating?

3. A great idea that can be translated into well-thought-out practice, coupled with all the necessary talent and a clear plan for the future, does not automatically mean that money will follow. If a particular sector of the economy is cold and its foreseeable future remains in doubt, financing is hard to come by. On the other hand, if money is being sought for a good or service that investors understand, like, and see good prospects for, the odds improve significantly.

CASE STUDY   Mark Palazzo, President of Pittsford Capital Group *(Continued)*

Once the initial hurdles have been cleared, the time comes to make a thorough review of the business plan. Mark advises that this be prepared in advance. It will have to be done anyway, and it is a positive reflection on anybody seeking funding if they can show they are serious and organized enough to come in at the beginning with a clear, realistic plan. In drawing up the plan, it is important that it be in good form and draw on the knowledge of other involved professionals, such as lawyers and accountants, as needed.

A common shortcoming of business plans is found in their estimates of future performance. Mark's experience has been that, "Many times projections they think are conservative we think are aggressive," resulting in a downward adjustment that is more in line with reality.

Another common shortcoming, usually because people have not thought far enough ahead, is the absence of an exit strategy. Investors who obtain a partial ownership interest in a business want to know how they are going to get their money back. Will the business be sold? Does it want to eventually do a stock offering and become a public company? People who have made a business out of their innovations have taken on a lot of risk and have devoted themselves to making a go of the enterprise. To think of exiting it as it is can be seen as the equivalent of abandoning a child. Of course, if the founder's stake increases along with the value of their venture, the exit becomes easier to take.

Even when all the conditions for becoming a worthy investment candidate have been satisfied, when the ideas look both great and practical, with solid management in place, and a good business plan that takes the firm to their likely exit(s), the deal can still collapse. Oftentimes business owners get scared off by the cost of financing, the amount of control they must yield, or the degree of the ownership interest they must exchange in return for the financing being sought. Another land mine can come from the relationships of the people involved in an enterprise. Whenever more than one person is responsible for decision making and have not clearly marked out their responsibilities or the boundaries of their relationships, both professional and personal, the potential exists for clashes that can sabotage their enterprise.

THE BUSINESS PLAN

ROAD MAP TO SUCCESS

A Tutorial and Self-paced Activity
Download or View a Text Version

BUSINESS PLAN OUTLINE

(See Spanish Version)

Below is an outline for a business plan. Use this model as a guide when developing the business plan for your business.

Elements of a Business Plan

- 1. Cover sheet
- 2. Statement of purpose
- 3. Table of contents

- I. The Business
  - A. Description of business
  - B. Marketing
  - C. Competition
  - D. Operating procedures
  - E. Personnel
  - F. Business insurance
  - G. Financial data

- II. Financial Data
  - A. Loan applications
  - B. Capital equipment and supply list
  - C. Balance sheet
  - D. Breakeven analysis
  - E. Pro-forma income projections (profit & loss statements)
    - Three-year summary
    - Detail by month, first year
    - Detail by quarters, second and third years
    - Assumptions upon which projections were based
  - F. Pro-forma cash flow
    - Follow guidelines for letter E.

- III. Supporting Documents
  - Tax returns of principals for last three years
  - Personal financial statement (all banks have these forms)

FIGURE 9.1   Business Plan Guide

- In the case of a franchised business, a copy of franchise contract and all supporting documents provided by the franchisor
- Copy of proposed lease or purchase agreement for building space
- Copy of licenses and other legal documents
- Copy of resumes of all principals
- Copies of letters of intent from suppliers, etc.

THE BUSINESS PLAN - WHAT IT INCLUDES

What goes in a business plan? This is an excellent question. And, it is one that many new and potential small business owners should ask, but oftentimes don't ask. The body of the business plan can be divided into four distinct sections: 1) the description of the business, 2) the marketing plan, 3) the financial management plan and 4) the management plan. Addenda to the business plan should include the executive summary, supporting documents and financial projections.

THE BUSINESS PLAN - DESCRIPTION OF THE BUSINESS

In this section, provide a detailed description of your business. An excellent question to ask yourself is: "What business am I in?" In answering this question include your products, market and services as well as a thorough description of what makes your business unique. Remember, however, that as you develop your business plan, you may have to modify or revise your initial questions.

The business description section is divided into three primary sections. Section 1 actually describes your business, Section 2 the product or service you will be offering and Section 3 the location of your business, and why this location is desirable (if you have a franchise, some franchisors assist in site selection).
  ○ 1. Business Description

When describing your business, generally you should explain:
  ○ 1. Legalities - business form: proprietorship, partnership, corporation. The licenses or permits you will need.
  ○ 2. Business type: merchandizing, manufacturing or service.
  ○ 3. What your product or service is.
  ○ 4. Is it a new independent business, a takeover, an expansion, a franchise?
  ○ 5. Why your business will be profitable. What are the growth opportunities? Will franchising impact on growth opportunities?
  ○ 6. When your business will be open (days, hours)?
  ○ 7. What you have learned about your kind of business from outside sources (trade suppliers, bankers, other franchise owners, franchisor, publications).

A cover sheet goes before the description. It includes the name, address and telephone number of the business and the names of all principals. In the description of your business, describe the unique aspects and how or why they

FIGURE 9.1 *(Continued)*

will appeal to consumers. Emphasize any special features that you feel will appeal to customers and explain how and why these features are appealing.

The description of your business should clearly identify goals and objectives and it should clarify why you are, or why you want to be, in business.

THE BUSINESS PLAN - 2. Product/Service

Try to describe the benefits of your goods and services from your customers' perspective. Successful business owners know or at least have an idea of what their customers want or expect from them. This type of anticipation can be helpful in building customer satisfaction and loyalty. And, it certainly is a good strategy for beating the competition or retaining your competitiveness. Describe:
- 1. What you are selling.
- 2. How your product or service will benefit the customer.
- 3. Which products/services are in demand; if there will be a steady flow of cash.
- 4. What is different about the product or service your business is offering.

THE BUSINESS PLAN - 3. The Location

The location of your business can play a decisive role in its success or failure. Your location should be built around your customers, it should be accessible and it should provide a sense of security. Consider these questions when addressing this section of your business plan:
- 1. What are your location needs?
- 2. What kind of space will you need?
- 3. Why is the area desirable? the building desirable?
- 4. Is it easily accessible? Is public transportation available? Is street lighting adequate?
- 5. Are market shifts or demographic shifts occurring?

It may be a good idea to make a checklist of questions you identify when developing your business plan. Categorize your questions and, as you answer each question, remove it from your list.

THE BUSINESS PLAN - The Marketing Plan

Marketing plays a vital role in successful business ventures. How well you market you business, along with a few other considerations, will ultimately determine your degree of success or failure. The key element of a successful marketing plan is to know your customers-their likes, dislikes, expectations. By identifying these factors, you can develop a marketing strategy that will allow you to arouse and fulfill their needs.

Identify your customers by their age, sex, income/educational level and residence. At first, target only those customers who are more likely to purchase

FIGURE 9.1 *(Continued)*

your product or service. As your customer base expands, you may need to consider modifying the marketing plan to include other customers.

Develop a marketing plan for your business by answering these questions. (Potential franchise owners will have to use the marketing strategy the franchisor has developed.) Your marketing plan should be included in your business plan and contain answers to the questions outlined below.
- o 1. Who are your customers? Define your target market(s).
- o 2. Are your markets growing? steady? declining?
- o 3. Is your market share growing? steady? declining?
- o 4. If a franchise, how is your market segmented?
- o 5. Are your markets large enough to expand?
- o 6. How will you attract, hold, increase your market share? If a franchise, will the franchisor provide assistance in this area? Based on the franchisor's strategy? how will you promote your sales?
- o 7. What pricing strategy have you devised?

Appendix I contains a sample Marketing Plan and Marketing Tips, Tricks and Traps, a condensed guide on how to market your product or service. Study these documents carefully when developing the marketing portion of your business plan.

THE BUSINESS PLAN - 1. Competition

Competition is a way of life. We compete for jobs, promotions, scholarships to institutes of higher learning, in sports-and in almost every aspect of your lives. Nations compete for the consumer in the global marketplace as do individual business owners. Advances in technology can send the profit margins of a successful business into a tailspin causing them to plummet overnight or within a few hours. When considering these and other factors, we can conclude that business is a highly competitive, volatile arena. Because of this volatility and competitiveness, it is important to know your competitors.

Questions like these can help you:
- o 1. Who are your five nearest direct competitors?
- o 2. Who are your indirect competitors?
- o 3. How are their businesses: steady? increasing? decreasing?
- o 4. What have you learned from their operations? from their advertising?
- o 5. What are their strengths and weaknesses?
- o 6. How does their product or service differ from yours?

Start a file on each of your competitors. Keep manila envelopes of their advertising and promotional materials and their pricing strategy techniques. Review these files periodically, determining when and how often they advertise, sponsor promotions and offer sales. Study the copy used in the advertising and promotional materials, and their sales strategy. For example, is their copy short?

FIGURE 9.1 *(Continued)*

descriptive? catchy? or how much do they reduce prices for sales? Using this technique can help you to understand your competitors better and how they operate their businesses.

THE BUSINESS PLAN - 2. Pricing and Sales

Your pricing strategy is another marketing technique you can use to improve your overall competitiveness. Get a feel for the pricing strategy your competitors are using. That way you can determine if your prices are in line with competitors in your market area and if they are in line with industry averages.

Some of the pricing strategies are:
- retail cost and pricing
- competitive position
- pricing below competition
- pricing above competition
- price lining
- multiple pricing
- service costs and pricing (for service businesses only)
  - service components
  - material costs
  - labor costs
  - overhead costs

The key to success is to have a well-planned strategy, to establish your policies and to constantly monitor prices and operating costs to ensure profits. Even in a franchise where the franchisor provides operational procedures and materials, it is a good policy to keep abreast of the changes in the marketplace because these changes can affect your competitiveness and profit margins.

Appendix 1 contains a sample Price/Quality Matrix, review it for ideas on pricing strategies for your competitors. Determine which of the strategies they use, if it is effective and why it is effective.

THE BUSINESS PLAN - 3. Advertising and Public Relations

How you advertise and promote your goods and services may make or break your business. Having a good product or service and not advertising and promoting it is like not having a business at all. Many business owners operate under the mistaken concept that the business will promote itself, and channel money that should be used for advertising and promotions to other areas of the business. Advertising and promotions, however, are the life line of a business and should be treated as such.

Devise a plan that uses advertising and networking as a means to promote your business. Develop short, descriptive copy (text material) that clearly identifies

FIGURE 9.1 *(Continued)*

your goods or services, its location and price. Use catchy phrases to arouse the interest of your readers, listeners or viewers. In the case of a franchise, the franchisor will provide advertising and promotional materials as part of the franchise package, you may need approval to use any materials that you and your staff develop. Whether or not this is the case, as a courtesy, allow the franchisor the opportunity to review, comment on and, if required, approve these materials before using them. Make sure the advertisements you create are consistent with the image the franchisor is trying to project. Remember the more care and attention you devote to your marketing program, the more successful your business will be.

A more detailed explanation of the marketing plan and how to develop an effective marketing program is provided in the Workshop on Marketing. See Training Module 3 - Marketing Your Business for Success.

THE BUSINESS PLAN - THE MANAGEMENT PLAN

Managing a business requires more than just the desire to be your own boss. It demands dedication, persistence, the ability to make decisions and the ability to manage both employees and finances. Your management plan, along with your marketing and financial management plans, sets the foundation for and facilitates the success of your business.

Like plants and equipment, people are resources-they are the most valuable asset a business has. You will soon discover that employees and staff will play an important role in the total operation of your business. Consequently, it's imperative that you know what skills you possess and those you lack since you will have to hire personnel to supply the skills that you lack. Additionally, it is imperative that you know how to manage and treat your employees. Make them a part of the team. Keep them informed of, and get their feedback regarding, changes. Employees oftentimes have excellent ideas that can lead to new market areas, innovations to existing products or services or new product lines or services which can improve your overall competitiveness.

Your management plan should answer questions such as:
- How does your background/business experience help you in this business?
- What are your weaknesses and how can you compensate for them?
- Who will be on the management team?
- What are their strengths/weaknesses?
- What are their duties?
- Are these duties clearly defined?
- If a franchise, what type of assistance can you expect from the franchisor?
- Will this assistance be ongoing?
- What are your current personnel needs?
- What are your plans for hiring and training personnel?
- What salaries, benefits, vacations, holidays will you offer? If a franchise, are

FIGURE 9.1 *(Continued)*

these issues covered in the management package the franchisor will provide?
○ What benefits, if any, can you afford at this point?

If a franchise, the operating procedures, manuals and materials devised by the franchisor should be included in this section of the business plan. Study these documents carefully when writing your business plan, and be sure to incorporate this material. The franchisor should assist you with managing your franchise. Take advantage of their expertise and develop a management plan that will ensure the success for your franchise and satisfy the needs and expectations of employees, as well as the franchisor.

THE BUSINESS PLAN - THE FINANCIAL MANAGEMENT PLAN

Sound financial management is one of the best ways for your business to remain profitable and solvent. How well you manage the finances of your business is the cornerstone of every successful business venture. Each year thousands of potentially successful businesses fail because of poor financial management. As a business owner, you will need to identify and implement policies that will lead to and ensure that you will meet your financial obligations.

To effectively manage your finances, plan a sound, realistic budget by determining the actual amount of money needed to open your business (start-up costs) and the amount needed to keep it open (operating costs). The first step to building a sound financial plan is to devise a start-up budget. Your start-up budget will usually include such one-time-only costs as major equipment, utility deposits, down payments, etc.

The start-up budget should allow for these expenses.

Start-up Budget

○ personnel (costs prior to opening)
○ legal/professional fees
○ occupancy
○ licenses/permits
○ equipment
○ insurance
○ supplies
○ advertising/promotions
○ salaries/wages
○ accounting
○ income
○ utilities
○ payroll expenses

An operating budget is prepared when you are actually ready to open for business. The operating budget will reflect your priorities in terms of how your

FIGURE 9.1 *(Continued)*

spend your money, the expenses you will incur and how you will meet those expenses (income). Your operating budget also should include money to cover the first three to six months of operation. It should allow for the following expenses.

Operating Budget

- personnel
- insurance
- rent
- depreciation
- loan payments
- advertising/promotions
- legal/accounting
- miscellaneous expenses
- supplies
- payroll expenses
- salaries/wages
- utilities
- dues/subscriptions/fees
- taxes
- repairs/maintenance

The financial section of your business plan should include any loan applications you've filed, a capital equipment and supply list, balance sheet, breakeven analysis, pro-forma income projections (profit and loss statement) and pro-forma cash flow. The income statement and cash flow projections should include a three-year summary, detail by month for the first year, and detail by quarter for the second and third years.

The accounting system and the inventory control system that you will be using is generally addressed in this section of the business plan also. If a franchise, the franchisor may stipulate in the franchise contract the type of accounting and inventory systems you may use. If this is the case, he or she should have a system already intact and you will be required to adopt this system. Whether you develop the accounting and inventory systems yourself, have an outside financial advisor develop the systems or the franchisor provides these systems, you will need to acquire a thorough understanding of each segment and how it operates. Your financial advisor can assist you in developing this section of your business plan.

The following questions should help you determine the amount of start-up capital you will need to purchase and open a franchise.
- How much money do you have?
- How much money will you need to purchase the franchise?

FIGURE 9.1 *(Continued)*

- How much money will you need for start-up?
- How much money will you need to stay in business?

Other questions that you will need to consider are:
- What type of accounting system will your use? Is it a single entry or dual entry system?
- What will your sales goals and profit goals for the coming year be? If a franchise, will the franchisor set your sales and profit goals? Or, will he or she expect you to reach and retain a certain sales level and profit margin?
- What financial projections will you need to include in your business plan?
- What kind of inventory control system will you use?

Your plan should include an explanation of all projections. Unless you are thoroughly familiar with financial statements, get help in preparing your cash flow and income statements and your balance sheet. Your aim is not to become a financial wizard, but to understand the financial tools well enough to gain their benefits. Your accountant or financial advisor can help you accomplish this goal.

Sample balance sheets, income projections (profit and loss statements) and cash flow statements are included in Appendix 2, Financial Management. For a detailed explanation of these and other more complex financial concepts, contact your local SBA Office. Look under the U.S. Government section of the local telephone directory.

FIGURE 9.1   *(Continued)*

more than $1 billion dollars a year on its vast portfolio, is the heavy-weight champion of patent licensing. It will probably continue in that position, too, having recently applied for patents on a new technique for quadrupling disk storage capacity, which it intends to license also.

Licensing can also be a solution to infringement cases that allows the patent holder and the alleged infringer to work out an agreement that is mutually beneficial. Domino's Pizza was sued for using heated delivery bags that R.G. Barry Corporation claimed infringed on its patent. The case was settled, with Domino's agreeing to pay $5 million for having used the technology and entering into a licensing agreement where they either buy the bags directly from R.G. Barry or pay R.G. Barry a licensing fee and buy them from their supplier.

It is not unheard of for people to obtain patents for the express purpose of licensing them. In many fields the cost, whether in money, time, effort, or a combination of the three, to produce an invention at the level necessary to enter a market is prohibitive. Knowing that at the outset enables you to tailor a patented innovation to a particular niche. Robert Levine and Stephen Wardlaw, a pair of Yale Medical School professors are a good example. In 1977 they showed a representative of Becton Dickinson and Company a prototype of a blood analyzer it had cost them $100 to build. The company had already invested millions in the effort to develop a blood analyzer of their own. When Levine and Wardlaw demonstrated that their table-top prototype worked as well as what the company had put millions of dollars into, they were able to enter into a licensing agreement with Becton Dickinson and Company. Today, they have been granted almost 400 patents on diagnostic equipment whose sales have totaled more than $1 billion. They have earned millions of dollars in royalties for these.

Licensing intellectual property is similar to raising money because in both cases outside parties have to be convinced that your invention will result in the future cash flows that make entering into an agreement with you a worthwhile endeavor. Following are four general steps to assist you in the licensing of your patent.

1. Identify potential licensors.

2. Make initial contacts to screen for the best candidates.

3. Put together and submit a package of material.

4. Assess offers and negotiate the license agreement.

1. Chances are that having the expertise to obtain a patent, along with the knowledge gained during the patent process, means that you already have a good idea of who the potential licensors are. In addition, you can do searches in the area of commerce your invention will inhabit and see who does related things. Trade journals and groups, conventions, associations, contacts in the industry, and any networks you are a part of all can provide good candidates. Another possibility is to employ an agent who, in exchange for a fee or an ongoing slice of your future royalties, will seek licensing opportunities for you. Because anybody can claim to be an agent, it is important to find one with a good reputation with credible references you can check.

2. Once you have developed a list, make initial contact by phone, e-mail, or letter, where you provide an initial query in order to judge their level of interest. Provided you have the candidates, the more queries the better. An initial query should be brief and to the point, explaining your invention, its market, and reasons why the person you have queried should be interested in it.

3. Based on the query responses that are promising, you should prepare a detailed package of material for them. This package should detail your background, expertise, and general qualifications for having ideas others will want to acquire rights to. Your invention should be explained in greater detail, with charts, brochures, and the like to clearly demonstrate what it does and why it should appeal to them.

A market analysis is very important, too, as it allows you to demonstrate that, while there are precedents for inventions similar to yours being very successful, yours has unique features that cause it to be even more appealing.

4. Assuming you receive offers as a result of your efforts, it is time to decide which is the best deal. The highest royalty rate alone, for example, is not enough basis on which to make a decision. It is also important to look at who is going to do the best job of promoting the invention they are licensing for you and how long they will stick with it, along with assessing them as a possible source of additional licensing agreements in the future. This process, and especially the contract that follows, should be pursued with a competent attorney who has experience in the area.

SELLING A PATENT

In order to identify, contact, and negotiate with, potential buyers of your patent the same steps as in the licensing section can be used. The difference in a sale is that you are permanently assigning your patent rights to somebody else. Because of that, a sales price that reflects all probable future benefits must be agreed upon. There is always the risk of parting with your intellectual property too cheaply, only to witness it going on to earn a fortune that will never find its way into your pocket. The purchaser of your patent has the opposite worry, of paying for something that never ends up providing a suitable return on investment. The great advantage for you as the seller is that once the patent is sold and the check clears, it is no longer your worry. In order to prevent later worry that you let it go too cheaply, be sure your attorney is skilled both at the mechanics of the agreement and in giving you guidance on what its perceived value is.

COPYRIGHTING YOUR CREATIONS

10

THE FREEDOM OF PROTECTION

The United States Constitution instructs Congress to "... make no law" that obstructs free speech, but it also gives Congress the authority to enact laws that "promote the progress of science and the useful arts, by securing for limited times to authors and inventors the exclusive right to their respective writings and discoveries." In 1790 Congress determined that copyright protection would last for 14 years, which could then be renewed for another 14-year term. In subsequent years, that period of time was increased, then increased again to its current limits by the Sonny Bono Copyright Term Extension Act in 1998: the life of the author plus 70 years or, for corporations who own copyrights, 95 years.

How are the freedoms to speak and create reconciled with the protections offered by copyrights? Copyrighted works are intellectual property and, as property, are given a legal status that allows their owners to prosecute those who use them without permission. The difficulty is that intellectual property is different by nature from physical property, like buildings and equipment, because more than one person can be in possession of it, or using some aspect of it, at any given time and they can be using it in conflicting ways. A recent copyright conflict serves to illustrate the issue.

Alice Randall is the author of *The Wind Done Gone,* a work written from the point of view of a slave who is the half-sister of Scarlett O'Hara, the character from the novel *Gone with the Wind,* by Margaret Mitchell. The heirs of Ms. Mitchell, who possess the copyright for *Gone with the Wind,* maintained that *The Wind Done Gone* infringed on that copyright. They initiated legal action and a federal judge stopped the publication of the new novel in order to give an appeals court time to decide on the case.

The Wind Done Gone does use characters, settings, and some passages from *Gone with the Wind*, but it provides takes on issues like race, power, social relations, and the Civil War that are very different, providing a parody its author claims to have written "... for all Americans, both black and white, so they could have a deep, hearty belly laugh," about the difficult Civil War period. Parody has always been such, putting a new twist on existing works and situations with the goal of saying something very different from, and usually contrary to, the original work, as when Weird Al Yancovic did a parody of the Michael Jackson song "Beat It," calling his "Eat It."

The difference between parody and infringement seems to lie in the very blurry distinction between using what somebody else has done as a platform to launch a new work and using existing creations in ways that are not significantly different and therefore become a wrongful use of another's intellectual property. The fact that *The Wind Done Gone* inspired a debate where the opposing sides each made excellent points illustrates just how difficult the distinction is to make. What makes a parody original enough to be considered a separate work in its own right, rather than merely being derivative of another, and therefore not eligible for a copyright? No set of directions for making clear distinctions exists. The injunction preventing publication of *The Wind Done Gone* was lifted by a federal appeals court and the book went on to be published, but that did nothing to settle the passionate disagreements that persist.

The intent of copyright law is to provide the authors of original creations exclusive rights over them. Composing a song, writing a book, authoring a computer program, or notating a work of choreography are all challenging endeavors, with their authors having no guarantee of ever gaining any rewards, beyond the satisfaction of creation, which, though it is a nice feeling, does not pay a lot of bills. The exclusive right to a work is a powerful motivator for artists. As with patent rights, it does not guarantee a paying audience, but it does deter theft of intellectual property and gives copyright owners recourse if a theft does occur.

With the Internet able to function like a gigantic copying machine (as seen with the Napster controversy), where individuals are able to make unlimited numbers of copies of copyrighted works and distribute and sell them just about anywhere, copyright issues will continue to be a challenge, especially in the enforcement. As an indication of the magnitude this issue has reached due to advances in technology, the Business Software Alliance estimates that over a third of all business software is copied illegally. The group estimates that worldwide theft of copyrighted software cost manufacturers of it nearly $12 billion in the year 2000, a figure that is sure to continue rising along with computer usage.

WHAT IS A COPYRIGHT?

A copyright provides legal protection for the creators of "original works of authorship." These include literary, dramatic, musical, and artistic creations, such as books, computer software, plays, songs, cartoons, choreography, photographs, and architecture. The protection covers works whether they are published or not and gives the owner, or joint owners if more than one person participated in the creation, the sole rights to make copies, produce derivative works based on the original, sell, rent or lease the work, transfer ownership to somebody else, and perform and display the work.

An original work is automatically copyrighted when it is first put in a tangible form and can be perceived by others, with the author(s) being the sole owner(s). The legal protection lasts for the life of the author, plus an additional 70 years. When copyrighted works are owned by those who have hired others to create them, the copyright lasts for the shorter of 95 years from publication or 120 years from creation.

As with patents, the first federal Copyright Act was enacted in 1790. It covered books, maps, and charts for a 14-year period, which was renewable for another 14 years. It is interesting to learn that, given the controversies of recent years surrounding the illegal reproduction and sale of copyrighted material, that the first copyright laws pertained only to United States citizens. Copyright protection did not extend to foreign works, as it does now.

The result was that foreign books were reprinted and sold at lower prices than if they had been protected by copyright, and the original authors were not paid for their work. Early in U.S. history, there were few American books being published, so there was a strong demand for foreign works, which made pirating them a lucrative business. Years later, American authors, particularly of software and musical works, have faced the same kinds of problems when their works are copied and sold in foreign countries that do not offer, or enforce, legal protections. Once a work is in digital form, it can be copied infinitely, with no solid mechanism in place to guarantee that the original author collects any royalties. Of course, the Internet benefits authors, too, by opening up new avenues for consumers to be exposed to them and purchase their works legally.

COPYRIGHT CRITERIA

Just because somebody has put together some material does not necessarily mean that it is eligible for a copyright. For example, information taken from public documents, such as a list of names from the phone book, cannot be copyrighted, nor can ideas, titles, procedures, names, familiar designs (or slight variations on them), or short slogans. If you write down a recipe for chocolate chip cookies that merely contains a list of common ingredients and procedures, you cannot copyright it. The key to securing a copyright is producing an original work in a tangible form, such as a book, photograph, drawing, or software program. So, if you come up with a unique approach to making chocolate chip cookies that you can detail in a novel form, a copyright can be secured.

Copyright law says, "In no case does copyright protection for an original work of authorship extend to any idea, procedure, process, system, method of operation, concept, principle, or discovery, regardless of the form in which it is described, explained, illustrated, or embodied in such work." In short, it is an author's unique expression of the above that is protected, not ideas, principles, or discoveries. For example, a few years ago there was a torrent of books on total quality management. If the first author who hit on it had been able to secure a copyright on the original idea, then no other books about it could legally have followed. As the law stands, however, as many authors who want to can write about it, so long as they do not copy exactly what another writer has already expressed.

The requirement for originality is fairly loose, and it has nothing to do with quality. If you listen to the radio regularly, you know that if a hit with an original sound comes out, a lot of similar sounding songs will quickly follow. In the early 1990s the band Nirvana had a huge hit with "Smells Like Teen Spirit." Almost the next day, it seemed, there were hundreds of bands trying to produce similar songs. They could not legally reproduce the same song, but plenty got away with coming awfully close.

Though originality is a requirement for securing a copyright, it is not a difficult hurdle to clear. A creation can be similar to others that have gone before and still be copyrighted, so long as it does more than just make a trivial change or modification. If you listen to blues music, you know how small the differences can be. Most blues is based on simple chord progressions and melodies, with many new songs sounding a lot like the old ones. What is unique, however, is the artist's ability to bring something to the form that causes clearly original work to emerge, despite sharing a host of common features with existing creations.

The same issue comes up frequently with computer programs. Many programs are written to perform word processing, data base, and spreadsheet functions that look nearly identical to the user. That is permissible because there is no restriction on works addressing the same subject. The reason programs that appear so much alike are able to be copyrighted is that, in the use of the languages that express what the program does, they are significantly different from the others and not mere derivatives.

COPYRIGHT REGISTRATION

Despite the fact that a copyright occurs automatically and there is no requirement that a work be formally registered, registering your work with the U.S. Copyright Office is an excellent idea. It is an easy task, too, merely requiring that you fill out a simple application form, write a check for $30, and send these, in the same package that contains 3 copies of your work, to the Copyright Office.

Depending on whether you are copyrighting a literary piece, a creative work in the visual arts, a set of software, or one of the many other forms of expression entitled to copyright protection, the specific requirements for the form the work submitted must take will vary. The best and most efficient way to obtain the specifics you need is to access the Copyright Office's web site at www.loc.gov/copyright. There you will find guides covering whatever form of copyright you are seeking, which can be downloaded and printed out.

Copyright circulars and announcements are also available from the Copyright Office by fax, (202) 707-2600. Copyright application forms can be found on, and printed out from, the web site just given. They are available for ordering by phone at (202) 707-9100. If you want to talk to a person who is an information specialist for the Copyright Office, one can be reached at (202) 707-3000. The mailing address for sending your completed application and accompanying material is:

Library of Congress
Copyright Office
101 Independence Avenue, S.E.
Washington, DC 20559-6000

Registration occurs on the date that the Copyright Office receives all the required material in proper form. Because they receive close to 600,000 applications a year, you will not receive confirmation of receipt unless you send the material by registered or certified mail and request a return receipt, but you will get a certificate of registration within a few months, which serves as proof of your copyright. Should the material you submit be lacking anything necessary, the Copyright Office will notify you. Because the process is so straight-forward, there is no reason to run into any trouble, so long as your work qualifies and you follow a few simple steps. In the year 2000, the Copyright Office received 588,498 claims for copyright and registered 515,612, so the odds are on your side if you follow some pretty easy directions.

PROTECTING YOUR COPYRIGHT

Copyright protection exists whether your work is published or un-published, and it does not cease when others acquire your work. Registering works you have authored is a good first step in protecting copyrights because it provides solid evidence that you are indeed the creator and clearly shows the date that fact became known to the Copyright Office.

Next, any copies of your work that are distributed in any fashion, be it a sale, loan, lease, or rental, should be clearly marked as yours. Otherwise, if your work is used by another, they can claim they did not know of the copyright. So be sure this documentation is visible. As an example, what follows are the elements necessary to serve notice of a copyright when the copies of the work are visually perceptible. Three things need to be present to make this type of copyright notice complete:

1. The word "Copyright," the abbreviation "Copr.," or a symbol with the letter C contained in a circle.
2. The year the work was first published.
3. The name of the person who owns the copy.

If a work has not been published, retain 1. and 2. and, instead of the date of publication, state "unpublished work" and provide the year the work was put into a fixed form.

Once your work becomes available to the public, especially if it is being sold and generates revenue, it is vital that the owner of a copyright keep track of how the work is being used, and by whom. Almost any kind of copyrighted work is much easier to copy and sell illegally than ever before. Vigilance on the part of the copyright holder and other interested parties, such as book or music publishers who earn their livings by selling copyrighted works of authors, is an absolute necessity.

If another party is duplicating copyrighted works without permission, or is selling them without authorization, then infringement has occurred. As a practical matter, not all infringement is worth pursuing. For example, if copying and distribution of your work is being done on a small scale, the matter may not be worth your while to pursue, or maybe you feel that the infringement is working to your benefit by increasing the public's exposure to your work. If, however, infringement is causing you harm or loss, then you should consider initiating legal action. Should you go this route, be sure to employ a competent attorney who is familiar with this area of practice.

FAIR USE

It is not unusual to hear part of a popular melody played in another song or to see a line from a literary work used in a different book. True, the original works were copyrighted at creation and their authors have exclusive rights to them, but not necessarily to every last bit. The concept involved here is "fair use," a limitation Congress has placed on the reach of copyrights.

Courts look at the following criteria when deciding cases involving questions of fair use:

1. The purpose and character of the use. If somebody is not using copyrighted material with the intent of making a monetary gain, a teacher in an educational institution who uses it to further class instruction, for example, they have more flexibility than another who is seeking profit. The profit seeker is still entitled to fair use, but must be very careful about how much copyrighted material to utilize, which brings us to the next criterion.

2. How substantial the portion used is in relation to the entire work. Using a bit or piece is generally safe, but the risks of infringement rise as the size of the borrowed excerpt does.

3. The nature of the copyrighted work. If a copyrighted work was intended for intellectual or educational purposes whose benefits are primarily social, usually quite a bit of leeway is allowed in using parts of it. When a copyrighted work was produced with the intention of making money, such as a popular song or movie, the copyright owners are probably going to be a lot less liberal about it, as will the courts.

4. How the copyrighted work's value is affected by the use. Sometimes the use of copyrighted material by another can actually benefit the copyright holder if it produces more interest in the work. If the value of a copyright is reduced, however, through loss of sales or anything else that diminishes or tarnishes it, then successful legal action is a greater possibility.

In 1961, the Report of the Registrar of Copyrights on the General Revision of the U.S. Copyright Law provided some examples of what courts have considered to be fair use. These are:

- "Quotation of excerpts in a review or criticism for purposes of illustration or comment;
- Quotation of short passages in a scholarly or technical work, for illustration or classification of the author's observations;
- Use in a parody of some of the content of the work parodied;
- Summary of an address or article, with brief quotations, in a news report;
- Reproduction by a library of a portion of a work to replace part of a damaged copy;
- Reproduction by a teacher or student of a small part of a work to illustrate a lesson;
- Reproduction of a work in legislative or judicial proceedings or reports;
- Incidental and fortuitous reproduction, in a newsreel or broadcast, of a work located in the scene of an event being reported."

Despite these guidelines, it is still hard to distinguish between fair use and infringement. No definite numbers are given as to the amounts of notes or words that can be used without permission, so what looks like a fair use to one person could just as easily appear as the theft of intellectual property to another. This happened frequently a few years back when it became common for the authors of rap songs to take recognizable samples from previously recorded material and incorporate them into their own creations. For the most part, rap artists are able to do this because, even with samples that are easy to recognize, they serve as quotes that are used in a new work, rather than as a repetition of what the original artist did, which would be infringement.

It is up to the copyright holder to decide how much, or little, use of their material they are willing to tolerate before doing something about it. In the event you want to use a portion of another's work and have any doubt about whether it constitutes fair use or not, the best course is to ask them for permission to use it. If the answer is no, proceed with caution, as legal trouble could be in your future. Because the fair use criteria leave plenty of room for interpretation on a case-by-case basis, finding a good attorney is a must if you are serious about pursuing the matter through legal avenues.

INFRINGEMENT

If you discover that somebody is infringing your copyright by using your original work of authorship for their own profit, there are legal measures you can take, but they must be instituted at your own initiative. As with patents, there is no mechanism, no special police force, in place to go after the offending parties. Also in common with patents, it is best to pursue legal matters with an attorney who is experienced in the area. Since that can be expensive, be clear on what you are trying to accomplish, and whether or not it is worthwhile, before proceeding.

Legal remedies provided by the Copyright Act include the following:

- A court could grant an injunction to prevent the continued infringement of a copyright.
- Illegal copies of copyrighted material may be impounded or destroyed.
- The infringer can be found liable for damages, lost profits, and cost incurred to pursue the matter legally.
- Should the infringement be judged criminal, the offending party can be fined and jailed.

As mentioned earlier in this chapter, judging whether a work is an infringement or merely a parody, example of fair use, or a sufficiently original work in its own right is difficult. Honda found this out the hard way. In 1994 they aired a commercial where one of their cars was being chased by a helicopter. The commercial featured a character with similarities to the James Bond character, which MGM holds the copyright on. MGM sued Honda and Honda's advertising agency, eventually winning a preliminary injunction that barred further airing of the commercial. The court decided that, rather than being an example of fair use, Honda might harm the value of MGM's copyright, saying "It is likely that James Bond's association with a low-end Honda model will threaten its value in the eyes of future upscale licensees."

INTERNATIONAL COPYRIGHTS

The amount or recognition and protection afforded patents outside their country of origin varies significantly. No mechanism exists that will automatically give you the same exclusive rights in other countries that are automatic in the United States.

As copying copyrighted materials became easier, so did the problem of pirated materials grow. In an economy that is increasingly information based, products that are based on ideas, such as software programs and musical creations, cost a lot of money in the initial creation process (think of the millions and millions of dollars necessary to develop a new version of Windows), but are cheap to reproduce. A new CD by a popular musical group requires a significant investment of time, energy, creativity, and money, so the company that produces it feels justified in charging $17 a copy when it comes out, even though making each CD subsequent to the first probably costs less than $1. Somebody in a country where copyright laws are lax, or not enforced, then, can simply make inexpensive copies of a CD, sell them for $2 or so apiece, and make plenty of money, just as computer programs that cost $100 in a store can be copied cheaply and sold at a profit far below the retail cost.

There are two primary international copyright conventions that the United States belongs to, the Berne Union for the Protection of Literary and Artistic Property and the Universal Copyright Convention. Along with these, the United States has entered into a variety of bilateral copyright agreements with other countries for the purpose of providing mutual copyright protection. If you need specific details on how particular countries treat U.S. copyrights, these are available from the Copyright Office.

EARNING ROYALTIES AND THE SALE OF COPYRIGHTS

Royalties are fees paid to the owners of copyrights by those using the intellectual property. The size of royalty payments is determined by the demand for the particular item. If you want to use the characters from the *Toy Story* movies as part of a promotion for your new business, be prepared to have their use come with a hefty price tag. But if you decide instead to use an unknown song by an obscure songwriter, the cost will be a lot less. Oftentimes authors are glad to see their works receive public exposure and freely give permission without needing any payment in return.

The sale of a copyright can be an effective means of getting money in the present that might take a much longer time to generate through royalties, provided you strike a good bargain. The advantage is that you get paid today and do not have to worry about the copyright any longer. The disadvantage is the risk of selling copyrights for an amount far less than their ultimate value proves to be. In all sales of copyrights, good legal help is a must to help you determine if you are receiving fair market value for your work.

Most authors of copyrighted works who are interested in marketing them to a large audience do so through companies with the resources to copy, distribute, and market the work, a daunting set of tasks to attempt on one's own. The author then receives a percentage of the sales price in the form of royalties. With the Internet it is possible for individuals to reach a large audience on their own and distribute their wares electronically, thereby enabling them to keep all the proceeds instead of a percentage, but that method has yet to prove as effective in generating sales as the traditional channels.

COPYRIGHTS AND THE WEB

Anybody who has a web site that is important to their business should copyright it. Web sites enable you to reach an almost limitless audience and if yours has features that enable you to do so in unique ways, do not risk losing full rights and protections in them.

Though computer code that is stored on a disc clearly meets the copyright requirement that an author's creation be "fixed in any tangible medium of expression, now known or later developed," web sites seem a little less certain. Is the web page that results from a computer program in a fixed form? And what of the fact that many of these pages are fluid, being added to and subtracted from on a regular basis? Fortunately, the Copyright Office regularly accepts registrations for web sites and seems very willing to adapt the law to the needs of novel expressions made with the aid of new technology.

The issue of whether or not a web site has been published or not is also unclear. A web site used for an intranet network, like one used at a place of employment for workers to communicate with each other, may not be seen as meeting the requirements of copyright law, which considers evidence of publication to be "the distribution of copies of phonorecords of a work to the public by sale, transfer of ownership, or by rental, lease or lending." Further, "A public performance or display of a work does not itself constitute publication." If the site is online and used with the intent of having people access it, chances are that it will be considered to have been published. Fortunately, so far it seems that if the copyright holder considers their web site to have been published, the Copyright Office will concur.

Considering how rapidly web sites become available to anybody with a computer and a modem, rapid registration is more important than it is for other forms of copyrightable creations. As discussed in earlier sections of this chapter, registration provides the copyright holder with better legal options, even though a work is automatically copyrighted at creation. In order to sue somebody for infringement, you must have registered your work with the Copyright Office within three months of the initial publication, or, at the very least, have done so before the infringement occurs. You can still collect actual damages without registration, but these may not amount to much. In fact, the possible actual damages may not even be enough to cover your legal fees.

Actual damages include losses suffered by the author or profits that the infringer used the author's creation to accumulate. Unless the infringer made a lot of money misappropriating the intellectual property in question, there probably will not be much to go after. If registration has been properly accomplished, however, the copyright holder can seek statutory damages up to $100,000, along with attorney fees and court costs. With registration being such an easy process, there is no reason to do anything other than take care of it as soon as possible.

CASE STUDY   Words to Eat by: The Dinosaur Bar-B-Que

The Dinosaur Bar-B-Que is a great example of how different forms of intellectual property can be integrated in a way where each enhances the other. In an upcoming chapter on trade secrets we go into some of the establishment's history and discuss the value of one of the owner's, John Stage's, sauces. These sauces, used in conjunction with great food, music, and service, are employed to build a highly regarded brand name, incorporated in a trademark (the topic of the next chapter) that is associated with a wonderfully unique pair of restaurants.

As a sort of guided exercise try typing dinosaurbar-b-que.com on your computer. Notice that the trademark is right there to assure you that you are at the right spot when the first page comes up. After all, there are lots of barbecue places on the Web, and it would be easy to hit on a few of the wrong ones before you made it to the real Dinosaur.

Without copyright and trademark protection, anybody could copy this site and use it to direct web surfers to their own businesses and products. But, with a copyrighted web site that features his registered trademark, John Stage can take legal action should anybody infringe on his intellectual property.

With a copyrighted web site John can provide information on upcoming bands playing, biker events, featured recipes, and the food he serves. If you click on the menu, you will notice how nicely it provides a flavor of the establishment and reinforces other aspects of the Dinosaur experience. In addition, the Dinosaur web site is an ideal place to show off, and take orders for, his sauces and his recently published cookbook.

Recently John Stage has had another successful copyrighting experience. He published a cook book, along with Nancy Radke, called *DINOSAUR BAR-B-QUE; An American Roadhouse*. Though having a copyright helps, it was the quality and reputation of the Dinosaur Bar-B-Que that caused the first printing of 25,000 copies to sell within a matter of a few short weeks, no small accomplishment for a largely barbecue based cookbook first published at the beginning of summer, a time when the market is choked with other (obviously inferior) books featuring similar types of recipes.

John Stage is not an expert on copyrighting; he does not need to be because by focusing on what he does best he can hire people who are. But he does recognize the value of his original creations and the need to give them the best possible protection. He has worked far too hard not to.

CASE STUDY   What's in a Name? Paychex in Print

Paychex is another example of an excellent trademark (more on them in the next chapter), where the name clearly indicates what they do and becomes an increasingly valuable piece of intellectual property as they continue to grow and do it exceptionally well. As does the Dinosaur, they have a web site of the same name, but what I want to highlight is how they also use different forms of intellectual property to complement each other and effectively promote the business.

Processing paychecks (one among many of Paycheck's services) does not bring to mind creativity and innovation for most people. It sounds like a pretty mundane function that just has to be ground out. In reality, that is not the case, and Paychex has done an excellent job of using copyrighted material not only to let potential clients know about them, but to demonstrate to existing and future clients that they are, indeed, a creative and innovative firm. By establishing that impression, Paychex becomes a more attractive choice for both payroll services and the additional functions they perform, along with establishing credibility in advance as an out of the box thinker and paving the way for acceptance of services still to come.

Figures 10.1–10.4 are examples of some particularly creative, and copyrighted, advertising Paychex has done. The only alteration made here is to blank out the number of clients they serve, simply because the old numbers are so much smaller than the present number of clients. Notice how well the first advertisement draws attention to a function that readers might normally pass over. The picture of the squirrel generates curiosity, then the wording keeps the reader engaged with its clever use of language and, before she knows it, the reader has gone through the entire piece, with the trademarked name at the end firming up the association among the company, what they do, and how creatively they let people know about it.

With its winterized turkey, the next advertisement does the quickest job of catching attention, then keeps it by referring to the concept in the print portion. The copy does an excellent job of showing the particular functions to be done as tedious and time consuming, while Paychex comes off looking efficient and creative, a business that is interesting in its ability and enthusiasm for performing tasks that are undesirable to everybody else, but not to them.

The same idea is seen in the third advertisement, featuring the cow with the barnyard in the background. My favorite of the Paychex advertisements is the last one, with the five beans followed by one that has sprouted. What is different here is that the professionals who recommend Paychex to their clients, CPA firms, are flattered by inferring that their superior judgment has resulted in their becoming more evolved than typical bean counters.

With copyright protection, these advertisements are off limits to anybody but Paychex. Anybody who wants to use them, including me, must get permission from the company. With Paychex having sole rights to their creative works, they enjoy the exclusive benefits. While this is very positive for them, it must be remembered that the reverse can also be true. There are plenty of copyrighted works, be they advertisements or otherwise, that create a negative impression in their audience and actually reduce the chance that the person who has come across the piece will become a consumer of the product it promotes. The Paychex advertisements, however, are an excellent example of how copyrighted intellectual property can enable a company to enhance its value.

YOU CAN GO NUTS OVER PAYROLL.

OR FEED IT TO PAYCHEX.

Why scamper from one payroll crisis to the next? Let Paychex free you up for more important matters. We're the nuts for any small business that needs payroll and payroll tax preparation services.

You'll find Paychex to be cost-effective and accurate for handling your clients' time-consuming, laborious paperwork. Plus, we make sure clients meet all deadlines to avoid costly penalties and we supply detailed records for accounting.

Best of all, our services are comprehensive — including automatic enrollment and electronic payroll tax deposits for your clients who must meet the new IRS "EFTPS" mandate.

Maybe that's why more than small- to mid-size businesses nationwide count on Paychex for payroll, payroll tax preparation and deposits. Companies also turn to Paychex for such benefits administration services as 401(k) programs and section 125 cafeteria plans.

Stop shelling out hundreds of hours on tedious payroll preparation. Call Paychex at 1-800-322-7292.

PAYCHEX®

911 Panorama Trail South, Rochester, NY 14625
www.paychex.com

FIGURE 10.1   Paychex Squirrel Ad

Reprinted with permission of Paychex, Inc. Paychex is a registered trademark of Paychex, Inc.

FIGURE 10.2   Paychex Turkey Ad
Reprinted with permission of Paychex, Inc. Paychex is a registered
trademark of Paychex, Inc.

FIGURE 10.3   Paychex Cow Ad

Reprinted with permission of Paychex, Inc. Paychex is a registered trademark of Paychex, Inc.

FIGURE 10.4   Paychex Bean Ad

**Reprinted with permission of Paychex, Inc. Paychex is a registered
trademark of Paychex, Inc.**

CASE STUDY   Staking Out New Territory: Bonadio & Co.

Patents are the devices that get most of the credit for protecting new innovations, but it is not unusual for business people to launch new endeavors that rely on the protections offered by copyrights.

Bonadio & Co. is a CPA firm that got its start in the late 1970s when Tom Bonadio left a large accounting firm to start a new business with a partner. With hardly any clients in the beginning, Bonadio & Co. had to be innovative in order to survive and grow. Fortunately for them, they were in a very conservative field where there was plenty of room for creativity available to anyone willing to spot, and take advantage of, opportunities. Tom saw marketing his business as an area that other CPA firms, at the time, ignored, so he made it a specialty and went on to attract a large client base, a base whose growth was furthered by Bonadio and Co.'s reputation for excellence in providing clients with a range of accounting services. Today, they are the largest independent CPA firm in Upstate New York.

Achieving success in their traditional areas of practice did not keep Bonadio & Co. from continuing to be alert to new opportunities. An example of just one of these came in 1997 when changes in the tax law spawned 529 plans, which were attractive new programs that allowed parents to put money aside in investment accounts for their children's future college expenses and avoid taxes until the money was withdrawn. A partner at Bonadio & Co., Joe Hurley, the head of the taxation division, recognized these plans for the great opportunity they were and quickly became an expert, no simple task considering tax plans can vary considerably from state to state. Before long he was publishing articles on the subject in a variety of newspapers and financial magazines, which were so good that outside firms began hiring him to give talks and act as a consultant.

Joe took the plunge of writing a book on 529 plans, called *The Best Way to Save for College*. Instead of going through the tortuous process of finding a publisher, Bonadio & Co. formed their own publishing company, BonaCom publications, and produced the book themselves. With a regular newsletter on 529 plans to go with it, along with the author's continuing to speak and write articles, the book began selling well right out of the gate. With copyright protection on their side, Bonadio & Co. were able to stake out new territory and give themselves a significant advantage over any potential competitors. Others were free to write books on the same subject, too, of course, but they could not duplicate Joe Hurley's, which meant they would have to play catch-up by creating an original new work if they wanted to keep competitive. And this was in an area where the amount of information to be absorbed by a newcomer could be daunting.

CASE STUDY   Staking Out New Territory: Bonadio & Co.
(Continued)

It should be remembered that a copyright, like a patent, is only worth-while if the creation it protects is of a high enough quality that it warrants guarding. Copyrighting a bad book makes no more sense than insuring a junked car. In the case of *The Best Way to Save for College,* Joe received such a favorable response, in the form of glowing reviews that portrayed his book as an indispensable guide to 529 plans, that copyright protection was a must.

The success of this copyrighted product inspired Bonadio & Co. to launch another, a web site designed to provide information on 529 plans, take orders for the book, accept subscriptions to the newsletter, and provide updates as changes in 529 plans were introduced. The popularity of the web site took off almost instantly, even catching a firm known for optimism by surprise. They saw what an opportunity this venture had grown into and spun off a new company devoted to it, with Joe Hurley as its CEO. The address is savingforcollege.com. It is an excellent example of the cross-fertilization that is possible with copyrights, where the web site promotes the book and newsletter, which each draws attention to the other, in addition to spreading the word about a unique CPA firm, the only one I know of that has developed its own successful dot-com company.

All of this was possible because Joe Hurley spotted an opportunity while in the employ of a firm with an innovative culture, then went on to build on his strengths with the aid of the protections afforded by copyrights. While engaged in producing his early copyrighted material on 529 plans (the columns he wrote), he could not possibly predict what his works of authorship would grow into. The quality of his copyrighted material opened up new markets that Bonadio & Co. were ready to enter, with even more ambitious uses of copyrighted creations.

THE TRADEMARK STORY

11

BRANDING YOUR PROPERTY

About six years ago Michael Doherty registered the domain name peta.org. Then he created a web site there (it has since moved) called People Eating Tasty Animals that made fun of the views of the animal rights group PETA. PETA apparently did not find the use of its name humorous and now there is a legal battle going on over whether Mr. Doherty was within his rights to use the domain name.

As with the example used to open Chapter 7, the issue again is how far a parody can go without violating intellectual property rules, in this case for a trademark instead of a copyright. Doherty claims the domain name was part of the parody. PETA, who has a registered trademark for the name, charges that the domain name promoted the false impression that they were associated with the web site.

Because trademarks are essentially brand names, their owners are understandably concerned that they be used to convey the intended impression. Creators of parody, just as understandably, feel that using a trademark in a humorous fashion, whether the owner believes it funny or not, is an important part of our right to free speech. Parodies are considered literary creations and are covered by the First Amendment. Infringing on a trademark, though, is illegal. As this case, which has not reached a final resolution as of this writing demonstrates, the distinction between the two can be a difficult one to draw.

WHAT IS A TRADEMARK?

Trademarks are used to identify and distinguish the goods and services of one producer from those of others. The goal of trademarking is to establish a powerful brand name that is synonymous with quality and value in the minds of consumers, making your product the natural first choice.

Trademarks can be symbols, words, names, sounds, devices, or any combination of these. In our daily lives we see hundreds of them, such as McDonald's golden arches, the Nike "swoosh," Mercedes' double star, the Apple Computer's bitten apple, and the Good Housekeeping seal of approval. Each of these trademarks is a valuable asset that firms will go to great lengths to protect. In effect, an established trademark provides constant advertising, without the expense.

For a new business a trademark can be a wonderful mechanism for establishing a positive image in the minds of consumers that sets the new business apart from competitors. Established firms rely on trademarks to keep their products in the public mind and, because trademarks have no time limit, can use them to extend the advantages patents bring long after the patents themselves expire.

THE BIRTH OF A TRADEMARK

Now that we know a little about what trademarks are, we will learn about the process of securing one by using a demonstration product, of my own. A few years ago, I became interested in brewing my own beer, so I went out and bought some books on it, invested in the necessary equipment, and started experimenting. Making good beer is not a complicated process, and before long I was producing what, to me, seemed to be pretty good stuff.

One night I was home by myself when I heard the sound of exploding glass in the kitchen. I ran into the kitchen, expecting to see a broken window and somebody coming through it. The windows were fine; my beer was not. I had bottled my latest batch and was letting it ferment in a kitchen cabinet. Now I saw that some of my precious beer was dripping out and onto the floor. Tragedy had struck, in the form of an exploding 24-ounce bottle.

Exploding bottles usually mean that the bottle was too full when it was capped, too much priming sugar was added, or the beer went bad. Careful enough to be on a bomb squad, I opened another bottle in the sink to test it. Sure enough, the beer had gone bad. Not just a little bad either; it tasted foul enough to kill off a herd of goats.

The taste inspired me to think of the perfect name for my beer. I would call it Lethal Injection Ale. Now, I had no intention of continuing to cook up lousy batches of the stuff on purpose, but, since the style I like has a pretty strong taste anyway, it appealed to me. This was a beer for serious beer consumers, who could handle heaping helpings of hops and malt, not something for those fainthearted drinkers of lite beer.

To go with the name, I thought a descriptive little picture would be nice. So I came up with a pencil drawing of a man sitting in a recliner, with a jug of beer mounted on a pole and the beer flowing into his arm through an IV. The picture was inside a circle that was formed by the beer's name, Lethal Injection Ale. (See Figure 11.1, a new version

FIGURE 11.1   Lethal Injection Ale Trademark

drawn by my nephew.) I used my computer to make some labels and started putting them on subsequent batches. That is as far as I went, but what if I wanted to take the next step and go into the business of selling my beer, assuming I could keep it from blowing up in the hands of my customers?

The first step is to make sure my inspiration for one really qualifies as a trademark. If the idea is merely a generic or descriptive mark, I am out of luck. So, if I tried to trademark "beer" or "strong ale," I would not succeed. Beer is an entire category of products, and strong ale is a simple description. The trademarks that hold up best in legal challenges are those that are fanciful or arbitrary, something that is not an obvious part or description of the product. In fact, even a term that had been successfully trademarked in the past can lose its status if it becomes too closely connected with the product itself. For example, Aspirin and Kleenex are no longer trademarks because, instead of describing the product, like the term Kodak film does, they came to stand for the product itself. In essence, when a trademark goes from being an adjective (descriptive) to a noun (the thing itself), it becomes a generic term that does not qualify for trademark protection. If Lethal Injection Ale ever went from being a brand name to standing for beer itself in the public mind, I, too, would lose my trademark.

Along with generic or descriptive terms, there are some other things to watch out for. For example, you cannot trademark a slogan that makes laudatory claims or just provides information, so I cannot trademark the phrase "New York's greatest beer." Nor could I trademark Lethal Injection Ale if somebody else was already using the name.

REGISTERING A TRADEMARK

If I really thought my trademark had value, I would register it with the Patent and Trademark Office. There is no rule that says I have to, but federal trademark registration is beneficial for a number of reasons. First of all, it gives notice to others that I have a claim on the trademark and is good evidence that I own it. So, if the day comes when somebody else decides to use my trademark without my permission, I can initiate legal action to stop them or collect a judgment based on documented evidence that I had the trademark first.

Even if nobody deliberately uses the trademark another already has placed in use, there are times when the idea occurs to somebody who has no idea of a prior claim. If you have a trademark you want to use and develop, then be sure it is not already in circulation. This is more important now than ever because, with the Internet and web sites, a duplicate trademark in another part of the country that never would have been discovered in years past, could easily be stumbled across today just in the course of doing a simple search.

Further, registering your trademark in the United States can be used as a first step in obtaining trademark registration in other countries and the domestic registration can be filed with the U.S. Customs Service to prevent goods that infringe on your patent from being imported from other countries.

Once I decide it is worthwhile to trademark Lethal Injection Ale and register it with the Patent and Trademark Office, I have some options. The old-fashioned way is write or call them and ask to be sent forms that I can fill out by hand, then mail back in. The easiest and most sensible way, though, is to take advantage of the Internet. At uspto.gov you can get all the forms you need, along with clear instructions for how to fill them out. Trademark applications are much simpler than those for patents and can be completed fairly quickly. An even better alternative than downloading the forms is to use the Trademark Electronic Application System (TEAS), found at teas.uspto.gov. TEAS allows you to complete the application online and submit it directly to the USPTO.

TEAS is easy to find at uspto.gov, is very simple to use, and the service provides you with complete instructions. As with applying for patents, be sure to do a prior search to make sure the mark is not already in use.

USING A TRADEMARK

Once a trademark has been registered, it is important to mark it clearly in use. This way, if you later discover the mark is being infringed on, the fact that your original was clearly labeled prevents the excuse of not knowing about it from being used. The superscript TM should be used before it is registered, then a capital *R* with a circle around it after the registration.

The stronger and more positive the association between a product and a trademark, the longer and larger are the potential benefits. After a patent expires, anybody can duplicate the technology. But if customers are used to buying a product based on a trademark they are comfortable and trust, the protection afforded can last many years beyond the limit of a patent.

TRADEMARKS ON THE WEB

In recent years there has been an explosion of trademarks on domain names used on the Internet. As with patents and copyrights, existing law, largely written before the Internet was a factor in commerce, has been adapted to the technology. Overall, the fit has been pretty good and the same standards apply as do traditional trademarks.

The difference now is that domain names can be viewed by more people, more readily, than was ever possible for traditional trademarks. This means that, once again, seeking protection for your intellectual property at the earliest possible opportunity is more important than ever.

Figure 11.2 is the guide for examiners at the USPTO who look at trademarks, which will give you a better idea of what they are looking for.

UNITED STATES DEPARTMENT OF COMMERCE
Patent and Trademark Office
OFFICE OF ASSISTANT COMMISSIONER FOR TRADEMARKS
2900 Crystal Drive
Arlington, Virginia 22202-3513

EXAMINATION GUIDE NO. 2-99

September 29, 1999

MARKS COMPOSED, IN WHOLE OR IN PART, OF DOMAIN NAMES

I. Introduction And Background

A domain name is part of a Uniform Resource Locator (URL), which is the address of a site or document on the Internet. In general, a domain name is comprised of a second-level domain, a "dot," and a top-level domain (TLD). The wording to the left of the "dot" is the second-level domain, and the wording to the right of the "dot" is the TLD.

> *Example*: If the domain name is "XYZ.COM," the term "XYZ" is a second-level domain and the term "COM" is a TLD.

A domain name is usually preceded in a URL by "http://www." The "http://" refers to the protocol used to transfer information, and the "www" refers to World Wide Web, a graphical hypermedia interface for viewing and exchanging information. There are two types of TLDs: generic and country code.

FIGURE 11.2   Trademark Examiner's Guide

Generic TLDs

Generic TLDs are designated for use by the public. Each generic TLD is intended for use by a certain type of organization. For example, the TLD ".com" is for use by commercial, for profit organizations. However, the administrator of the .com, .net, .org and .edu TLDs does not check the requests of parties seeking domain names to ensure that such parties are a type of organization that should be using those TLDs. On the other hand, .mil, .gov, and .int TLD applications are checked, and only the U.S. military, the U.S. government, or international organizations are allowed in the domain space. The following is a list of the current generic TLDs and the intended users:

.com	commercial, for profit organizations
.edu	4 year, degree granting colleges/universities
.gov	U.S. federal government agencies
.int	international organizations
.mil	U.S. military organizations, even if located outside the U.S.
.net	network infrastructure machines and organizations
.org	miscellaneous, usually non-profit organizations and individuals

Country Code TLDs

Country code TLDs are for use by each individual country. Each country determines who may use their code. For example, some countries require that users of their code be citizens or have some association with the country, while other countries do not. The following are examples of some of the country code TLDs currently in use:

.jp	for use by Japan
.tm	for use by Turkmenistan
.tv	for use by Tuvalu
.uk	for use by the United Kingdom

Proposed TLDs

Due to growing space limitations, several new TLDs have been proposed, including the following:

.arts	cultural and entertainment activities
.firm	businesses
.info	entities providing information services
.nom	individual or personal nomenclature
.rec	recreation or entertainment activities
.store	businesses offering goods to purchase
.web	entities emphasizing activities related to the web

While these proposed TLDs are not currently used on the Internet as TLDs, applicants may include them in their marks.

FIGURE 11.2 *(Continued)*

Applications for registration of marks composed of domain names

Since the implementation of the domain name system, the Patent and Trademark Office (Office) has received a growing number of applications for marks composed of domain names. While the majority of domain name applications are for computer services such as Internet content providers (organizations that provide web sites with information about a particular topic or field) and online ordering services, a substantial number are for marks used on other types of services or goods.

When a trademark, service mark, collective mark or certification mark is composed, in whole or in part, of a domain name, neither the beginning of the URL (http://www.) nor the TLD have any source indicating significance. Instead, those designations are merely devices that every Internet site provider must use as part of its address. Today, advertisements for all types of products and services routinely include a URL for the web site of the advertiser. Just as the average person with no special knowledge recognizes "800" or "1-800" followed by seven digits or letters as one of the prefixes used for every toll-free phone number, the average person familiar with the Internet recognizes the format for a domain name and understands that "http," "www," and a TLD are a part of every URL.

Applications for registration of marks consisting of domain names are subject to the same requirements as all other applications for federal trademark registration. This Examination Guide identifies and discusses some of the issues that commonly arise in the examination of domain name mark applications.

II. Use as a Mark

A. Use Applications

A mark composed of a domain name is registrable as a trademark or service mark only if it functions as a source identifier. The mark as depicted on the specimens must be presented in a manner that will be perceived by potential purchasers as indicating source and not as merely an informational indication of the domain name address used to access a web site. *See In re Eilberg*, 49 USPQ2d 1955 (TTAB 1998).

In *Eilberg*, the Trademark Trial and Appeal Board (Board) held that a term that only serves to identify the applicant's domain name or the location on the Internet where the applicant's web site appears, and does not separately identify applicant's services, does not function as a service mark. The applicant's proposed mark was WWW.EILBERG.COM , and the specimens showed that the mark was used on letterhead and business cards in the following manner:

WILLIAM H. EILBERG
ATTORNEY AT LAW

820 HOMESTEAD ROAD, PO BOX 7
JENKINTOWN, PENNSYLVANIA 19046
215-883-4600
FAX. 215-883-4603
EMAIL WWW.EILBERG.COM

PATENTS TRADEMARKS
AND COPYRIGHTS

WWW.EILBERG.COM

FIGURE 11.2 *(Continued)*

The Board affirmed the examining attorney's refusal of registration on the ground that the matter presented for registration did not function as a mark, stating that:

> [T]he asserted mark, as displayed on applicant's letterhead, does not function as a service mark identifying and distinguishing applicant's legal services and, as presented, is not capable of doing so. As shown, the asserted mark identifies applicant's Internet domain name, by use of which one can access applicant's Web site. In other words, the asserted mark WWW.EILBERG.COM merely indicates the location on the Internet where applicant's Web site appears. It does not separately identify applicant's legal services as such. *Cf. In re The Signal Companies, Inc.*, 228 USPQ 956 (TTAB 1986).
>
> This is not to say that, if used appropriately, the asserted mark or portions thereof may not be trademarks or [service marks]. For example, if applicant's law firm name were, say, EILBERG.COM and were presented prominently on applicant's letterheads and business cards as the name under which applicant was rendering its legal services, then that mark may well be registrable.

Id. at 1956.

The examining attorney must review the specimens in order to determine how the proposed mark is actually used. It is the perception of the ordinary customer that determines whether the asserted mark functions as a mark, not the applicant's intent, hope or expectation that it do so. *See In re Standard Oil Co.*, 275 F.2d 945, 125 USPQ 227 (C.C.P.A. 1960).

If the proposed mark is used in a way that would be perceived as nothing more than an address at which the applicant can be contacted, registration must be refused. Examples of a domain name used only as an Internet address include a domain name used in close proximity to language referring to the domain name as an address, or a domain name displayed merely as part of the information on how to contact the applicant.

> *Example*: The mark is WWW.XYZ.COM for on-line ordering services in the field of clothing. Specimens of use consisting of an advertisement that states "visit us on the web at www.xyz.com" do not show service mark use of the proposed mark.
>
> *Example*: The mark is XYZ.COM for financial consulting services. Specimens of use consisting of a business card that refers to the service and lists a phone number, fax number, and the domain name sought to be registered do not show service mark use of the proposed mark.

Refusal of registration

If the specimens of use fail to show the domain name used as a mark and the applicant seeks registration on the Principal Register, the examining attorney must refuse registration on the ground that the matter presented for registration does not function as a mark. The statutory bases for the refusals are:

FIGURE 11.2 *(Continued)*

For trademarks: Trademark Act §§1, 2 and 45, 15 U.S.C. §§1051, 1052, and 1127

For service marks: Trademark Act §§1, 2, 3 and 45, 15 U.S.C. §§1051, 1052, 1053 and 1127

If the applicant seeks registration on the Supplemental Register, the examining attorney must refuse registration under Trademark Act §23, 15 U.S.C. §1091.

B. Advertising One's Own Products or Services on the Internet is not a Service

Advertising one's own products or services is not a service. *See In re Reichhold Chemicals, Inc.*, 167 USPQ 376 (TTAB 1970); TMEP §1301.01(a)(ii). Therefore, businesses that create a web site for the sole purpose of advertising their own products or services cannot register a domain name used to identify that activity. In examination, the issue usually arises when the applicant describes the activity as a registrable service, e.g., "providing information about [a particular field]," but the specimens of use make it clear that the web site merely advertises the applicant's own products or services. In this situation, the examining attorney must refuse registration because the mark is used to identify an activity that does not constitute a "service" within the meaning of the Trademark Act. Trademark Act §§1, 2, 3 and 45, 15 U.S.C. §§1051, 1052, 1053 and 1127.

C. Agreement of Mark on Drawing with Mark on Specimens of Use

In a domain name mark (e.g., XYZ.COM or HTTP://WWW.XYZ.COM), consumers look to the second level domain name for source identification, not to the TLD or the terms "http://www." or "www." Therefore, it is usually acceptable to depict only the second level domain name on the drawing page, even if the specimens of use show a mark that includes the TLD or the terms "http://www." or "www." *Cf. Institut National des Appellations D'Origine v. Vintners Int'l Co., Inc.*, 954 F.2d 1574, 22 USPQ2d 1190 (Fed. Cir. 1992) (CHABLIS WITH A TWIST held to be registrable separately from CALIFORNIA CHABLIS WITH A TWIST); *In re Raychem Corporation*, 12 USPQ2d 1399 (TTAB 1989) (refusal to register "TINEL-LOCK" based on specimens showing "TRO6AI-TINEL-LOCK-RING" reversed). *See also* 37 C.F.R. §2.51(a)(1) and TMEP §807.14 *et. seq.*

Example: The specimens of use show the mark HTTP://WWW.XYZ.COM. The applicant may elect to depict only the term "XYZ" on the drawing page.

Sometimes the specimens of use fail to show the entire mark sought to be registered (e.g., the drawing of the mark is HTTP://WWW.XYZ.COM, but the specimens only show XYZ). If the drawing of the mark includes a TLD, or the terms "http://www.," or "www.," the specimens of use must also show the mark used with those terms. Trademark Act §1(a)(1)(C), 15 U.S.C. §1051(a)(1)(C).

Example: If the drawing of the mark is XYZ.COM, specimens of use that only show the term XYZ are unacceptable.

D. Marks Comprised Solely of TLDs for Domain Name Registry Services

If a mark is composed solely of a TLD for "domain name registry services" (e.g., the services currently provided by Network Solutions, Inc. of registering .com domain names), registration should be refused

FIGURE 11.2 *(Continued)*

under Trademark Act §§1, 2, 3 and 45, 15 U.S.C. §§1051, 1052, 1053 and 1127, on the ground that the TLD would not be perceived as a mark. The examining attorney should include evidence from the NEXIS® database, the Internet, or other sources to show that the proposed mark is currently used as a TLD or is under consideration as a new TLD.

If the TLD merely describes the subject or user of the domain space, registration should be refused under Trademark Act §2(e)(1), 15 U.S.C. §2(e)(1), on the ground that the TLD is merely descriptive of the registry services.

E. Intent-to-Use Applications

A refusal of registration on the ground that the matter presented for registration does not function as a mark relates to the manner in which the asserted mark is used. Therefore, generally, in an intent-to-use application, a mark that includes a domain name will not be refused on this ground until the applicant has submitted specimens of use with either an amendment to allege use under Trademark Act §1(c), or a statement of use under Trademark Act §1(d), 15 U.S.C. §1051(c) or (d). However, the examining attorney should include an advisory note in the first Office Action that registration may be refused if the proposed mark, as used on the specimens, identifies only an Internet address. This is done strictly as a courtesy. If information regarding this possible ground for refusal is not provided to the applicant prior to the filing of the allegation of use, the Office is in no way precluded from refusing registration on this basis.

III. Surnames

If a mark is composed of a surname and a TLD, the examining attorney must refuse registration because the mark is primarily merely a surname under Trademark Act §2(e)(4), 15 U.S.C. §1052(e)(4). A TLD has no trademark significance. If the primary significance of a term is that of a surname, adding a TLD to the surname does not alter the primary significance of the mark as a surname. *Cf. In re I. Lewis Cigar Mfg. Co.*, 205 F.2d 204, 98 USPQ 265 (C.C.P.A. 1953) (S. SEIDENBERG & CO'S. held primarily merely a surname); *In re Hamilton Pharmaceuticals Ltd.*, 27 USPQ2d 1939 (TTAB 1993) (HAMILTON PHARMACEUTICALS for pharmaceutical products held primarily merely a surname); *In re Cazes*, 21 USPQ2d 1796 (TTAB 1991) (BRASSERIE LIPP held primarily merely a surname where "brasserie" is a generic term for applicant's restaurant services). *See also* TMEP §1211.01(b).

IV. Descriptiveness

If a proposed mark is composed of a merely descriptive term(s) combined with a TLD, the examining attorney should refuse registration under Trademark Act §2(e)(1), 15 U.S.C. §1052(e)(1), on the ground that the mark is merely descriptive. This applies to trademarks, service marks, collective marks and certification marks.

> *Example*: The mark is SOFT.COM for facial tissues. The examining attorney must refuse registration under §2(e)(1).

> *Example*: The mark is NATIONAL BOOK OUTLET.COM for retail book store services. The examining attorney must refuse registration under §2(e)(1).

The TLD will be perceived as part of an Internet address, and does not add source identifying significance to the composite mark. *Cf. In re Page*, 51 USPQ2d 1660 (TTAB 1999) (addition of a telephone prefix

FIGURE 11.2 *(Continued)*

such as "800" or "888" to a descriptive term is insufficient, by itself, to render the mark inherently distinctive); *In re Patent & Trademark Services Inc.*, 49 USPQ2d 1537 (TTAB 1998) (PATENT & TRADEMARK SERVICES INC. is merely descriptive of legal services in the field of intellectual property; the term "Inc." merely indicates the type of entity that performs the services and has no significance as a mark); *In re The Paint Products Co.*, 8 USPQ2d 1863 (TTAB 1988) (PAINT PRODUCTS CO. is no more registrable as a trademark for goods emanating from a company that sells paint products than it would be as a service mark for retail paint store services offered by such a company); *In re E.I. Kane, Inc.*, 221 USPQ 1203 (TTAB 1984) (OFFICE MOVERS, INC. incapable of functioning as a mark for moving services; addition of the term "Inc." does not add any trademark significance to matter sought to be registered). *See also* TMEP §1209.01(b)(12) regarding marks comprising in part "1-800," "888," or other telephone numbers.

V. Generic Refusals

If a mark is composed of a generic term(s) for applicant's goods or services and a TLD, the examining attorney must refuse registration on the ground that the mark is generic and the TLD has no trademark significance. *See* TMEP §1209.01(b)(12) regarding marks comprised in part of "1-800" or other telephone numbers. Marks comprised of generic terms combined with TLDs are not eligible for registration on the Supplemental Register, or on the Principal Register under Trademark Act §2(f), 15 U.S.C. §1052(f). This applies to trademarks, service marks, collective marks and certification marks.

Example: TURKEY.COM for frozen turkeys is unregistrable on either the Principal or Supplemental Register.

Example: BANK.COM for banking services is unregistrable on either the Principal or Supplemental Register.

The examining attorney generally should not issue a refusal in an application for registration on the Principal Register on the ground that a mark is a generic name for the goods or services unless the applicant asserts that the mark has acquired distinctiveness under §2(f) of the Trademark Act, 15 U.S.C. §1052(f). Absent such a claim, the examining attorney should issue a refusal on the ground that the mark is merely descriptive of the goods or services under §2(e)(1), and provide an advisory statement that the matter sought to be registered appears to be a generic name for the goods or services. TMEP §1209.02.

VI. Marks Containing Geographical Matter

The examining attorney should examine marks containing geographic matter in the same manner that any mark containing geographic matter is examined. *See generally* TMEP §§1210.05 and 1210.06. Depending on the manner in which it is used on or in connection with the goods or services, a proposed domain name mark containing a geographic term may be primarily geographically descriptive under §2(e)(2) of the Trademark Act, 15 U.S.C. §1052(e)(2), or primarily geographically deceptively misdescriptive under §2(e)(3) of the Trademark Act, 15 U.S.C. §1052(e)(3), and/or merely descriptive or deceptively misdescriptive under §2(e)(1) of the Trademark Act, 15 U.S.C. §1052(e)(1).

Geographic matter may be merely descriptive of services provided on the Internet

When a geographic term is used as a mark for services that are provided on the Internet, sometimes the geographic term describes the subject of the service rather than the geographic origin of the service.

FIGURE 11.2 *(Continued)*

Usually this occurs when the mark is composed of a geographic term that describes the subject matter of information services (e.g., NEW ORLEANS.COM for "providing vacation planning information about New Orleans, Louisiana by means of the global computer network"). In these cases, the examining attorney should refuse registration under Trademark Act §2(e)(1) because the mark is merely descriptive of the services.

VII. Disclaimers

Trademark Act §6(a), 15 U.S.C. §1056(a), provides for the disclaimer of "an unregistrable component" of a mark. The guidelines on disclaimer set forth in TMEP §1213 *et. seq.* apply to domain name mark applications.

If a composite mark includes a domain name composed of unregistrable matter (e.g., a merely descriptive or generic term and a TLD), disclaimer is required. *See* examples below and TMEP §§1213.03.

If a disclaimer is required and the domain name includes a misspelled or telescoped word, the correct spelling must be disclaimed. *See* examples below and TMEP §§1213.04(a) and 1213.09(c).

A compound term composed of arbitrary or suggestive matter combined with a "dot" and a TLD is considered unitary, and therefore no disclaimer of the TLD is required. *See* examples below and TMEP §1213.04(b).

Mark	Disclaimer
XYZ BANK.COM	BANK.COM
XYZ FEDERALBANK.COM	FEDERAL BANK.COM
XYZ GROCERI STOR.COM	GROCERY STORE.COM
XYZ.COM	no disclaimer
XYZ.BANK.COM	no disclaimer
XYZBANK.COM	no disclaimer

VIII. Material Alteration

Amendments may not be made to the drawing of the mark if the character of the mark is materially altered. Trademark Rule 2.72, 37 C.F.R §2.72. The test for determining whether an amendment is a material alteration was articulated in *Visa International Service Association v. Life-Code Systems, Inc.*, 220 USPQ 740 (TTAB 1983):

> The modified mark must contain what is the essence of the original mark, and the new form must create the impression of being essentially the same mark. The general test of whether an alteration is material is whether the mark would have to be republished after the alteration in order to fairly present the mark for purposes of opposition. If one mark is sufficiently different from another mark as to require republication, it would be tantamount to a new mark appropriate for a new application.

Id at 743-44.

Each case must be decided on its own facts. The controlling question is always whether the new and old form of the marks create essentially the same commercial impression. TMEP §807.14(a).

FIGURE 11.2 *(Continued)*

Example: Amending the mark PETER, used on kitchen pots and pans, from PETER to PETER PAN would materially change the mark because adding the generic word PAN dramatically changes the meaning of the mark – from a person's name, to a well known storybook character's name.

Adding or deleting TLDs in domain name marks

Generally, for domain name marks (e.g., COPPER.COM), the applicant may add or delete a TLD to the drawing of the mark without materially altering the mark. A mark that includes a TLD will be perceived by the public as a domain name, while a mark without a TLD will not. However, the public recognizes that a TLD is a universally-used part of an Internet address. As a result, the essence of a domain name mark is created by the second level domain name, not the TLD. The commercial impression created by the second level domain name usually will remain the same whether the TLD is present or not.

Example: Amending a mark from PETER to PETER.COM would <u>not</u> materially change the mark because the essence of both marks is still PETER, a person's name.

Similarly, substituting one TLD for another in a domain name mark, or adding or deleting a "dot" or "http://www." or "www." to a domain name mark is generally permitted.

Example: Amending a mark from XYZ.ORG to XYZ.COM would <u>not</u> materially change the mark because the essence of both marks is still XYZ.

Adding or deleting TLDs in other marks

If a TLD is not used as part of a domain name, adding or deleting a TLD may be a material alteration. When used without a second level domain name, a TLD may have trademark significance. *See* TMEP §807.14(a).

Example: Deleting the term .COM from the mark .COM ? used on sports magazines would materially change the mark.

IX. Likelihood of Confusion

In analyzing whether a domain name mark is likely to cause confusion with another pending or registered mark, the examining attorney must consider the marks as a whole, but generally should accord little weight to the TLD portion of the mark. *See* TMEP §1207.01(b) *et. seq.*

X. Marks Containing The Phonetic Equivalent of A Top Level Domain

Marks containing the phonetic equivalent of a TLD (e.g., XYZ DOTCOM) are treated in the same manner as marks composed of a regular TLD. If a disclaimer is necessary, the disclaimer must be in the form of the regular TLD and not the phonetic equivalent. *See* TMEP §1213.09(c).

Example: The mark is INEXPENSIVE RESTAURANTS DOT COM for providing information about restaurants by means of a global computer network. Registration should be refused because the mark is merely descriptive of the services under Trademark Act §2(e)(1), 15 U.S.C. §1052(e)(1).

Example: The mark is XYZ DOTCOM. The applicant must disclaim the TLD ".COM" rather than the phonetic equivalent "DOTCOM."

FIGURE 11.2 *(Continued)*

CASE STUDY   Paychex: From Small Label to Major Brand

Paychex, seen also in Chapter 10, is another excellent example of intellectual property being used to help promote and protect a great innovation. The company was founded in 1971 by Thomas Golisano to provide payroll services for small businesses. He had worked in the same field for another company prior to going out on his own. During that time, he developed a more efficient means of providing payroll services to small firms, a market payroll companies had ignored in the belief there was no money to be made there. Tom knew better and developed a method that proved it. He pitched his ideas to the company he was working for; they passed on it so he went out on his own. Today, that company is long gone while Paychex is thriving, widely regarded as one of the best run firms in the world with a stock whose record of performance is extraordinary.

In the beginning Tom's company consisted of himself, one other employee, and 40 customers. It took about five years of incredibly hard work, going through times when even having enough money to operate was in question, before Paychex really started to take off, but then it did. Right from the start, Tom knew the opportunity was tremendous. The vast majority of firms in existence were small businesses that the large payroll companies continued to ignore, with CPAs doing the payrolls but, even there, not seeing them as a significant source of revenue. In fact, lots of CPAs were happy to refer their payroll clients to Tom.

In 1989 Paychex had 100,000 clients; in 1995 that number had increased to 210,000; today they are at approximately 400,000 clients (and still growing rapidly) and offer an array of services in addition to payrolls. Along the way, Paychex has received countless glowing reviews in business and financial magazines for their rapid growth, excellent management, innovative offerings, and the ever-increasing value of their stock, among other things. These were best summed up in the year 2000 when Forbes Global ranked Paychex #1 on their A-list of the 400 best companies in the world, divided into 40 sectors in the Business Services section.

For Tom Golisano and Paychex, going from being a struggling small firm to becoming the best in the world at what they do has been a spectacular ride. It seems almost too much to believe, but when you meet Tom and get acquainted with his company, it makes sense.

The Paychex name is a registered trademark of extraordinary value (the logo can be seen In Figure 11.3, displayed on the front page of the Paychex annual report for 2000). Beginning with the obvious, it refers to the original function of the company without being so descriptive as to jeopardize the trademark status. In addition, the name is associated with Tom Golisano, a man who started the company with his $3,000 life savings and is now on the list of the 200 wealthiest men in the world, a man whose wealth is matched by the generosity shown in how he shares it with a host of worthy causes. Paychex can literally be taken to mean "best at what they do," the trademarked name of a company that recognized a new market, developed it, and not only grew as its business did, but consistently added an array of related products to their core services. At root, what gave the trademark value was perception, guts, innovation, and hard work.

FIGURE 11.3   Paychex Annual Report Cover and Trademark
Reprinted with permission of Paychex, Inc. Paychex is a registered
trademark of Paychex, Inc.

CASE STUDY   People's Pottery: Made in America

Though People's Pottery was founded in the early 1970s, it was not until 1996 that the company embarked on the remarkable growth that has seen them expand from 2 to 50 stores. The secret ingredient? Jim and Carla Froehler, a couple with more than 20 years' experience apiece in retail, who recognized what a great concept People's Pottery was and bought it.

The defining mission of People's Pottery has remained consistent since the beginning: to feature and sell high quality works of American artists. As the chain has grown, so, too, have the opportunities for the artists associated with it. The talents of the original owner and the Froehlers have resulted in the People's Pottery trademarked name becoming synonymous with excellent service, wonderful works by an array of talented artists, taste, and an appealing shopping experience. (See Figure 11.4.)

So strong is their brand that shoppers on a quest for a gift will enter the store and, when asked by a sales associate if they are looking for anything in particular, will say that the person they are on a gift quest for had merely told them, "Just get me anything from People's Pottery." Now there is a terrific example of faith in a brand name. Usually that shopper, if they are new to the store, becomes a fan, also. I can testify to how important this is because my wife is one of those people, which means I can be assured of getting her something she will be very fond of, using the brand as a crutch for my impaired shopping sense.

PEOPLE'S POTTERY

Shop The
Catalog

About
People's
Pottery

Store
Locations

Departments

Contact

QTVR

A tradition for over 25 years.
PEOPLE'S POTTERY®
Handmade in America.

People's Pottery is a store like no other. Totally unique in every way. Yet uncommonly familiar. The kind of store that, when you see it for the first time, you know "this is so obviously right". Merchandise of unmistakable quality. One-of-kind treasures so unrivaled that it would be impossible not to find something anyone would cherish.

Founded 1972: The Original Ithaca Storefront Circa 1867.

FIGURE 11.4   People's Pottery Web Page and Trademark
Reprinted with permission.

DEEP IN THE VAULT: THE VALUE OF TRADE SECRETS

12

THE COLONEL'S NOTEBOOK

In the early 1970s Tom and Cherry Settle purchased their home from Harland Sanders, the founder of Kentucky Fried Chicken (KFC). Almost 30 years later they came across a note in their basement, which had been handwritten in a date book owned by Mr. Sanders, that featured a recipe containing 11 herbs and spices.

The Settles wanted to auction the note, so they asked KFC, now owned by Tricon Global Restaurants Inc., to verify that it was the Colonel's handwriting. Imagine how shocked they were when the company filed a lawsuit against them that was intended to keep them from selling the recipe.

After examining the note, KFC dropped the lawsuit and announced that the note was "nowhere close" to the original recipe, which has been a closely guarded secret for 62 years. As drastic as their actions might appear, bear in mind that only a few key employees know the entire recipe and they are bound by strict confidentiality agreements. KFC's secret recipe is an exceptionally valuable piece of intellectual property. After all, anybody can cook chicken with some combination of 11 herbs and spices, but KFC has built a major brand with a particular combination that has probably not been duplicated. Sure, figuring out most, or maybe even all, of the ingredients could likely be done, but there is probably a ratio or method involved that nobody outside the company has hit on yet. If somebody had, they could make and market the same chicken themselves, or sell the information to competitors, who could start going after KFC's customer base.

Consider the case of Coca-Cola's syrup formula, a secret that is kept locked in a vault and is said to be known to only two people in the company. Hundreds of competing colas have been launched since Coca-Cola set up shop, but most are long gone now, while Coca-Cola has grown into a hugely successful brand. Publish that formula, though, and almost instantly there would be a myriad of producers of identical colas, with Coke potentially experiencing a drop in market share and rapidly deteriorating profit margins.

Another good example is the special sauce that accompanies Mc-Donald's Big Mac. To me, it tastes like Russian salad dressing, and most of us could surely develop a similar sauce, but it would not be the same as McDonald's. It's that sauce that transforms two hamburger patties and an extra half a roll into something unique and desirable enough that millions of them are consumed every year, all over the globe.

TRADE SECRETS VS. PATENTS

If trade secrets are so important, yet lose their value once an outsider figures out the mystery, why not patent them and have offensive rights against anybody who uses the ideas? Patent protection lasts only for 20 years from the date of application. After that the intellectual property in question is no longer off limits and becomes fair game. Also bear in mind that patent applications describing how the article in question works are public property that are easily accessible. So, even though that patent bars a competitor from doing the same thing, they may glean insight from it that allows them to develop, and patent, something similar they can use to gain part of your market.

Because there are no application requirements to meet, a broad range of intellectual property can be treated as trade secrets, such as tangible and intangible processes, ways of organizing teams to accomplish tasks, formulas, techniques, methods, patterns, designs, chemical formulas, mechanisms, compositions, and the list could continue. For important intellectual property that does not meet the criteria for other forms of protection, such as that offered by patents and copyrights, a trade secret can be a valuable alternative.

Trade secrets can have ongoing value even if a patent for a product they are related to has expired. For example, the patent GD Searle had for its Nutrasweet brand of artificial sweetener (aspartame) has expired, but because they have kept the manufacturing knowledge they have gained over the years as a trade secret, they have maintained their dominance because competitors have not been able to develop a method for producing the artificial sweetener as cheaply as GD Searle can.

WHAT IS A TRADE SECRET?

A trade secret is information that has economic value to its owner, who takes appropriate measures to keep it secret, and is not generally known outside the owner's enterprise. The Uniform Trade Secrets Act, in effect in most states, with the others having similar laws on their books, defines trade secrets as "information, including a formula, pattern, compilation, program, device, method, technique, or process that derives independent economic value from not being generally known and not being readily ascertainable and is subject to reasonable efforts to maintain secrecy."

Following is a list of the conditions usually drawn on to determine if a piece of intellectual property is a trade secret or not.

- How broadly the information is known to those outside a particular enterprise.
- How many employees know the information.
- The measures in place and used to maintain the secret.
- The economic value the trade secret has to its owner and the owner's competition.
- The resources (time, money) that went into developing the trade secret.
- How easily the information could be acquired by those not authorized to possess it.

As we saw with the example of the patents developed by Bluetie, inventions that are not ready to be patented, or will never be patented, can be effectively protected as trade secrets. As we saw earlier, during their stealth phase, when Bluetie was developing the technology for Secure Send but was not ready to patent it, treating the technology involved as a trade secret kept it away from the wrong eyes until patent protection became available.

Say, for example, that you are developing an online business that will be based on a method for using computer software to match single people with other singles they will actually like. But you have not progressed to the point where you feel comfortable filing a patent application, or have not decided if you even want to share the information with the world in the form of a published patent application. It is worthwhile to treat your invention as a trade secret to prevent somebody else from preempting you, or from a description of it becoming prior art that will invalidate your application if you do decide to patent but fail to file soon enough. Or maybe you have a secret list of consumers ready and willing to buy $30 light bulbs from any telemarketer who calls and solicits them. You cannot patent a list of names, so you had better keep the list to yourself and keep working those phones.

A trade secret does not have to meet the kinds of criteria patents, copyrights, and trademarks are subject to. It merely needs to provide an economic advantage, or possible advantage, to its owner in the commercial marketplace.

OBTAINING TRADE SECRET STATUS

Unlike patents, where an application is required, or copyrights and trademarks, where registration is a must, even though not mandated, nothing must be filed in order to be entitled to the legal protections that come with the trade secret status. To be a trade secret, the intellectual property in question must possess value and be owned by somebody who takes reasonable steps to keep it confidential.

A trade secret does not need to be novel or unique in the sense an invention must be to satisfy the requirements for a patent, so long as others do not know about it. If information used to be a trade secret belonging to another, then was stolen or became known to the public, it cannot qualify now as somebody else's secret.

As an illustration of obtaining trade secret status, go back again to that secret list of buyers willing to spring for high-priced light bulbs. The economic value can readily be seen in the sales results, and further verified by comparing it to normal customer lists that fail to produce such a spectacular result. Once this has been established, the next step is to take adequate measures to keep it a secret. Even if you have absolute trust in everybody you work with, if you keep the list on your desk in plain sight and a thief wanders in off the street, recognizes it as the gold mine it is, pockets it, and runs out the door to start his own bulb business, you will not, based on your lack of effort, be able to demonstrate that you went to the necessary trouble to protect your property.

MAINTAINING A TRADE SECRET

In the June 2000 issue of the journal *Security*, Scott Charney, a principal at PriceWaterhouseCooper and a former head of the Computer Crimes

Section of the U.S. Department of Justice, said of the year 1999, "The documented loss of proprietary information exceeds $45 billion and 60 percent of network sites have been breached by intruders. These facts reveal a chilling level of vulnerability in the corporate community." At a time when intellectual property is recognized as having more value than ever before, when it is not unusual for even single trade secrets to be worth millions of dollars, the biggest threat to maintaining them is theft, be it by outsiders or people within the firm itself.

If somebody is able to figure out your secret, whether through reverse engineering or a lucky guess, there is nothing to be done about it; the secret is out. The law offers only remedies if trade secrets are misappropriated, as when a spy breaks into your office, cracks the safe, and steals the process you developed for producing great tasting chocolate that contains no calories. What to do? Institute measures to protect your trade secrets.

It is against state and federal law to steal or misappropriate trade secrets. Most states have adopted the Uniform Trade Secrets Act, which allows claimants to seek remedies under civil law, and those that have not have similar protections in place. In 1996 Congress enacted the Economic Espionage Act, which allows for criminal charges at the federal level for the theft of trade secrets, technologies, research, or other information possessed by businesses in the United States. Specific items included in the above classifications are "patterns, plans, compilations, program devices, formulae, designs, prototypes, methods, techniques, processes, programs, or codes, whether tangible or intangible, and whether or how stored, compiled or memorialized ... if it's reasonably protected and has value." Some recent international agreements and treaties also address the theft of trade secrets.

Theft can be accomplished in a variety of ways. Provided the information was adequately protected, illegal thefts, according to federal law, come in the form of copying, sketching, duplicating, drawing, photographing, transmitting, uploading, downloading, delivering, mailing, or any other means of communicating information of value a firm has taken good precautions to keep secret. According to the FBI, most trade secret theft is done by insiders, primarily current or former employees who are disgruntled.

The owners of trade secrets that were misappropriated can pursue a number of legal remedies, including damage awards, royalty payments, the return or destruction of pirated property, and awards of attorney fees, along with seeking fines and jail time for the offending party. In order to have the benefit of legal recourse, however, it is vital that the conditions necessary for qualification as a trade secret be met.

Even if a case of trade piracy is successfully pursued, it is doubtful that any recovery made will match the cost of the aggravation and economic loss brought on by the loss of a trade secret. The best approach is to protect your trade secrets well enough to minimize the chances of losing them. The most common measures firms take are the following:

- Have employees and others with access to sensitive information sign nondisclosure agreements that prohibit them from disclosing trade secrets to all unauthorized parties.

- Require that key personnel sign noncompete agreements that prevent them from going to work for a rival for a specified period of time or in a defined geographic area.

- Limit access to, and the ability to copy, trade secrets to the fewest possible people.

- Institute security measures that prevent unauthorized access to premises and information systems.

- Do reference and background checks on new employees.

- Educate employees about what trade secrets are and how they should be handled.

- Conduct exit interviews with employees who are leaving with accumulated trade secret knowledge and remind them of their continued responsibility to maintain confidentiality.

- Develop a coherent and effective information management system.

Though it sounds paradoxical, another way to protect trade secrets is to publish parts of them. If you are concerned that somebody is going to file a patent for an invention that uses a technology you have maintained as a trade secret, or you just want to block the possibility of it happening, defensive publishing can be effective. If you publish a part, or parts, of a trade secret, yet not enough to give the whole thing away, a prior art document has been created that will prevent a patent for the same creations to be granted.

CASE STUDY   Dinosaur Bar-B-Que: The Secret's in the Sauce

The first Dinosaur Bar-B-Que restaurant was founded by John Stage and his partners in Syracuse, NY, in 1988. It was built on the success John won as a caterer whose primary focus was biker events. Prior to 1983, John had no restaurant or catering experience, but he was a natural as a cook and possessed a powerful curiosity about different kinds of foods and techniques, along with an affinity for learning, experimenting, teaching himself, and putting his own stamp on what he makes. What really brings all the elements together can be summed up in his own words, "My cooking reflects life experiences."

As a biker, he had found the food to be terrible at the events he had attended. The idea behind going into catering was simply to produce food he liked, knew was good, and would appeal to the market he intended to serve. Sure enough, he was right. Soon after going into business for himself in 1983, John quickly became an in-demand caterer with a reputation for bringing great food at very reasonable prices.

As a successful caterer John heard over and over again from people who tried his food that he should open his own restaurant. When he opened that first Dinosaur Bar-B-Que, it was designed for quick service and take-out. An instant hit, it wasn't long before he added a bar, expanded the restaurant into a larger, full-service establishment, and made it into a place known for terrific food that also regularly booked great blues bands that couldn't be heard anyplace else nearby.

One of the many things his customers raved about was his sauce. John had never cared much for the usual commercial sauces that relied too much on sweetener and liquid smoke. He preferred a taste with a "roundness of flavor that complements instead of overwhelms," which was hard to find elsewhere. Since he had already developed one that his customers kept coming back for and begged him to sell outside his restaurant, he decided to bottle and market it. Though most of the ingredients in it were common to other barbecue sauces, John used a set of spices whose content, combinations, and ratios were unique. When he contracted out to have the sauce made and bottled for him to sell, he kept the recipe a trade secret.

To do this John had most of the sauce made at one location, then had his spice blend shipped in from another location and added in. Both companies involved had to sign confidentiality agreements that bound them to keep their knowledge of his sauce to themselves, even though using the different locations helped to make sure that only he knew how to put together the whole recipe correctly. So far, there have been no problems keeping the recipe secure. John says that if somebody really wanted to and was willing

(Continued)

CASE STUDY   Dinosaur Bar-B-Que: The Secret's in the Sauce
(Continued)

to pay to have it analyzed, they could figure out the recipe. The bigger hurdle, though, would be in building the brand recognition that leads people to reach for his sauce from among a shelf full of competitors' because they have faith in the good reputation he has earned through years of producing great food.

Capitalized on a trade secreted flavor, coupled with his unique trademark on the label, John's sauce quickly became a hit in supermarkets throughout the Northeast, with strong pockets all over the country and even a few abroad. On the strength of his first sauce, John has added six more (see the display of them on the Dinosaur web site) and now sells them through catalogs and over the Internet, in addition to retail locations.

Whether it be in deciding on the best approach to keeping a trade secret, registering a trademark, or obtaining a contract, John recommends using the services of a good attorney. With all the sweat a business like his takes to making a go of it, there is no sense taking on any risk of doing your enterprise harm by venturing into an area you are not fully equipped to handle. "Do what you do and pay somebody good to do what they do. That way you can focus on what you're best at." Finally, trade secrets and other forms of intellectual property can be a big help. But they will not be of much value unless they are part of a venture that is developed, maintained, and operated well enough that this intellectual property becomes so attractive that other people are willing to pay for the privilege of sharing it with you.

CASE STUDY Bluetie: The Secret of Speed

Though still a young company, Bluetie has been very active in the patent process and will continue to be for many years to come. In their world, nobody truly expects a patent to give them a 20-year advantage; things move too fast. The innovation you patented two years ago could suddenly become obsolete, then nobody would even want to infringe on it. The best that can be hoped for is protection that lasts long enough to establish a patented product in the market without having a competitor make off with the technology your firm worked so hard, and spent so much, to make viable. If a patent in Bluetie's environment has solid value for 3 to 5 years, it is doing itself proud.

As valuable as the patented technologies in the suite of business services they offer are, what may prove to be of greater and more lasting value are some of the things that go into developing them, which Bluetie carefully maintains as trade secrets. Concerning the creation of new applications and services, Bluetie employs unique methods for organizing and performing the necessary tasks that enable them to complete the development of new technologies in time frames that are extraordinarily short. In an industry where speed to market is vital, these trade secrets give them a significant advantage.

Much of this information is in the form of approaches and techniques that would not meet the criteria for a patent. Some of it may in terms of being business processes, but if Bluetie patented these, an important part of their intellectual property would become available to anybody who wanted to use it.

David Koretz estimated that 90% of Bluetie's value was in the form of intangible assets. These assets are not static; they are continually used to produce new products and methods that keep increasing the value of the firm as they come to fruition. By sharing their trade secrets Bluetie would risk not only what they have in the present, they would also risk the realization of future opportunities.

COMMON QUESTIONS ABOUT THE PATENT PROCESS

13

Q: *What is a patent?*

A: A patent is an exclusive property right granted to an inventor that lasts for 20 years from the date of application (14 years for design patents). The patent holder has "the right to exclude others from making, using, offering for sale, of selling" the patented item in the United States, or importing it.

Q: *What government agency decided what patents are?*

A: Congress was given the power in the Constitution ". . . to promote the progress of science and useful arts, by securing for limited times to authors and inventors the exclusive right to their respective writings and discoveries." By its authority, Congress designates the United States Patent and Trademark Office as being responsible for administering laws related to the granting of patents.

Q: *Who can apply for a patent?*

A: Usually only the inventor, or joint inventors, can apply for a patent. Some exceptions are as follows: If the inventor is dead, her legal representatives may apply. If the inventor is insane, an application can be made by a legal guardian. In the case of a joint patent, if one party cannot be found or refuses to apply, the joint parties, or those with a proprietary interest, can apply in her place. Employees of the Patent and Trademark Office may not apply for a patent.

Q: *What can be patented?*

A: The law states that anybody who "invents or discovers any new and useful process, machine, manufacture, or composition of matter, or any new and useful improvement thereof, may obtain a patent."

Q: *What do the terms used mean?*

A: A process is an act or method and usually pertains to industrial or technical processes, though business method processes can be included, too, such as one-click shopping. A machine is just that. Manufacture covers things that can be made and a composition of matter covers mixtures of ingredients and chemical compositions and compounds. To be new, an invention cannot already be in use, patented, or described anywhere. Improvements on existing creations can qualify as new. Usefulness is a broad term taken to mean that the invention has a specific purpose.

Q: *What cannot be patented?*

A: Suggestions, abstract ideas, laws of nature, physical phenomena, illegal items, and inventions already existing or described. Further, in order to get a patent, an inventor must be able to describe how the invention works so that it is apparent to a patent examiner that it really will does. Just hoping is not enough.

Q: *Where can I get a patent application and instructions for how to complete it?*

A: Patent applications can be ordered from the USPTO or downloaded from its web site, along with all necessary instructions. Completed applications can either be mailed traditionally or submitted using the USPTO's electronic filing system.

Q: *What is the meaning of "patent pending" and "patent applied for?"*

A: It is a term manufacturers put on items to let others know that a patent application has been filed.

Q: *Does the USPTO share information in patent applications?*

A: Not right away. A patent application may be published 18 months after being submitted, and, once a patent has been granted, patents are freely accessible to anybody who wants to see them. Patents can be accessed online and copies ordered from the USPTO site.

Q: *If more than one person participated in creating a new invention, who gets the patent?*

A: If they all participated, a joint patent will be issued. If only one person of the group contributed all the ideas and the others merely followed directions, the one with the ideas will be granted the patent.

Q: *Do I have to hire a lawyer in order to file a patent application?*

A: No, but unless you are very familiar with the process, using a competent lawyer is a must for anything worth patenting. Lawyers who specialize in this area have accumulated a range of expertise, contacts, and experience it would be nearly impossible to duplicate. Though patent applications are not difficult to fill out, simple mistakes, like failing to word a claim broadly enough, can weaken your patent and cause you myriad difficulties in the years following the granting of your patent.

Q: *How do I find a good attorney?*

A: While the USPTO does not recommend particular attorneys or control the fees they charge, they do publish a directory that is available to you where all registered attorneys who are recognized by the USPTO can indicate if they are accepting new clients. The best source is the recommendations of people who have employed patent attorneys with good results in the past. Not just any attorney will do; get one who specializes in patent law. The USPTO guide can be purchased from their office in either paper or digital formats (uspto.gov).

Q: *How do I get in touch with the United States Patent and Trademark Office?*

A: They have a very complete web site that can be accessed with the address given previously, or you can reach them by conventional mail at: United States Patent and Trademark Office, Crystal Plaza 3, 2021 Jefferson Davis Plaza, Arlington, VA.

Q: *What is the mission of the USPTO?*

A: To administer patent laws, examine patents, grant patents when appropriate, maintain records of patents and patent applications, record assignments of patents, supply copies of patent documents (such as applications, informational publications, and previously applied for and issued patents), along with a range of additional administrative duties.

Q: *What does the USPTO do to enforce patents or decide cases of infringement?*

A: Nothing; the above are matters that will have to be decided in the legal system.

Q: *Can the USPTO help me to develop and market a patent?*

A: They do not, but they will put a notice in their *Official Gazette* that your patent is available to be sold or licensed.

Q: *Do I have to submit a model of my invention along with the patent application?*

A: Very rarely will this be required. Because a description of how your invention works is required as part of the application, a model is usually not needed.

Q: *Do drawings of inventions need to be submitted as part of the application?*

A: If a drawing(s) is needed for a patent examiner to understand how the invention works, then it must be submitted. Specific requirements for these are available from the USPTO.

Q: *What is a provisional application for a patent?*

A: A provisional application allows for an earlier filing date of a patent, costs less than a traditional application, and allows the applicant to use the term "patent pending." An applicant filing a provisional application has 12 months to file a complete nonprovisional application.

Q: *Can patent applications be amended after they are filed?*

A: Yes. An amendment can be used to correct errors and show better relationships between claims.

Q: *How long does it take between filing an application and having it granted?*

A: The timing varies, but the average is a little more than 18 months.

Q: *What are the chances of my patent being granted without a hitch?*

A: It is not unusual for the USPTO examiners to ask for additional clarifications and information, nor is it unheard of for an applicant not to have all aspects of a patent granted. Approximately 72% of all patent applications result in patents being granted.

Q: *Is there anything I can do if my application is denied?*

A: Yes, you can appeal the ruling. Check the USPTO site for specifics of the procedure.

Q: *Who decides if patents are granted or not?*

A: Patent examiners employed by the USPTO. They are broken up into groups according to their area of specialization. When your application is received, it is assigned to the appropriate group.

Q: *What is "prior art"?*

A: It is any description of your invention that exists before you file your application. Usually, you or your lawyer will search for prior art before filing an application. Patent examiners also search for prior art. If prior art is found, you will not be granted a patent.

Q: *Where do I search for prior art?*

A: To be on the safe side, it is usually best to have an experienced attorney or professional searcher do it for you, as it is easy to miss prior art references if you are not familiar with where to look. In addition to online databases, the USPTO has a searchable data base of issued, applied for, and expired patents. They also maintain Patent and Trademark Depository libraries in cities throughout the United States, along with their primary facilities, The Scientific and Technical Information Center and The Patent Search Room, both in Arlington, Va. Check the web site for specific information and locations.

Q: *What are the fees?*

A: Figure 13.1 is a listing, taken from the USPTO web site, of the applicable fees.

UNITED STATES PATENT AND TRADEMARK OFFICE
Effective October 1, 2001

Any fee amount paid on or after October 1, 2001, must be paid in the revised amount. The fees subject to reduction for small entities that have established status (37 CFR 1.27) are shown in a separate column.

For additional information, please contact the General Information Services Division at (703) 308-4357 or (800) 786-9199.

Patent Fees	**PCT Fees**	**Trademark Fees**
Application Filing Fees	**National Stage**	**Processing Fees**
Post-Allowance Fees	**International Stage**	**Service Fees**
Maintenance Fees	**PCT Fees to WIPO or EPO**	**Fastener Quality Act Fees**
Miscellaneous Fees		
Application Extension Fees		
Appeals/Interference Fees		
Petition Fees		
Service Fees		
Enrollment Fees		
Finance Service Fees		
Computer Service Fees		

Fee Code	37 CFR	Description	Fee	Small Entity Fee (if applicable)
Patent Application Filing Fees				
101/201	1.16(a)	Basic filing fee—Utility	740.00	370.00
131/231	1.16(a)	Basic filing fee—Utility (CPA)	740.00	370.00
102/202	1.16(b)	Independent claims in excess of three	84.00	42.00
103/203	1.16(c)	Claims in excess of twenty	18.00	9.00
104/204	1.16(d)	Multiple dependent claim	280.00	140.00
105/205	1.16(e)	Surcharge—Late filing fee or oath or declaration	130.00	65.00
106/206	1.16(f)	Design filing fee	330.00	165.00
132/232	1.16(f)	Design filing fee (CPA)	330.00	165.00
107/207	1.16(g)	Plant filing fee	510.00	255.00
133/233	1.16(g)	Plant filing fee (CPA)	510.00	255.00
108/208	1.16(h)	Reissue filing fee	740.00	370.00
134/234	1.16(h)	Reissue filing fee (CPA)	740.00	370.00
109/209	1.16(i)	Reissue independent claims over original patent	84.00	42.00
110/210	1.16(j)	Reissue claims in excess of 20 and over original patent	18.00	9.00
114/214	1.16(k)	Provisional application filing fee	160.00	80.00
127/227	1.16(l)	Surcharge—Late provisional filing fee or cover sheet	50.00	25.00
139	1.17(i)	Non-English specification	130.00	

(Continued)

FIGURE 13.1   List of Fees, U.S. Patent and Trademark Office

Fee Code	37 CFR	Description	Fee	Small Entity Fee (if applicable)
Patent Post–Allowance Fees				
142/242	1.18(a)	Utility issue fee	1,280.00	640.00
143/243	1.18(b)	Design issue fee	460.00	230.00
144/244	1.18(c)	Plant issue fee	620.00	310.00
195	1.18(d)	Publication fee for early, voluntary, or normal publication	300.00	
196	1.18(d)	Publication fee for republication	300.00	
Patent Maintenance Fees				
183/283	1.20(e)	Due at 3.5 years	880.00	440.00
184/284	1.20(f)	Due at 7.5 years	2,020.00	1,010.00
185/285	1.20(g)	Due at 11.5 years	3,100.00	1,550.00
	1.20(h)	Surcharge—Late payment within 6 months	130.00	65.00
187	1.20(i)(1)	Surcharge after expiration— Late payment is unavoidable	700.00	
188	1.20(i)(2)	Surcharge after expiration— Late payment is unintentional	1,640.00	
Miscellaneous Patent Fees				
179/279	1.17(e)	Request for continued examination (RCE) (see 37 CFR 1.114)	740.00	370.00
098	1.17(i)	Processing fee, except in provisional applications	130.00	
194	1.17(i)	Request for voluntary publication or republication	130.00	
169	1.17(k)	Request for expedited examination of a design application	900.00	
112	1.17(n)	Requesting publication of SIR— Prior to examiner action	920.00*	
113	1.17(o)	Requesting publication of SIR— After examiner action	1,840.00*	
126	1.17(p)	Submission of an Information Disclosure Statement	180.00	
123	1.17(q)	Processing fee for provisional applications	50.00	
146/246	1.17(r)	For filing a submission after final rejection (see 37 CFR 1.129(a))	740.00	370.00
149/249	1.17(s)	For each additional invention to be examined (see 37 CFR 1.129(b))	740.00	370.00
145	1.20(a)	Certificate of correction	100.00	
147	1.20(c)(1)	Request for ex parte reexamination	2,520.00	
099	1.20(c)(2)	Request for inter partes reexamination	8,800.00	
148/248	1.20(d)	Statutory disclaimer	110.00	55.00

*Reduced by basic filing fee paid.

FIGURE 13.1 *(Continued)*

Fee Code	37 CFR	Description	Fee	Small Entity Fee (if applicable)
Patent Application Extension Fees				
115/215	1.17(a)(1)	Extension for response within first month	110.00	55.00
116/216	1.17(a)(2)	Extension for response within second month	400.00	200.00
117/217	1.17(a)(3)	Extension for response within third month	920.00	460.00
118/218	1.17(a)(4)	Extension for response within fourth month	1,440.00	720.00
128/228	1.17(a)(5)	Extension for response within fifth month	1,960.00	980.00
Patent Appeals/Interference Fees				
119/219	1.17(b)	Notice of appeal	320.00	160.00
120/220	1.17(c)	Filing a brief in support of an appeal	320.00	160.00
121/221	1.17(d)	Request for oral hearing	280.00	140.00
Patent Petition Fees				
122	1.17(h)	Petitions to the Commissioner, unless otherwise specified	130.00	
138	1.17(j)	Petition to institute a public use proceeding	1,510.00	
140/240	1.17(l)	Petition to revive unavoidably abandoned application	110.00	55.00
141/241	1.17(m)	Petition to revive unintentionally abandoned application	1,280.00	640.00
091	1.17(t)	Acceptance of an unintentionally delayed claim for priority	1,280.00	
089	1.18(e)	Filing an application for patent term adjustment	200.00	
090	1.18(f)	Request for reinstatement of term reduced	400.00	
111	1.20(j)(1)	Extension of term of patent	1,120.00	
124	1.20(j)(2)	Initial application for interim extension (see 37 CFR 1.790)	420.00	
125	1.20(j)(3)	Subsequent application for interim extension (see 37 CFR 1.790)	220.00	

Fee Code	37 CFR	Description	Fee
Patent Service Fees			
561	1.19(a)(1(i)	Printed copy of patent w/o color, regular service, delivery by USPS, PTO Box, or electronic means	3.00
084	1.19(a)(1)(i)	Patent Application Publication (PAP)	3.00
562	1.19(a)(1)(ii)	Printed copy of patent w/o color, next business day delivery to PTO Box	6.00

(Continued)

FIGURE 13.1 *(Continued)*

Fee Code	37 CFR	Description	Fee
Patent Service Fees (*Continued*)			
564	1.19(a)(2)	Printed copy of plant patent, in color	15.00
565	1.19(a)(3)	Color copy of patent (other than plant patent) or SIR containing a color drawing	25.00
566	1.19(b)(1)(i)	Certified copy of patent application as filed, regular service	15.00
567	1.19(b)(1)(ii)	Certified copy of patent application, expedited local service	30.00
568	1.19(b)(2)(i)	Copy of patent-related file wrapper and paper contents of 400 or fewer pages	200.00
085	1.19(b)(2)(ii)	Additional fee for each additional 100 pages or portion thereof	40.00
086	1.19(b)(2)(iii)	Additional fee for certification of patent-related file wrapper and paper contents	25.00
087	1.19(b)(3)(i)	Copy of first compact disc in a single order of file wrapper and paper contents	55.00
088	1.19(b)(3)(ii)	Each additional compact disc in the single order of section 1.19(b)(3)(i)	15.00
569	1.19(b)(4)	Certified or uncertified copy of document, unless otherwise provided	25.00
570	1.19(b)(5)	For assignment records, abstract of title and certification, per patent	25.00
571	1.19(c)	Library service	50.00
572	1.19(d)	List of U.S. patents and SIRs in subclass	3.00
573	1.19(e)	Uncertified statement re status of maintenance fee payments	10.00
574	1.19(f)	Copy of non-U.S. document	25.00
577	1.21(c)	Disclosure document filing fee	10.00
578	1.21(d)	Local delivery box rental, annually	50.00
579	1.21(e)	International type search report	40.00
580	1.21(g)	Self-service copy charge, per page	0.25
581	1.21(h)	Recording each patent assignment, agreement or other paper, per property	40.00
583	1.21(i)	Publication in *Official Gazette*	25.00
584	1.21(j)	Labor charges for services, per hour or fraction thereof	40.00
585	1.21(k)	Unspecified other services, excluding labor	AT COST
586	1.21(l)	Retaining abondoned application	130.00
587	1.21(n)	Handling fee for incomplete or improper application	130.00
589	1.296	Handling fee for withdrawl of SIR	130.00
Patent Enrollment Fees			
609	1.21(a)(1)(i)	Application fee (non-refundable)	40.00
619	1.21(a)(1)(ii)	Registration examination fee	310.00
610	1.21(a)(2)	Registration to practice	100.00

FIGURE 13.1 *(Continued)*

Fee Code	37 CFR	Description	Fee
Patent Enrollment Fees (Continued)			
611	1.21(a)(3)	Reinstatement to practice	40.00
612	1.21(a)(4)	Copy of certificate of good standing	10.00
613	1.21(a)(4)	Certificate of good standing—suitable for framing	20.00
615	1.21(a)(5)	Review of decision of Director, Office of Enrollment and Discipline	130.00
616	1.21(a)(6)(i)	Regrading of seven or fewer questions	230.00
620	1.21(a)(6)(ii)	Regrading of eight or more questions	460.00

GENERAL FEES

Fee Code	37 CFR	Description	Fee
Finance Service Fees			
607	1.21(b)(1)	Establish deposit account	10.00
608	1.21(b)(2)	Service charge for below minimum balance	25.00
608	1.21(b)(3)	Service charge for below minimum balance restricted subscription deposit account	25.00
617	1.21(m)	Processing each payment refused or charged back	50.00
Computer Service Fees			
618		Computer records	AT COST

Fee Code	37 CFR	Description	Fee	Small Entity Fee (if applicable)
PCT Fees—National Stage				
956/957	1.492(a)(1)	IPEA—U.S.	710.00	355.00
958/959	1.492(a)(2)	ISA—U.S.	740.00	370.00
960/961	1.492(a)(3)	PTO not ISA or IPEA	1,040.00	520.00
962/963	1.492(a)(4)	Claims meet PCT Article 33(1)–(4)—IPEA—U.S.	100.00	50.00
970/971	1.492(a)(5)	For filing where search report prepared by EPO or JPO	890.00	445.00
964/965	1.492(b)	Claims—extra independent (over three)	84.00	42.00
966/967	1.492(c)	Claims—extra total (over twenty)	18.00	9.00
968/969	1.492(d)	Claims—multiple dependent	280.00	140.00
154/254	1.492(e)	Oath or declaration after twenty or thirty months from priority date	130.00	65.00
156	1.492(f)	English translation after twenty or thirty months from priority date	130.00	
PCT Fees—International Stage				
150	1.445(a)(1)	Transmittal fee	240.00	
151	1.445(a)(2)	PCT search fee—no U.S. application	700.00	

(Continued)

FIGURE 13.1 *(Continued)*

Fee Code	37 CFR	Description	Fee	Small Entity Fee (If applicable)
PCT Fees—International Stage (Continued)				
153	1.445(a)(2)	PCT search—prior U.S. application	450.00	
152	1.445(a)(3)	Supplemental search per additional invention	210.00	
190	1.482(a)(1)	Preliminary examination fee—ISA was the U.S.	490.00	
191	1.482(a)(1)	Preliminary examination fee—ISA not the U.S.	750.00	
192	1.482(a)(2)	Additional invention—ISA was the U.S.	140.00	
193	1.482(a)(2)	Additional invention—ISA not the U.S.	270.00	
PCT Fees to WIPO or EPO				
800		Basic application fee (first thirty pages)	382.00*	
801		Basic supplemental fee (for each page over thirty)	9.00*	
803		Handling fee	137.00*	
899		Designation fee per country	82.00*	
802		International search (EPO)	846.00*	

Fee Code	37 CFR	Description	Fee
Trademark Processing Fees			
361	2.6(a)(1)	Application for registration, per class	325.00
362	2.6(a)(2)	Filing an Amendment to Allege use under § 1(c), per class	100.00
363	2.6(a)(3)	Filing a Statement of Use under § 1(d)(1), per class	100.00
364	2.6(a)(4)	Filing a Request for a Six-month Extension of time for Filing a Statement of Use under § 1(d)(1), per class	150.00
365	2.6(a)(5)	Application for renewal, per class	400.00
366	2.6(a)(6)	Additional fee for filing renewal application during grace period, per class	100.00
380	2.6(a)(21)	Correcting a deficiency in a renewal application	100.00
367	2.6(a)(7)	Publication of mark under § 12(c), per class	100.00
368	2.6(a)(8)	Issuing new certificate of registration	100.00
369	2.6(a)(9)	Certificate of correction, registrants error	100.00
370	2.6(a)(10)	Filing disclaimer to registration	200.00
371	2.6(a)(11)	Filing amendment to registration	100.00

*WIPO and EPO fees subject to periodic change due to fluctuations in exchange rate. Refer to the *Official Gazette of the United States Patent and Trademark Office* for current amounts.

FIGURE 13.1 *(Continued)*

Fee Code	37 CFR	Description	Fee
Trademark Processing Fees (Continued)			
372	2.6(a)(12)	Filing § 8 affidavit, per class	100.00
381	2.6(a)(14)	Additional fee for filing § 8 affidavit during grace period, per class	100.00
382	2.6(a)(20)	Correcting a deficiency in a § 8 affidavit	100.00
373	2.6(a)(13)	Filing § 15 affidavit, per class	200.00
375	2.6(a)(15)	Petition to the Commissioner	100.00
376	2.6(a)(16)	Petition for cancellation, per class	300.00
377	2.6(a)(17)	Notice of opposition, per class	300.00
378	2.6(a)(18)	Ex parte appeal, per class	100.00
379	2.6(a)(19)	Dividing an application, per new application (file wrapper) created	100.00
Trademark Service Fees			
461	2.6(b)(1)(i)	Printed copy of each registered mark, regular service, dely. by USPS, fax, or PTO Box	3.00
462	2.6(b)(1)(ii)	Printed copy of each registered mark, next bus. day dely. to PTO Box or fax dely.	6.00
464	2.6(b)(4)(i)	Certified copy of registered mark, with title and/or status, regular service	15.00
465	2.6(b)(4)(ii)	Certified copy of registered mark, with title and/or status, expedited local service	30.00
466	2.6(b)(2)(i)	Certified copy of trademark application as filed, regular service	15.00
467	2.6(b)(2)(ii)	Certified copy of trademark application as filed, expedited local service	30.00
468	2.6(b)(3)	Certified or uncertified copy of trademark-related file wrapper and contents	50.00
469	2.6(b)(5)	Certified or uncertified copy of trademark document, unless otherwise provided	25.00
470	2.6(b)(7)	For assignment records, abstracts of title and certification per registration	25.00
480	2.6(b)(9)	Self-service copy chage, per page	0.25
481	2.6(b)(6)	Recording trademark assignment, ageement or other paper, first mark per document	40.00
482	2.6(b)(6)	For second and subsequent marks in the same document	25.00
484	2.6(b)(10)	Labor charges for services, per hour or fraction thereof	40.00
485	2.6(b)(11)	Unspecified other services, excluding labor	AT COST
488	2.6(b)(8)	X-SEARCH terminal session time, per hour	40.00
Fastener Quality Act Fees			
650	2.7(a)	Recordal application fee	20.00
651	2.7(b)	Renewal application fee	20.00
652	2.7(c)	Late fee for renewal application	20.00

FIGURE 13.1 *(Continued)*

INDEX

United States Patent Office, 51
Universal Copyright Convention, 213
Usefulness requirement, x, 65–66
Utility patent:
    description of, 4, 120
    fees, 122
    instructions for application, 123–137

Value of intellectual property, 7–9, 18
Van Bortel, Kitty, 45–46
Venice, Italy, exclusive rights in, 48
Venture capital company case study,
    190–191
Voting machine (Edison), 149, 150–152

Wardlaw, Stephen, 201
Washington, George, 51
Web sites:
    Baby Jogger, 61
    copyright and, 214–215, 216

Delphion.com, 92
Dinosaur Bar-B-Que, 216
IP.com, 146
patent search, 91–92
Saving for College, 223
Small Business Administration, 189
trademarks and, 228–229, 230–238
United States Copyright Office,
    208
United States Patent and Trademark
    Office, 62, 87, 228
Wind Done Gone, The (Randall), 204–205
Winslow, Samuel, 51
Woods, Tiger, 46–47

Xerox, FutureColor, 3

Yancovic, Weird Al, 205

Zovant (Eli Lilly), 8–9